TRAIN
JOURNEYS
OF THE
WORLD

A SPECTACULAR VOYAGE OF DISCOVERY ALONG **30** OF THE WORLD'S MOST EXCITING RAIL ROUTES

BARNES
&NOBLE
BOOKS
NEW YORK

The Publishers would like to thank the following individuals for their help in the planning and preparation of this book: Neil Ambrose, Chris Bane, Hilary Bradt, Jeremy Collin, Dr S Dandapani of SD Enterprises Ltd, Alfonso Di Ianni, Paul Duncan, Paul Godwin, Elisabeth Grace, Gary Grainger at VIA Rail Canada Inc, Ralph Holzwarth, Fabienne Kalifat, Peter and Virginia Letcher, Elysabeth Logan, Marie Lorrimer, Rod MacFadyen, Caroline Marchetti, Polly Phillimore, Bonnie Randall, Jackie Rathband, Caroline Rathbone at VSOE, Melinda Regnell, Martine Simon, Keith Stimpson, Bernard Stonehouse, Peter Tremlett, Richard Turner, Gavin Wynford-Jones

The following groups and companies helped us with travel arrangements, flights, fares and accommodation, and without them the book could not have happened:
Italy: Citalia; *Turkey:* Turkish Consulate, Geneva; *Austria and Germany:* Austrian Federal Railways; Austrian National Tourist Office; German Federal Railways; German National Tourist Office; tourist offices of Konstanz, Bregenz and Linz; *Norway:* Norwegian State Railways Ltd, London; Color Line, Newcastle upon Tyne; *Spain:* Judith Greeven at Sugden McCluskie; Iberian Airways; *India:* Connemara Hotel, Madras; Taj Garden Retreat, Upper Coonor; Savoy Hotel, Ootacamund; British Airways; Taj Group of Hotels; *Myanmar:* Ministry for Transport & Communications, Yangon; *Mexico:* Sr Javier Rivas, Secretaría de Tourismo; Mexican Tourist Office, London; Balderrama Hoteles y Tours, Los Mochis; Chihuahua Gobierno del Estado, Chihuahua; Ferrocarriles Nacionales de México, Region Norte, Chihuahua; *Chile:* Adrian Turner, Traucomontt Tours/Andean Leisure; *Japan:* Japanese National Tourist Office, London; *New Zealand:* Brendon Wilson and New Zealand Rail Ltd; *South Africa:* the Management and Public Relations Office of Spoornet; *and for routes throughout the world:* Dave Clark and Longhaul Leisurail of Peterborough; British Rail International

Copy Editor: Susan Gordon

This edition published by Barnes & Noble, Inc., by arrangement with The Automobile Association, Fanum House, Basingstoke, Hampshire RG21 2EA

1993 Barnes & Noble Books
Reprinted with amendments 1995

ISBN 1-56619-207-2

This book was produced using QuarkXPress™, Aldus Freehand™ and MicrosoftWord™ on Apple Macintosh™ computers.

Colour origination by L.C. Repro and Sons Ltd, Aldermaston.
Printed and bound in Spain by Graficromo S.A.

The contents of this book are believed correct at the time of printing. Nevertheless, the Publishers cannot accept responsibility for errors or omissions, or for changes in details given.

Contents

THE TRANS-SIBERIAN EXPRESS
INTOURIST MOSCOW USSR

14592

Gültig zur Beförderung
zwischen zwei
Bahnhöfen der Linien
Wien Westbf.-Meulen-
Wien F.J.B.-Tulln,
Wien Sbf.-Leobersdorf,
Kaltenleutgeben
Nordbf.-Gänsern-
dorf oder Stockerau und
Wr. Verbindungsbahnen
oder umgekehrt
Unmarkiert ungültig.
W II S —-50
14592

An Introduction to the World of Rail

PAUL ATTERBURY

❖

The Growth of the Railways

ON 14 JUNE 1842 Queen Victoria, writing from Buckingham Palace in London, said: 'We arrived here yesterday morning, having come by the railroad from Windsor, in half an hour, free from dust and crowd and heat, and I am quite charmed with it.' From the moment of her first experience of train travel, as an anxious passenger along 18 miles of the recently opened Great Western Line, the Queen became an enthusiastic supporter of the railways and remained so throughout her reign. Victoria's enjoyment of trains was tempered, however, by her well-known fear of excessive speed, and she was always insistent that the royal train should never exceed 40 miles per hour (65kph).

Britain was the cradle of the railway age, and the rapid spread of the network across the country, and its growth in other parts of the

world, was greatly encouraged by this royal patronage. Closely related as they were, the royal families of Europe were quick to follow the young British queen's lead, notably in Germany and Russia. Ludwig of Bavaria enjoyed one of the most luxuriously appointed royal carriages ever made, a veritable baroque palace on wheels whose fittings included a water-closet cushioned in swansdown. Russia's first public railway was a short 15-mile (24km) link between St Petersburg and the royal resort at Tsarskoe Selo, opened in 1837, but the Russian emperors saw the railway as an important vehicle for economic development and political control.

Queen Victoria's enthusiasm was not always shared by her ministers. In the early days of the railways the Duke of Wellington is reported to have commented: 'I see no reason to suppose that these machines will ever force themselves into general use.' Indeed, throughout the early decades of the 19th century the vices and virtues of the railway were hotly debated all over the world by the people whose lives it touched – the churchmen, politicians, scientists, soldiers, industrialists, professional men (and, occasionally, women), by writers and artists. For some the railway was the work of the Devil, for others it held the key to the future. Either way, the advance of the railway across the world proved unstoppable. The train quickly became the most significant event of the already eventful 19th century.

EARLY DAYS

Despite the novelty of travel for Queen Victoria in 1842, railways of one form or another had existed in many countries at least since the 17th century, and were commonly used to transport bulk products such as coal

BELOW, the opening of the Stockton-to-Darlington railway. In a modern world where the railway is part of everyday life, this 19th-century print is a reminder of the intense excitement at the novelty of it all

over short distances. These were primitive affairs with wooden, stone or cast-iron rails and single wagons hauled by people or horses, and it was not until the late 18th century and the dawn of the industrial age that the steam engine appeared, initially as a stationary power source hauling wagons by ropes and cables. In the early 1800s the first experiments were made with self-propelled steam engines. These crude machines were rapidly improved by their engineer-builders, and in 1825 the first ever steam-hauled public railway was opened between Stockton and Darlington, in England, heralding the start of the railway era.

Where Britain led, other countries were quick to follow. During the 1830s the first long-distance lines were planned and built, and from the 1850s the international rail network grew at an astonishing rate, to reach some 750,000 miles (1,206,975km) by the turn of the century. What had started on a domestic scale in England was soon striding across the frontiers of the world.

The first international railway achievement was the linking of the capitals of Europe, despite the considerable differences – economic and political – that had hitherto kept them apart. From Europe the network spread outwards, gaining in the process the ability to cross continents as well as countries. By the latter part of the 19th century it offered practical and reliable transport across North and South America, around India, and from Europe across the Middle East and Asia to China. It was the train that made it possible for Phineas Fogg to win his bet and travel around the world in 80 days. Perhaps the only failure in the railway-builders' great scheme was in Africa, where the projected line from Cairo to the Cape was never completed. Even the Channel tunnel linking Britain and France was part of a grand Victorian plan for international rail travel, and its completion represents the final triumph of 19th-century internationalism over a hundred years of political intriguing.

ALL ABOARD THE PASSENGER TRAIN
The legacy of all this was an astonishingly diverse network of scheduled passenger and freight services radiating out from national and international centres. At first primitive in their standards and rather slow, passenger services began to acquire that distinctly romantic aura, the echoes of which linger on today. Sleeping and dining cars arrived, pioneered by George Pullman in America, and speed, reliability and standards of safety improved, thanks to development in track, locomotive and rolling

stock technology, signalling and communications. Accidents, of course, were frequent in these early days, but each one highlighted weaknesses in the system which could be avoided in the future. New development companies sprang up to build particular lines and run particular routes, and they quickly thrived, amalgamated or went bust.

Even quite basic railways in developing countries had their share of express and Pullman trains, and the railway had the flag-carrying status enjoyed by the airlines today. The classic long-distance services began to acquire names – the Orient-Express, the Talgo, the Trans-Siberian, the Broadway Limited and so on – names of distinction which are carved deeply into the mythology of rail travel.

Equally significant was the development of tourism. The world's first outing by train was organized in the 1840s by a young Englishman named Thomas Cook, to enable 500 people from Leicester to travel to a temperance meeting in Loughborough – and more than 150 years later his name is still synonymous with rail travel all over the world. From the 1860s many railways concerned themselves directly with tourism, opening new lines and stations and organizing special trains to serve the particular needs of this new breed of pleasure traveller. Many holiday regions of Britain and elsewhere owe their existence entirely to the railway.

ABOVE, *a satirical sketch from Victorian times, entitled 'Sunday on the Union Pacific Railway', suggests that home comforts in travel were taken to excess*

ABOVE, railway art of the 1920s was stylish and distinctive, emphasizing the power, movement and beauty of the train itself rather than the destinations to which it travelled

IMPACT ON SOCIETY

At home, the railway gradually dominated all areas of industry, trade and business. In turn this was to affect almost every aspect of people's daily lives. Trains represented a straightforward and relatively cheap form of transport, available, after the imposition of certain government controls on pricing, to virtually everyone. And, unlike any other form of mass transport before or since, the railway was able to make its way directly to the heart of the towns and villages that lay along its route.

This revolutionary impact on society is widely reflected in the literature of the period. The great novelist Charles Dickens, for example, was an inveterate train traveller, and along with many eminent contemporaries he wrote extensively about trains and train travel, in both fact and fiction. His vast programme of lecture tours and readings was only made possible by the speed and ease of rail travel. In the 20th century, railway writing has diversified, reflecting the train's enhanced social standing in the period when it was the epitome of smart and elegant travel, and a primary vehicle for romance, intrigue and adventure. Such themes have also been extensively explored, with great success, in the international field of cinema.

THE IMPORTANCE OF FREIGHT

Railways were invented to transport bulky materials, and that use is still the mainstay of most of the world's railway track today. In the heyday of the railway, freight operations were diverse, with every local station having its own freight yard capable of handling domestic, individual, business and commercial freight of every conceivable kind throughout the network. Everything went by train – newspapers and mail, milk, fish, vegetables and flowers, animals alive and dead, machinery and commercial products, military equipment, building materials and much else beside – simply because there was, until the 1950s, no viable alternative.

DECLINE AND REBIRTH

It was not really until after 1945 that the private car, the commercial vehicle and, increasingly, the aeroplane began to make serious inroads into the markets that the train had dominated so successfully for 100 years. The 1960s and 1970s witnessed a drastic reduction in the amount of both freight and passenger traffic carried by the railways of the developed world, and as a result many countries greatly reduced their networks and services. The pattern of decline continued, and the railways of the United States and Europe, by now either state-owned or highly subsidized, concentrated their efforts and their resources on bulk freight, short-haul and commuter passenger services. For a time, many of the long-distance and international routes so painstakingly developed during the 19th century seemed doomed to disappear. However, during the last decade the railways have been revived by a spectacular new generation of high speed trains which offer rapid, economical and environmentally friendly inter-city transport. At the same time, simpler and more traditional railways have continued to play an important role in the social and economic infrastructure of the developing world.

Important in this recent rebirth of interest has been the increase in leisure traffic, where the emphasis is on the train itself. Taking pleasure in a train journey is now a significant international pastime, with the result that some of the long-distance routes, including the Trans-Siberian, the Indian-Pacific across Australia, and the Coastal Starlight along the west coast of the US, are largely devoted to tourist traffic, and are heavily booked far in advance. New 'classic' routes such as the Ghan (Australia) have been opened up, and old ones, including the Venice Simplon-Orient-Express and the Trans-Canada, have been revived and revitalized. Vintage engines and carriages have been brought out of mothballs and junk-yards, and lovingly restored to provide a glimpse of luxurious train travel of the past but with all modern conveniences.

Hundreds of thousands of miles of railway are still in use throughout the world, but the longer journeys are increasingly exploited for the experience itself, rather than just as a means of getting from A to B. The trains and the people they carry, the lands they pass through and the views from the window, the slow pattern of change as day follows day – these are the elements that make such journeys attractive to the modern traveller.

In their essential nature, trains have not changed much since they first appeared. Design, speed, comfort and standards of safety may have altered, but they are still the practical, and often enjoyable, mass transit system introduced to the world in 1825.

The Railway Pioneers and their Legacy

ALTHOUGH CUT STONE trackways were used by both Greeks and Romans, the true ancestors of the modern railway were probably the wooden tramways widely used in mines in Germany and central Europe from the 16th century. The wagons, propelled by man- or horse-power, featured the flanged iron wheels that are characteristic of most railways. By the 18th century iron rails were coming into use, generally mounted on stone blocks, and quite extensive networks built up in mining regions. The world's first railway viaduct, the Causey Arch, was built in 1727 on one such network in County Durham, in the north of England. Its designer, Ralph Wood, can claim to be the first identifiable railway engineer.

The Surrey Iron Railway, opened in 1803, was one of the world's first public railways. Wagons were pulled by horses along a well built, double set of tracks fully equipped with points and other technical elements essential to the reliable running of a regular service.

However, a more important event was to take place in the following year, when the world's first steam-powered railway locomotive successfully hauled a heavy load of wagons along an iron tramroad near Merthyr Tydfil in South Wales. This machine had been built by a Cornishman, Richard Trevithick, and represented the culmination of several years of experiments undertaken by him to develop the applications of steam power. In 1808 Trevithick demonstrated an improved version on a specially laid circular track in London, charging members of the public a shilling a head to be transported in wagons hauled by the steam locomotive.

THE GREAT NAMES

Trevithick was the first of a dynasty of British engineers whose skills, imagination and perseverance were at the heart of the development of railways all over the world. Engineers emerged from many different backgrounds (often mining), but all were quick to appreciate that the steam locomotive was the key to all subsequent developments.

In the early 19th-century the north-east of England was the centre for technical innovation and it was here, beside the Wylam Colliery Railway, that George Stephenson was born in 1781. Inspired by the machines built by William Hedley that clanked their way past his doorstep, Stephenson had built his first locomotive by 1815, and in his capable hands the technology developed in leaps and bounds.

In 1825 Stephenson's *Locomotion* went into service on the Stockton & Darlington Railway. Next came the Liverpool & Manchester Railway, also in northern England. In this project George Stephenson and his son Robert were responsible not only for the locomotives but also for the planning and construction of the line itself, with its viaducts, cuttings, bridges and other engineering features. In 1829 their engine *Rocket* was judged to be the winner of the famous Rainhill locomotive trials, proving itself capable of hauling loads at over 30 miles per hour (48kph). This efficient machine set a standard for railway engines that spread widely throughout Europe.

In France, trains hauled by Stephenson-type locomotives were in service by 1830. Germany's first public steam railway opened in 1835 between Nürnberg and Fürth, and also featured a Stephenson engine, exported from Britain complete with its driver. The engineer for this line was Friedrich List, a German who had previously built coal railways in the US and who later went on to plan and construct Germany's first long-distance railway, from Leipzig to Dresden.

The 1830s and 1840s were a boom time for

ABOVE TOP, *Trevithick's circular demonstration railway was set up at Euston, London, and offered passengers the chance to ride behind a steam engine for the first time*

ABOVE, *Richard Trevithick – a railway pioneer of vision*

ABOVE, *the influence of the great British engineer Isambard Kingdom Brunel is not confined to the railways – his name is also linked with shipping*

railway expansion all over the world, and it was at this time that individual engineers really made their mark. Robert Stephenson went on from strength to strength, responsible not only for the London-to-Birmingham line, with all the major cuttings, tunnels, embankments and viaducts that route entailed, but also for the main lines to Scotland and across Wales to Holyhead. The latter route was built to carry the Irish Mail train, and its highlight was the bridge across the Menai Strait, carrying the trains high above the water in wrought-iron tubes of rectangular section, the longest of which were 460 feet (140m) and weighed 1587 tons (1612 tonnes).

The other great figure to emerge at this time was Isambard Kingdom Brunel, a British engineer of extraordinary imagination, who is probably best known in railway circles for building the Great Western line from London to Bristol. This featured Brunel's favoured 7ft track gauge, chosen for comfort and high-speed running. At the time the standard gauge was 4ft 8½ ins, and for some years a battle raged between the engineers who favoured one or the other. In the end, Stephenson's gauge won the day, but Brunel's broader gauge remained in use in western Britain until 1892, and broader gauges are still used in other parts of the world today.

Adventurous in his use of materials and technology, Brunel created many remarkable structures, including the Royal Albert Bridge which carries his line high above the River Tamar into Cornwall. The revolutionary technology of this structure, with its delicate lattice-work of stressed metal, led directly to other great railway bridges, such as those crossing the Forth, the St Lawrence and Sydney Harbour.

If Britain was at the heart of railway development, it was not slow to export both skills and technology. Many British engineers worked abroad (including Joseph Locke, in France), and railways as far apart as South America, Africa, India, China and Japan were planned and constructed by British engineers, with finance raised by British banks. The British locomotive builders were similarly dominant, and throughout the 19th century the products of factories in Scotland and the north of England could be found at work in the most remote corners of the world.

Britain's main rival at this time was the United States, where the famous Baldwin locomotives were developed. At the end of the 19th century both Germany and France entered the fray, and international railway building became an important foreign policy objective for countries with either imperial ambitions or a desire to influence international politics.

THE IMPACT OF THE RAILWAY BUILDERS

It is hard today to grasp the physical impact of the railway age because its achievements have so often been overshadowed by subsequent developments – seen beside a new motorway or airport, a railway seems small and insignificant. Yet at the time of their building, railways appeared as immense works of frenetic endeavour, whose impact on their environment was often depicted in cataclysmic terms. A railway construction site was seen by contemporary writers as total chaos, its effect on a landscape previously unaltered for centuries frequently paralleled with earthquakes and other natural disasters of colossal magnitude. Some 150 years later such structures seem part of that landscape, their hard edges softened by nature.

Equally hard to grasp today is the nature of the work involved. Most of the world's railways were built by teams of men armed only with picks, shovels and wheelbarrows. The great cuttings were carved out, the embankments built up barrow load by barrow load, the tunnels hacked out inch by inch, and often with heavy loss of life. Only at the end of the 19th century did mechanical equipment such as steam-powered excavators come into general use, too late for most of the railways.

An early guide issued by the London & Birmingham Railway placed railway building far above other man-made structures, including the Great Wall of China:

Thus has sprung into existence in a few years, a piece of human workmanship of the most stupendous kind; which, when considered with respect to its scientific character, magnitude, utility, its harmony of arrangement, and mechanical contrivance, eclipses all former works of art. Compared to it, how shabby a structure would be the celebrated Roman wall [Hadrian's Wall], or even the more extensive one of the Chinese; as for the Egyptian pyramids, they, so far from being fit to be mentioned in comparison with the railway, are merely uncouth monuments of the ignorance and superstition of their founders...merely evidences of much physical force, having but little aid from science or taste.

Such attitudes illustrate the feeling of their time, with a universal sense of achievement and the reflection of the onward march of the human race towards order, harmony and the control of the forces of nature.

RAILWAY ARCHITECTURE

Landscape has always presented challenges rather than barriers to the railway engineer. Where waters were too wide to bridge, ferries carried complete trains from port to port in places as far afield as Italy, Scandinavia, and around the Great Lakes of North America. Where high mountains blocked the way, solutions were found in tunnelling and in building high-level tracks – the highest ever built linked Chile with Bolivia and passed 15,834 feet (4826m) above sea level, and there were at least 14 other lines above 10,000 feet (3000m) in South America, the United States and Switzerland.

It is the tunnels which represent perhaps the finest architectural achievement of the railway builders. The earliest were dug by hand, and it was not until the 1860s that the first boring machines were able to simplify the enormous labour involved. The greatest of all is the Channel tunnel, under the sea between France and England, a magnificent achievement due to be completed over a century after its first serious conception. The 12⅓ miles (20km) of the Simplon tunnel through the Alps between Switzerland and Italy should always remain one of the man-made wonders of the world. There are many other tunnels of note, at least 5 miles (8km) long, in Italy, Switzerland, France, the United States, Australia, New Zealand and Canada.

Bridges and viaducts, whether of timber, brick, stone, metal or concrete, have always been the structures which, above all else, seize the imagination. Their visual appeal is direct, and the best combine strength with functional elegance. The wealth of statistics surrounding these structures can be overwhelming. The Forth Bridge in Scotland, for example, absorbed 54,000 tons (54,900 tonnes) of steel in the building of its great cantilevered lattice work, and 6,500,000 rivets to hold it all together. The three steel towers supporting the bridge are taller

LEFT, *leaving steam far behind and breathing new life into the concept of rail travel – two of France's high speed TGV locomotives*

than St Paul's Cathedral in London, and the trains cross the water 160 feet (49m) above sea level. Just as impressive in their own way were the timber viaducts favoured by Brunel for the railways of Cornwall, a type also used extensively in North America. But in aesthetic terms, nothing can rival the delicate concrete viaducts that are such a feature of the railways of France and Switzerland.

The most characteristic bridging type is the multi-arched viaduct, and these are still among the most dramatic relics of the railway age. The sight of up to 40 great arches in brick or stone, striding away across a valley and carrying a train up to 100 feet (30m) in the air, is still enough to make any journey

THE FORTH BRIDGE
ON THE
LONDON AND NORTH EASTERN RAILWAY OF ENGLAND AND SCOTLAND

memorable. In the mountainous regions of Switzerland and South America some viaducts spring straight from the mouth of a tunnel, so that the train emerges from a dark hole to fly straight across a chasm. Even when disused and overgrown, a viaduct retains its power.

Any discussion of railway architecture would be incomplete without a mention of the stations that are an important legacy of the 19th century. Stations were a completely new building type, without precedent, and their rapid emergence from the 1830s underlined the social changes that the railway was bringing in its wake. Architecturally adventurous, exploiting new technology, often impressive in scale and visual detail, the railway station changed radically the appearance not only of the big cities, but also towns and small villages. The station came to symbolise the new freedom, a gateway to new horizons, and the architecture tried to reflect this in designs suitably novel and impressive – setting a tradition for novelty which continued well into the 20th century. Then, as now, the big rail terminal was complete and self-sufficient, fully equipped with shops and restaurants, hotels and washing facilities, police stations and post offices, to fulfil the needs – real and imaginary – of all travellers.

The Story of the Locomotive

WHEN RICHARD TREVITHICK watched his primitive locomotive lumbering along a cast-iron plate way in South Wales in 1804, he can scarcely have imagined that he was setting in motion a machine that was to revolutionize public transport. Over the next 25 years this crude, ungainly and painfully slow locomotive was refined and improved by engineers including William Hedley, Timothy Hackworth and, ultimately, George Stephenson, whose *Rocket* of 1829 established the pattern for everything which followed. This engine had a multi-tube boiler, external cylinders, driving wheels linked by connecting rods, and a firebox force-fed by a draught created by exhaust steam – all elements still to be found on locomotives today.

Over the next 30 years, as the machine was further refined, it acquired the characteristic shape still familiar today: a long boiler mounted between the driving wheels, with the cylinders and chimney at the front and a rear-mounted driving position, all travelling ahead of a separate vehicle, or tender, carrying supplies of fresh water and fuel, and with larger driving wheels centrally placed between subsidiary wheels or bogies, the latter flexibly mounted to spread the weight and allow the locomotive to negotiate a curving track.

Improvements came in many forms. Stephenson himself developed the Planet type loco, with its inside cylinders mounted beneath the boiler and driving a cranked axle. In the United States engineers such as the Norris brothers and Matthias Baldwin of Philadelphia developed the characteristic North American locomotive with its rear-set driving wheels, generous cabin, tall chimney and cow-catcher – a shape familiar from so many Western movies. In 1854 a Belgian, Eugene Walschaerts, invented the vale gear that bears his name, while in France Henri Giffard perfected the injector, a far more efficient method of forcing water directly into the boiler by means of steam. Thomas Crampton pioneered the large, single driving wheel, a style of locomotive popular in France and Germany which was later refined by Patrick Stirling, whose splendid express engines remain some of the most elegant of all time.

THE HEYDAY OF STEAM

Many are the great names of the 19th and early 20th centuries, men who, driven by commercial pressures, steadily improved the reliability, the power, and above all the speed of Stephenson's basic railway engine. In the 1830s locomotives like *Rocket* had taken just over two hours to cover the 38 miles (61km) between Liverpool and Manchester. A century or so later, Sir Nigel Gresley's magnificent streamlined *Mallard* set a new world record for steam trains by travelling along a measured stretch of track in the north of England at 126 miles per hour (203kph), a record that has never been beaten.

In many ways locomotives such as *Mallard*, *The Flying Scotsman*, and the fine French Pacifics designed by André Chapelon represented the apogee of the steam age. By the 1930s all the hopes of visionaries such as Stephenson and Brunel had been fulfilled and the steam-powered railway was dominant throughout the world.

In some countries the emphasis was on speed, and streamlining was common for express locomotives. Elsewhere it was the sheer power of steam that ensured its dominance. In the US the so-called Union Pacific 'Big Boys' of 1941 were among the biggest locos ever built – immense Mallet-type engines with 16 driving wheels, capable of hauling 7000-ton trains over huge distances and across rugged terrain. At the

LEFT, the archetypal American steam locomotive carried its own distinctive modifications, as this 19th-century print rather simplistically showed, from the giant smoke stack to the thrusting cow-catcher

same time, lesser relatives operated countless thousands of freight and local services worldwide. In many countries a vital part of this network was played by the narrow-gauge lines, some of which survive today. The gauges vary considerably and, typically of the diversity of which the steam engine was capable, each line had its own specially built locomotives and rolling stock. Where economy and simplicity of construction were all-important, the steam railway could supply the answer – on narrow gauges, on monorail, on elevated or underground urban railways and on agricultural lines. When coal was not available the locomotive could be adapted to be fired by oil, wood, peat, hay or even crop-trimmings such as sugar cane. For the simplest country railways, the steam engine could be built into a carriage, to form a kind of railcar.

STEAM IN DECLINE

After World War II steam at last began to yield before the combined challenge of diesel and electricity. At the same time, increasing coal prices further undermined its position. Despite attempts by locomotive designers to produce ever more efficient and economical machines, from the late 1950s onwards the steam engine began to disappear. By the early 1970s main line steam had effectively disappeared from western Europe, North America, Australia and many parts of South America and the Far East. It was able to

survive only in countries where coal was cheap and readily available, and labour costs low. Even today, steam is still in widespread use in parts of Africa, and in India and China – indeed, until quite recently China was still building new steam locomotives.

The inexorable disappearance of steam around the world has, however, been matched by an equally inexorable rise in enthusiasm for these venerable relics. No other machine has ever aroused such intense passion in the hearts and minds of its supporters. The steam age past will remain a part of the railway present for many years to come, imagination and reality running on parallel tracks.

ELECTRIFICATION

Although the idea of electrically powered trains goes back to the 1830s, it was not practically applied until the early 1880s, to a local line near Berlin. Once established, electrification spread rapidly on urban, local and commuter lines throughout Europe, the power being supplied either from overhead cables or from a third rail. The first important electrically powered main line railway was opened in Switzerland, and then, with a new generation of powerful electrical locomotives, main line electrification spread quickly during the 1920s and 1930s, particularly in France, Germany, Switzerland and Austria. In the 1950s the British too, along with many other countries, began to expand rapidly their networks of main line electric trains.

Always quiet, clean and efficient, the electric locomotive also had a great potential for speed. This was first exploited to the full by the

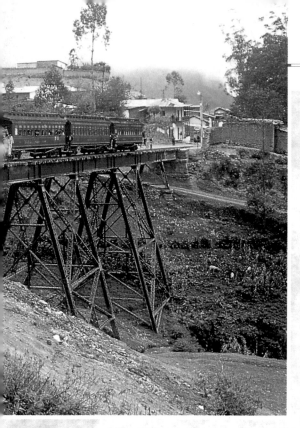

the passengers. It is thanks to these high-speed electric trains that railways are now enjoying a renaissance world-wide, as part of a carefully co-ordinated and integrated transport infrastructure.

DIESEL POWER

Steam's other great rival was the mechanical engine, fuelled either by petrol or diesel oil. Owing to difficulties in transmitting its power potential directly to the wheels, diesel was slow to make an impact.

However, in the 1950s and mid-1960s strong, dependable locomotives were developed that were cheap and easy to operate. This success was based on the application of the diesel-hydraulic and the diesel-electric principle, whereby the diesel engine was turned into a mobile generating plant for a secondary power source. The technique had been pioneered in Sweden as early as 1913, but it was not until the 1930s that General Motors in the United States developed a reliable and powerful machine.

Today, diesel power is ubiquitous, and growling locomotives are to be found performing every kind of railway duty in all countries of the world, from humble freight-shunting to high-speed passenger traffic.

Japanese when they opened their new Tokaido line in 1959. Buller trains on this line began to run at speeds of at least 150mph (240kph). Speeds crept up generally, but the real breakthrough came with the opening of the first of France's TGV lines, which established that trains could travel at up to 300mph (480kph) without prejudicing the safety or the comfort of

BELOW, *A far cry from Stephenson's 'Rocket', one of Germany's state of the art Inter City Europe high-speed trains awaits departure*

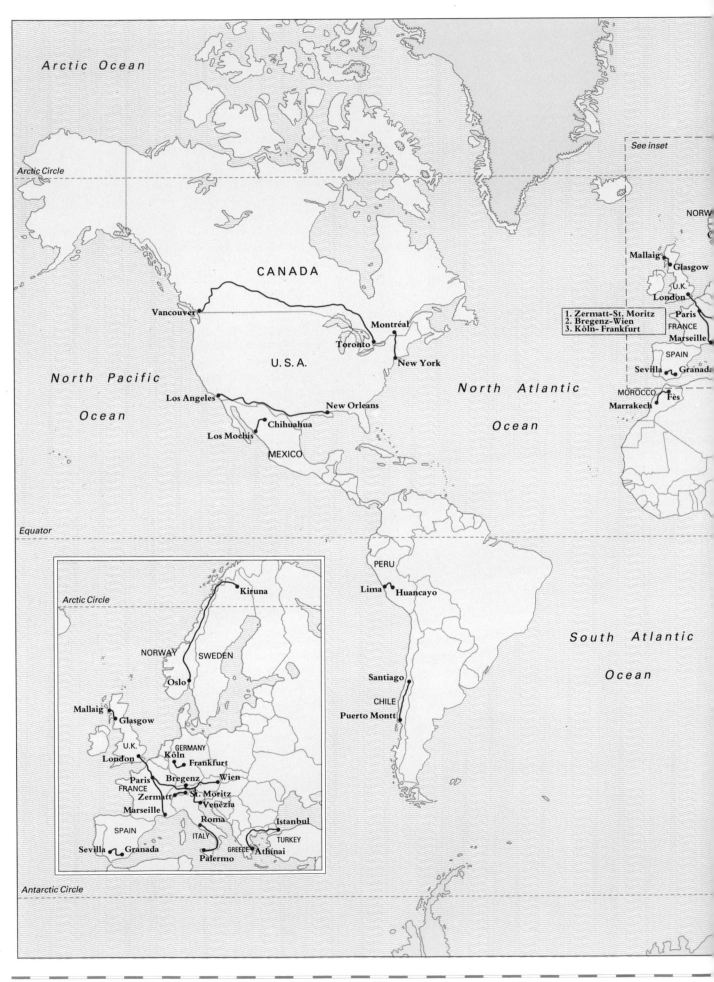

Arctic Ocean

Arctic Circle

CANADA

Vancouver

Montréal

Toronto

U.S.A.

New York

North Pacific

Ocean

Los Angeles

New Orleans

Chihuahua

Los Mochis

MEXICO

North Atlantic

Ocean

See inset

NORW

Mallaig
Glasgow
U.K.
London
Paris
FRANCE
Marseille
SPAIN
Sevilla   Granada
MOROCCO   Fès
Marrakech

1. Zermatt–St. Moritz
2. Bregenz–Wien
3. Köln–Frankfurt

Equator

PERU

Lima   Huancayo

South Atlantic

Ocean

Santiago

CHILE

Puerto Montt

Arctic Circle

Kiruna

NORWAY   SWEDEN

Oslo

Mallaig
Glasgow

U.K.
London

GERMANY
Köln
Frankfurt

Paris   Bregenz   Wien
FRANCE
Zermatt   St. Moritz
Marseille   Venézia

SPAIN   Roma   Istanbul
ITALY   TURKEY
Sevilla   Granada   GREECE   Athínai
Palermo

Antarctic Circle

16

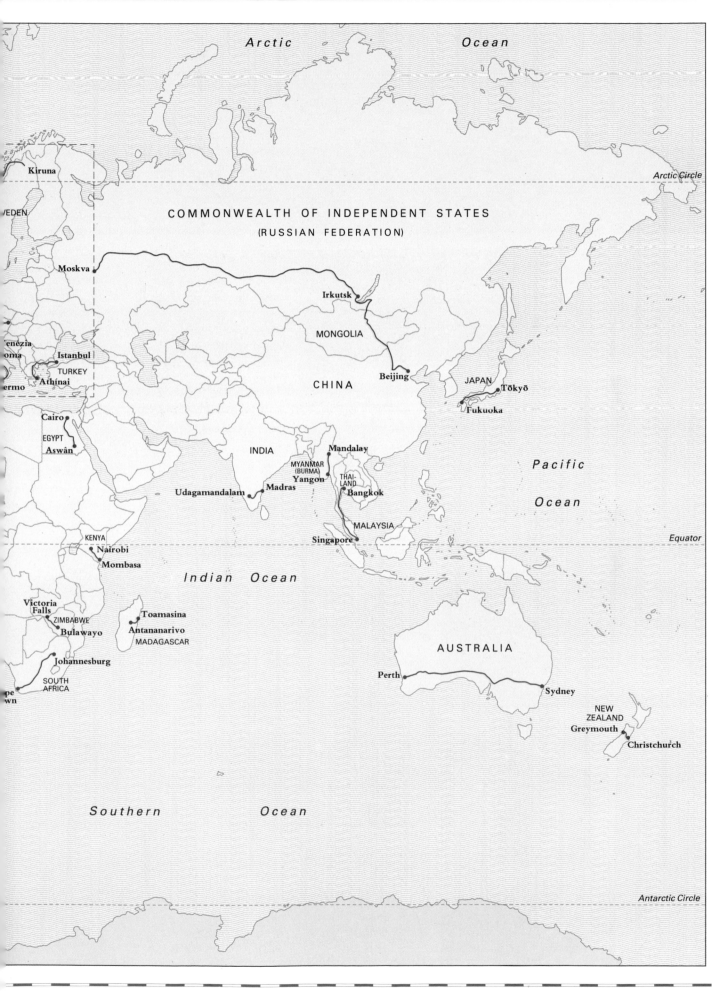

I N KEEN ANTICIPATION of one of the last great travelling experiences left today, I had arrived at Victoria Station long before any of the other passengers and, it seemed, before most of the crew. This at least gave me a chance to examine the train in some detail. The engine for this first section of the journey, to Folkestone, is one of British Rail's 'top link' locomotives, but it is the carriages that are quite different from anything today's rail traveller would otherwise experience. These are smart, cream and umber Pullman dining-carriages, from the original American design, with fittings and furniture of the highest standard: damask table cloths, fresh flowers, Sheffield silver and dishes by Wedgwood or Limoges.

I was taking all this in over coffee and a complimentary glass of champagne when the other passengers began to arrive, several of the ladies in 1920s-style cloche hats and theatrical flapper skirts.

The daytime dress for travel is best described as 'smart casual', while in the evening, black tie or formal suits are required from the gentlemen and formal dinner dresses are expected for the ladies.

Before long passengers discover that for many of their fellows the journey is a form of

■ The British Pullman train departs from London's Victoria Station, and after rumbling through the London suburbs crosses the orchard and oast-house dotted county of Kent while lunch is served. The train runs directly to Folkestone Harbour Station, where passengers embark on the Hoverspeed SeaCat for Boulogne.
The Continental VSOE train passes by the dome of the Basilica of Notre-Dame at Boulogne and runs on through Amiens, capital of Picardy, to Paris. Passports have been gathered up at Boulogne, and the staff handle all frontier crossings during the night while the train rolls on across France, passing through Troyes and

Mulhouse, and across the Swiss frontier at Basel to Zurich. Trains returning from the alternative route to Budapest travel through Germany via Munich, but the route described here is the original one and continues around Lake Zurich and on across Switzerland into Liechtenstein at Buchs, and then briefly across south-west Germany into Austria, crossing the frontier at Feldkirch.
Most of the passengers will be having breakfast as the train begins to climb the Arlberg Pass and enters the Arlberg tunnel to emerge at St Anton before running on through beautiful scenery to

Innsbruck, where lines go east to Budapest or south to Italy.
The train reaches Innsbruck by noon and forges on across Austria to the Brenner Pass, which marks the border between Austria and Italy.
By the time coffee is on the table after lunch, the Dolomites are in view, and on the last lap of the journey the train passes through Trento to Verona, terminating at the Santa Lucia Station at the head of Venice's Grand Canal.

Across Europe on the Venice Simplon-Orient-Express

ROBIN NEILLANDS

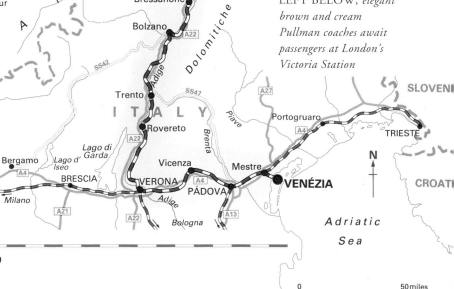

The ride on the Venice Simplon-Orient-Express from London to Venice or Budapest is not concerned with either the destination, the towns and cities *en route* or the countryside passing by. People ride on the VSOE to sample a more gracious way of travel and to play their part in a living re-creation of the golden age of rail. This journey is a journey into the past, into the history of the Orient-Express, and as we travel from London to Venice by Paris, Zurich, Innsbruck and Verona, we shall also travel back in time, beyond the turn of the 20th century, and see how this romantic and magical train ride came to be conceived and, more recently, revived.

ABOVE, *a stylish poster for the most famous train in the world*

LEFT TOP, *the elaborate golden crest of the Orient-Express*

LEFT BELOW, *elegant brown and cream Pullman coaches await passengers at London's Victoria Station*

celebration; people may be travelling on the VSOE as part of their honeymoon, or to mark their retirement or a special anniversary. Most are not hard up for a dollar or two, but others may have saved up for years to make this journey, and the mix of passengers is wide.

The journey to Folkestone through the green country of Kent was as pleasant as ever, and gave time for a look at the whole history of luxury train travel. To do that we have to go back a bit, to 1864, at the height of the American Civil War, when a young American

BELOW, *there are two sittings for dinner, one on either side of Paris*

engineer, George Pullman, created a train that was to transform travel across the vast American continent. Pullman had created a hotel on wheels of which the most significant features were seats that could be made up into beds at night and the introduction of dining-cars.

James Allport, General Manager of Britain's Midland Railway, invited Pullman to come to Britain and thus, in the mid-1870s, the Pullman Palace Car Company commenced operations, serving meals on board a train between London and Brighton, the first all-Pullman train in Europe. This was followed by a boat service, extending Pullman's service across the Channel, but meanwhile another innovative gentleman had appeared on the scene.

This was Georges Nagelmackers, a Belgian who had seen Pullman's trains in the United States and realised their potential for Europe, where there was an obvious need for trains that could provide meals and overnight accommodation for journeys of several days. Nagelmackers raised money where he could and his trains first went into service in 1876, under the banner of his new company, the Compagnie Internationale des Wagons-Lits.

FIRST CLASS SERVICE

Our own journey to Venice stopped at this point as the train arrived at Folkestone. Passengers transfer to the Hoverspeed SeaCat for a speedy 45-minute catamaran run across the English Channel. On the other side it takes only minutes to cross the *quai* and the platform to the gleaming, blue-and-gold train in the classic Orient-Express livery introduced in 1919, and there a host of white gloved attendants are waiting to usher passengers aboard for the main part of the journey.

The locomotive was to be changed six times during the journey, across the national boundaries and across the three types of electrification. The train has three restaurant cars, a Piano Bar carriage (complete with bar and baby grand), 11 sleeping cars, and two baggage and service cars for the crew and the passengers' luggage. The private compartments are most lavishly equipped in the best possible taste, but are not roomy. Each has a washbasin concealed in a cabinet, hot and cold water, towels, a plug for electric razors, and heating controls. Some compartments even have safes.

There are no showers or bathrooms.

The refurbished train we see today has been redesigned by the French designer Gerard Gallet, but owes most of its commercial success to the present owner, the American millionaire, James B Sherwood. Sherwood has wide business interests and owns, among other good things, the Hotel Cipriani in Venice. In 1977 – the year the original Orient-Express gave up the ghost – Sherwood bought two of the 1920s sleeping cars at a Sotheby's auction at Monte Carlo, in the face of some steep bidding from the King of Morocco. He then spent the next few years and a marvellous amount of money in finding and restoring other historic railway carriages.

By the time it ceased service in 1977 the Orient-Express had become a pale and shabby relic of its former self, and was used as a cheap way across Europe for migrant workers and itinerant backpackers. Sherwood had quite a different idea; he wanted to make the Orient-Express into a travelling experience, and sitting in the bar car, listening to piano selections from shows of the 1920s, I began to realise that Mr Sherwood had succeeded.

There are two sittings for dinner, one on either side of Paris. All the furniture and fittings are modelled on those used on the Wagons-Lits in 1903, right down to the lamps and the cutlery. The four-course dinner offered such dishes as sautéed *filet de bouef* with truffles and quails stuffed with *foie-gras* and for a small

supplement – and by this time who cares? – travellers can also choose from the à la carte... plus a superb collection of vintage wines and champagnes. Outside the window the countryside of northern France was flashing past, and before long the suburbs of Paris were appearing on either side. If Olga the Beautiful Spy or some characters from an Agatha Christie mystery were ever to appear, then this was surely the moment.

LITERARY CONNECTIONS

The name of Miss Christie is now inextricably woven into the history of the Orient-Express but this is almost by accident. Miss Christie never wrote a book called *Murder on the Orient-Express*. That title came later. Miss Christie's book was called *Murder on the Calais Coach*

which, admittedly, does not sound so good. The title referred to the de luxe Wagon-Lit which ran from Calais to the banks of the Golden Horn at Istanbul and, incidentally, that was a sleeping car train without the day-Pullman that was used in the film.

To date, the Orient Express has inspired six cinema films, 19 books, several television documentaries and at least one piece of music, a foxtrot called 'Orient-Express' which appeared in 1933. This snappy little number did not appear to be in the repertoire of the pianist who played the baby grand in the bar after dinner as the train thundered on across France, through the province of Burgundy to the distant frontier of Switzerland.

The 1000-mile plus journey would delight the young founder of the Wagons-Lits Georges

LEFT, *lalique glass panels adorn the dining car*

BELOW, *cleverly designed cabinets in each compartment conceal the washing facilities*

ABOVE, *the Orient-Express passes through some of the most spectacular scenery in Europe*

FAR RIGHT, *cabin stewards will deliver breakfast to your compartment*

Nagelmackers, who ran the first Orient-Express train out of Paris on 4 October 1883. This consisted of a luggage van, two luxurious sleeping cars and a well-appointed dining-car with a smoking lounge attached; all this for the 40 passengers, while the crew were jammed into a van at the rear. This train was the first to be called the 'Orient-Express' and the inaugural run made newspaper headlines across the world.

I awoke briefly at Zurich, where the morning papers and the breakfast croissants were loaded on board. The stop was brief and we set off again across the north of Switzerland, along the shores of the lakes, under the loom of the snow-tipped mountains for the tiny principality of Liechtenstein, centre of the numbered-account industry.

At one time the train left Switzerland directly into Italy via the Simplon tunnel which opened in 1906. The tunnel, 12 miles and 537 yards (20.163km) in length and the longest railway tunnel in the world, became the engineering wonder of the age. The Simplon tunnel put Paris much closer to Venice and Milan and offered a more southerly route to what was then Constantinople. Nagelmackers died in 1905, a year before the Simplon opened, and never saw his dream come to full fruition. In his day the trans-Europe express terminated on the Danube at Giurgiu, about 45 miles beyond Bucharest. From there the passengers had to cross the river by ferry and take a much less luxurious train to Varna on the Black Sea, where they boarded a ship for the overnight voyage to Constantinople.

By breakfast time we were in Austria, winding up through the Arlberg Pass and through the Arlberg tunnel, which delivered us back into the sunshine at St Anton, finest and most fashionable of all the Austrian ski resorts. As we came into the station, skiers were still curving down the steep slopes of the Valluga, high above the town.

to Vienna, capital of the Austro-Hungarian Empire, another casualty of the Great War, and so on to Budapest, the capital of modern Hungary and one of the most attractive cities in Eastern Europe. That would be the excuse for another journey but for now I followed the Smart Set south, over the Brenner Pass into Italy.

The Great War was a tragedy for millions but the Orient-Express, though interrupted by the conflict, had a part to play in its conclusion. In November 1918, the German delegation discussing the Armistice signed the surrender documents in Wagons-Lits car No 2419, brought for the purpose to a siding at Compiègne. The carriage remained there as a monument and its role was not forgotten; in 1940 the German Chancellor, Adolph Hitler, used the carriage as his chosen setting for the capitulation of France.

The late night revels had taken their toll, and not everyone on board was as bright as a trivet over breakfast, but by mid-morning the cups of coffee were giving way to another 'what-the-hell?' glass of champagne and the piano was giving a few exploratory tinkles.

A CHOICE OF ROUTES

In 1910 this route, which at first went only to Milan and then to Venice, was extended to Trieste. This was the start of the heyday of the Orient-Express, for the British aristocracy and the Smart Set had discovered Venice and were eager to escape the English winter for a rented *palazzo* in the 'Serenissima'. A tradition was born. The Great War of 1914 killed it.

At Innsbruck, the modern Orient-Express offers a choice of routes, south to Italy and the end of the line at Venice as in the Edwardian times, or the longer haul across the Salzburgerland

ABOVE, *the historic city of Venice, journey's end for the Orient-Express, has been described as the greatest work of art yet created*

FAR RIGHT, *passengers may come and go, but the magnificent Train Bleu rolls on*

Once across the Brenner, the end of this story and of this journey is almost at hand, as the train leaves the Alps and heads south towards the Dolomites and the Adriatic, weaving its way along mountain valleys towards Trento.

After World War I there was a great revival of train travel. In 1921 the train began a direct service to Istanbul, the journey taking only 56 hours from Paris and offering the now traditional three nights on board the train. Many of the carriages in the present train were originally built at this time and were used on that classic journey. The train ran on, a transport for the great and the good for the next 19 years, easily warding off competition from the growing airline industry, until war flung itself across the tracks again in 1939.

After World War II the train was back on the rails. By the December of 1945, four months after the atomic bomb fell on Hiroshima, a simpler 'Simplon-Orient-Express' was running again as far as Trieste. The Cold War often interrupted the service but never entirely stopped it, and by the 1950s the train was running a semi-First Class service all the way to Istanbul and Athens two to three times a week. The great age of rail travel was over, however, and the Orient-Express was in a relentless decline; the service ceased entirely in 1977.

A TRIUMPH OF ROMANCE

It was now mid-afternoon on the second day of my journey and the train was hurrying to its destination across the flatlands west of Venice, passing through the romantic city of Verona,

Shakespeare's setting for *Romeo and Juliet* – and you can't get much more romantic than that. Then came the crossing over the Mestre causeway into Venice, before we slowed to our final halt at the Santa Lucia Station, where the steps lead out on to the Grand Canal and the Serenissima in all her glory unfolds before you. There is no city in the world like Venice; it is impossible to think of building such a place today. We lack the courage, the confidence, and the creativity to embark on anything so uniquely splendid.

And like this journey, the story of the Orient-Express has a triumphant ending. The old, tattered and battered Orient-Express ceased service in May 1977 and James Sherwood began the task of reconstruction just five months later, when he bought the two sleeper carriages in Monte Carlo. The rest of this odyssey took another five years.

Hunting all over Europe, Sherwood eventually found another 35 suitable and historic sleeping cars and carriages, many of them in Spain where the golden age of rail had lingered on awhile. Some were in railway museums, others were in the hands of private collectors or being used by catering companies as mobile restaurants. The reconstruction of the nine Pullman cars which

make up the British section was carried out by craftsmen at Carnforth in Lancashire, while the conversion and rebuilding of the Wagons-Lits carriages on the continent was given to the Bremer Wagonbau firm in Germany and the Wagons-Lits workshops at Oostende.

It took a long time, a great deal of commitment and an incredible amount of money, but on 25 May 1982 James Sherwood saw his dream come true as the restored and gleaming Orient-Express pulled out of Victoria Station and started on the journey described here, all the way across Europe to the matchless city of Venice.

On any historic journey the traveller goes in two directions, forward through space, backwards through time. Were it not for the history of this journey and that of the men who made it possible, then for all its luxury, the evocative Orient-Express would simply be a pastiche or a sham. In fact it is neither of those things; it is a survivor, a glorious relic from a more glorious age. As I left the Santa Lucia Station, a little sad that the journey was over, I looked back and saw the staff swarming aboard, preparing the Orient-Express for the return journey, taking another set of travellers on another journey through time and space.

PRACTICAL INFORMATION

■ Trains run between London and Venice in both directions, twice weekly. The journey takes 32 hours, covering a distance of 1065 miles (1714km). Early booking is always advisable.

■ Alternative destinations are Vienna or Budapest, and there are plans to extend this route to other European cities. There is also a separate route from Dusseldorf through to Venice. It is possible to travel shorter distances, from London to Paris or Innsbruck for example, or even to go on day excursions within the United Kingdom. The Eastern & Oriental Express travels between Singapore and Bangkok. Border controls are handled by the train staff but travellers will need a full passport and whatever visa they normally require for entering any of the countries en route, ie, France, Switzerland, Germany, Austria, Italy and Hungary.

■ Full details can be obtained from any travel agent. The journey can be booked through travel agents or with the operators, the Venice Simplon-Orient-Express (VSOE), who rent the track on which the train travels. Contact the company for an illustrated brochure and for reservations: Venice Simplon-Orient-Express, Sea Containers House, 20 Upper Ground, London SE1 9PF. Tel: (0171) 928 6000. Fax: (0171) 620 1210.

■ In the US, contact Venice Simplon-Orient Express, 1155 Avenue of the Americas, New York, NY 10036. Tel: 212 302 5055 or T/F 800 2371236. Fax: 212 302 5073.

The Glacier Express through Switzerland

ROBIN NEILLANDS

The Glacier Express, one of Switzerland's greatest thrills, is a train that runs between two of the world's best-known ski centres, Zermatt under the loom of the mighty Matterhorn and the classic resort of St Moritz in the Engadin. The excitement of the route lies not just in its scenic beauty, which certainly matches anything else the continent of Europe has to offer, but also in the mind-boggling marvels of its engineering. Bewildering almost beyond belief, these are best outlined with a few statistics: the tortuous route of this narrow gauge railway embraces no less than 91 tunnels, 291 bridges and countless hairpin bends – only rarely is the famous red train on an even keel.

WITH A FEW HOURS to spare before catching the mid-morning train from Zermatt, I began my journey with a trip up the Gornergrat mountain railway for breakfast at the top, looking out across the valley to the sharp spike of the Matterhorn.

If not the tallest, at 14,688 feet (4477m), the Matterhorn is certainly the most impressive mountain in Europe. It still claims about a dozen lives a year and most of the victims lie in the graveyard at Zermatt, alongside the graves of the first group of climbers to reach the summit in 1865. This climb was led by an Englishman, Edward Whymper, and his seven-man team reached the top without undue difficulty. On the way down, however, four of the party fell 1000 feet (300m) to their deaths. Europe was shocked at the tragedy and Queen Victoria tried to have mountaineering banned, but climbers still come to the Matterhorn, as many as 60 a day in the height of the summer.

Zermatt is a pretty but curious town, entirely devoted to the tourist trade, skiing in winter, mountain walking and climbing in summer.

RIGHT, *the Gornergrat mountain railway is a breathtaking diversion, riding up from Zermatt and past the Matterhorn*

FAR RIGHT, *sections of the Glacier Express railway route are carved through the solid rock of the Swiss Alps*

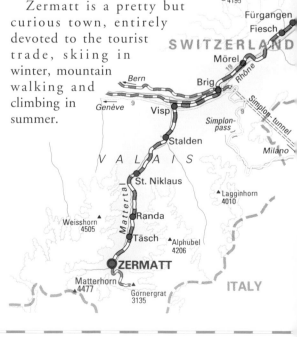

Cable cars and rack railways take people to the summits but there are no cars in the town itself. People get about on foot or bicycle, on horse-drawn sledges that sprout wheels in summer, or on the local electric buses. The town is run by a closed corporation drawn from the 'Burgergemeinde', the old families of Zermatt, many of whom have been there since the Middle Ages. I had my breakfast and skied back down in time to pick up the train for Täsch. Swiss trains leave to the second. Indeed, so efficient and popular is Swiss Rail that it is the only railway system in the world with a thriving fan club, at home and abroad.

The Glacier Express comes together as the train travels along the route. The train itself is not a 'special' and only two or three of the coaches leaving the station at Zermatt were going all the way to St Moritz. The track from Zermatt is dual purpose – built for rack-and-pinion as well as for normal use – and slopes away steeply down the mountainside.

The train's big windows offer wonderful views and

■ Although Switzerland is small and the most mountainous country in Western Europe, it musters an amazing 3100 miles (4988km) of railway, belonging to Swiss Federal Railways and a number of private networks, and another 4786 miles (7701km) of postbus services, as well as the lake steamers and mountain railroads, all of which are fully integrated into the national transport system. The Glacier Express is the way to travel across the roof of Europe, through the mountains and under the glaciers between Zermatt and St Moritz; through the Furka tunnel, across the

Oberalp Pass and over the Landwasser bridge, between the Valais and the Engadin – and it is equally enjoyable taken in either direction. The rivers under the numerous bridges along the way flow off in almost every direction, to the North Sea, the Black Sea, the Mediterranean and the Adriatic, and it is well worth taking a map, of at least 1:100,000 scale, in order to identify the various rivers, lakes, valleys and mountain peaks as they pass by on either side.
The route is made up of a number of private Swiss railway networks and dates back to 1899 when the first

track was laid from Visp into Täsch and Zermatt. In 1904 the line was completed up to St Moritz and in 1912 the Chur-to-St Moritz main line was extended to Reichenau and up the valley to the town of Disentis.
In 1915 the second link went in with the opening of the line from Furka to Oberalp and then to Gletsch, Disentis, Brig and Visp to complete the route. The main parts are now electrified but the same route is followed.

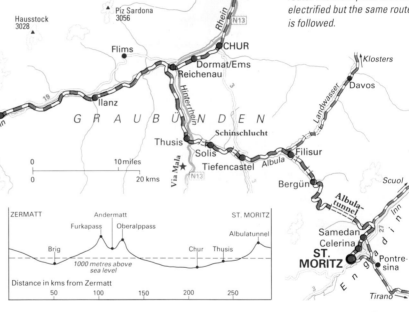

within a few hundred yards the Matterhorn vanished round a corner and the journey had really begun. The Second Class accommodation looked comfortable, but crowded. The Swiss are careful with their money and my First Class carriage was practically half empty.

The gradient to Täsch is only about 1:50, though that seemed steep enough to start the day, and the track is interspersed even here with much steeper rack-and-pinion sections over the various bridges spanning the mountain torrents, which were in full spate at this time. A number of skiers and motorists picking up their cars got out at Täsch and the train continued past St Niklaus, where the valley walls are so steep and narrow that in winter the village sees the sun only now and again. The 1:8 gradients down the

bridges at Stalden are the steepest on the entire journey, and we had already fallen over 1800 feet (600m) since leaving Zermatt. My ears were popping regularly as the train rocked down into a broader valley and the town of Visp. The man sitting opposite me looked up from his map, nodded at the river and said 'The Rhône'.

HEART OF THE ALPS

Visp is a main railway junction and a pretty little town, almost painfully neat in the best Swiss fashion, and here more of the Glacier Express arrived and was attached to our carriages. I tried to get out to watch this process, following the well-established traveller's rule that if you can get your feet on the ground at any station you can say you have visited the town, but I was hounded back on board by an outraged conductor who told me I could get out where my ticket permitted, at Andermatt, and not before.

The bright-red, shiny engine pulled us on to Brig, which at 2100 feet (700m) is the second lowest point on the journey. It was from here that the Simplon route across the Alps was pioneered by Napoleon, and the Simplon Pass still draws people to this little town. When the pass is closed it is possible to put cars on to a train for the 12-mile (20km) journey through the Simplon tunnel.

Brig would be a very good place to stop for the night: it is another of those pin-bright towns, dominated by a castle that was built in the 17th century by Baron Stockalper, the most successful businessman in the entire history of the Valais. I was told this by the conductor who was examining my ticket and was clearly anxious to make amends. The people of the Valais remember a businessman like other nations remember their great explorers or scientists.

The train now follows the Rhône on a branch line beside the river, to look across the valley and see the main track plunging into the Simplon tunnel. Rarely does the train go more than 20mph (32kph), but now it began to get up a fair amount of speed. We were still climbing steadily, however, as I sat down to lunch in the dining-car.

Here I was given one of the famous Glacier Express wineglasses that has a rim higher on one side than the other. The glass can be turned to keep the wine from spilling out as the train dips and sways – a feature which proved immediately useful as the track began a very steep climb between the stations at Mörel and Fiesch. The lunch itself was very good: a salad, some veal with rosti, a slice or two of cheese and a bottle of Arbois. For those who do not wish to dine, or cannot get a table in the dining-car, a roving trolley offers hot snacks, rolls, coffee and beer.

As we ate, the train crossed a wide bend in the river on a high viaduct, apparently heading

FAR LEFT, *a skiers' paradise in winter, the region around Andermatt seems impossibly lush and green in summer*

LEFT, *the dramatic 17th-century baroque palace, the Stockalperschloss, dominates the historic town of Brig*

BELOW, *passing below a tiny mountain village, the Glacier Express in its bright red livery brings a splash of warmth to a wintery landscape*

FAR RIGHT, *journey's end – the fashionable winter resort town of St Moritz*

BELOW, *with the train hugging the mountainside, much work has been done to protect the line from avalanches*

directly for the sheer cliff on the far side before making another of those now familiar swerves. It then began to zig-zag – and there is no other word for it – up the face of the mountain, using the rack-and-pinion to get a grip on the steep track. People were hanging on and the food-trolley wheels were locked for the ascent. There are three of these steep rack-and-pinion sections in the six miles up to Fürgangen, with an average gradient of 1:11.

The line flattened out for a while after Münster and rocked down to Oberwald. Up to here the country had been, in Swiss terms, fairly open, with the Rhône Valley forging a path through the mountains. At Oberwald all this comes to an end and I was not the only one to wonder at the tenacity of the Swiss railway engineers who had first conceived the idea of ramming a railway line through these enclosing mountains. 'Through' is the word, for just outside Oberwald the famous Furka Basistunnel begins. The climb to the tunnel is another steep ascent but the compensation is the marvellous view across to the Rhône Glacier which gives this train its name.

The climb from Oberwald to the mouth of the tunnel at Muttbach is about 5 miles (8km), during which the track rises about another 2600 feet (800m) but this fairly short tunnel, about 2 miles (3km) long through the top of the mountain, saved the engineers hacking their way up for another 330 yards (300m) to the top of the Furka Pass which carries the road. (The Furka Tunnel has since been replaced by the Albula, the longest single track tunnel in the world.)

At the far end of the tunnel, at Realp, the train soars downhill for a short distance to Andermatt, where I had decided to spend the night. This section of the line was once swept by avalanches and closed by deep snow in winter, but the introduction of avalanche bridges over the line and regular snow-ploughing has now made it safe and it remains open in all but the very worst conditions. The Rhône had now vanished and we were in the region of the Rhein. The track crosses the Reuss Valley and drops steeply for another 2600 feet (800m) through the village of Hospental into Andermatt. It was 15.30hrs and I had travelled long enough for one day. The Oberalp lay ahead but that could wait until tomorrow.

PLAYGROUND OF THE RICH

Andermatt, like Zermatt, is a ski and mountaineering resort, set at 4747 feet (1447m) above sea level, in a mountain valley above the St Gotthard Pass. There are over 300 miles (500km) of mountain walks around the town, and a lake fed by tumbling streams. There are a good number of hotels and for anyone who is enjoying the trip and wants to make it last, it is an excellent place for an overnight stop.

Andermatt is also a rail junction where trains leave for Lugano or Zurich. There are also more alpine trains or postbuses running through the mountains over the Furka Pass or the Susten Pass to Interlaken or Gletsch.

Next afternoon, the train was hardly out of the station when it started to climb a switchback route across and beside the road, up and up the side of the valley and then around the edge of the Oberalpsee, the lake, and under an avalanche tunnel to the Oberalp Pass at 6699 feet (2048m).

The gradient on the way up the mountain east of Andermatt averages 1:30 and there are a couple of rack-and-pinion sections on the way, but at the top the views are superb; this really is the 'roof of Europe'. The descent down the far side of the pass seems almost equally steep. The mountainside is barren and the train is under an avalanche shield for much of the way. The train clatters through Sedrun and then comes into Disentis, a fair-sized town with some pleasant inns and very good walks. A host of people boarded for the next, particularly spectacular, section of the route toward Chur.

Disentis lies at 3750 feet (1143m), a long way down from the Oberalp Pass. Here another of the Swiss railway companies, the Rhaetian Railway, takes charge of the train. We had now arrived in the Grisons (Graubünden), the most eastern, largest and most thinly populated of all the Swiss cantons and the only one where three languages of Switzerland are spoken, German, Italian and Romansh.

The restaurant car was now serving tea, a very civilized thing to do in that rather barren mountain setting. It might have been the tea, or the sun pouring in from the west, but as we rolled up the valley towards Chur the countryside along the Rhein began to soften and change, becoming greener and more gentle. There was still snow above the tree-line but the fruit trees in the farms around Trun and Ilanz were already showing hints of blossom. To the Romans, Ilanz was the first town on the Rhein.

A little further on, just when it seems safe to sit back, the rugged mountains begin again in the gaunt but spectacular Gorge of Flims. The railway runs beside the river here so that the cliffs tower above, a mass of crumbling rock that a sneeze might dislodge. The now familiar Rhein below is joined at Reichenau by another foaming stream, the Hinterrhein. Here the line diverts to Chur, capital of the Grisons, after which the Glacier Express presses on back up the Hinterrhein Valley towards Thusis and Tiefencastel.

The problems of building a railroad through these mountains were exceptionally taxing, and for this reason the final section of the route is as fascinating as any so far. The climb from the junction at Reichenau is fairly steep, rising about 5800 feet (1770m) in 50 miles (80km), with the gradient getting steeper all the time. The engineers were unable to get a fair run at it,

because the mountains are riven with gorges and steep cliffs that force the track into endless contortions. The Hinterrhein gushes out of one cleft in the rocks, the Via Mala, fed at this point by another lively tributary, the River Albula.

The construction difficulties at this point delayed the work for seven years before a solution was found in 1904. This was to enter the Schyn Ravine (Schinschlucht) and cross the Hinterrhein, climbing through a long series of tunnels to Solis and then going out over the Solis bridge, where the track is over 300 feet (90m) above the river. Many of my fellow passengers were on their feet now, cameras clicking, but I am no lover of heights and stayed where I was as the train curved through more tunnels, forcing its way ever-upward through the rock, on what is said, with reason, to be the most exciting part of the whole route.

It becomes rather too exciting at the bridge at Landwasser, the view featured on all the posters. This was white-knuckle stuff for some of us, as the train shot out of a dark tunnel apparently into thin air, to cross the Landwasser bridge, far too high above the river. Somebody screamed.

Just past here a branch line goes off to Davos but the Glacier Express is now scenting home and climbs on to Bergün in the Albula Valley through two more tunnels, leading into an open mountain valley. This relief does not last long. Within minutes we were climbing again, looping around to gain height, more like an aircraft than a train. There is tunnel after tunnel

now, and bridge follows bridge over ravines and torrents, the track still climbing – a seemingly impossible feat of construction.

Now comes the Albula tunnel, which 1000 men laboured to build between 1898 and 1902, still the highest tunnel in Europe at 5970 feet (1820m) above sea level and run like an arrow through the mountain. On the far side lies Samedan, capital of the Engadin, the valley of the River Inn or En, flat enough to have an airfield where light planes were hauling gliders up into the sky. Then suddenly, we were in the Engadin, wide and grassy and dotted with lakes, another world from the one of cliffs and chasms through which we had been climbing for the last three hours.

Samedan is the junction for the resort of Pontresina, which looks across the valley to Celerina and St Moritz, and we are running along the flat valley (yes, a flat valley) beside the lake and coming to a halt in the town of St Moritz, famed for its winter sports and its 'Champagne climate'.

I got off the train, feeling quite exhausted. This last section of the journey up from Chur is more of an assault than a train journey, for the scenery and the constant twisting and turning of the track are battering at the senses all the way. From the station I made my way directly to my hotel and had a very large drink. Next day I would hire some skis and put in a little time on the Corviglia, but I had had more than enough of heights for the moment.

PRACTICAL INFORMATION

■ The train runs all year and can be boarded at any station along the route. It currently runs three times a day in each direction, but with some exceptions. The journey covers about 180 miles (290km) and takes 7½ hours.

■ It is essential to book as far ahead as possible. It is also advisable to book a dining-car table well ahead, either at local ticket offices, through some Swiss National Tourist Offices (SNTO), or by contacting the Rhaetische Bahn, Bahnhofstrasse 25, CH-7002, Chur. Tel: 081-21 91 21. Fax: 081-22 85 01.

■ The trip is always beautiful, but June or September can be especially recommended, when the crowds have yet to arrive and the mountains are looking lovely.

■ Many tour operators include a trip on the Glacier Express as part of a touring holiday in Switzerland. Information on the Glacier Express and details of a variety of valuable rail passes are available from SNTO worldwide or from international rail offices. The SNTO in London is at: Swiss Centre, Swiss Court, Leicester Square, London W1V 8EE. Tel: (0171) 734 1921. Fax: (0171) 437 4577. In the US the SNTO is at Swiss Centre, 608 5th Avenue, New York, NY 100200. Tel: 212 757 5944. Fax: 212 262 6116.

Riding the TGV from Paris to Marseilles

PAUL ATTERBURY

With their development of the TGV network, the French have carried the train into the 21st century. The pioneering route was that opened between Paris and Lyon, and it was the success of this that ensured the continuing expansion of high speed train travel. The journey between Paris and Marseilles is the best of all worlds for it combines the speed, comfort and convenience of the TGV with a route rich in echoes of cultural and social history. The landscape is interestingly varied, the line closely following the Rhône southwards from Lyon and passing through the classic Rhône Valley towns. The real appeal of the journey, however, is the traditional lure of travelling south in search of the sun.

ABOVE AND FAR RIGHT, *the Train à Grande Vitesse, France's successful answer to high speed travel in the 20th century*

RIGHT, *setting off on any train journey can be an adventure, but the route to the south is especially rich in history*

Taking the train southwards from Paris to the Mediterranean is to travel in the footsteps of history. It is a route full of ghosts, for so many people both famous and forgotten made this journey, hoping to find something better, or at least something different in the sunshine of the Côte d'Azur. Down the line from Paris came Van Gogh, Gauguin, Cézanne and a host of other artists whose work was radically changed by the light and colour of Provence and the Mediterranean. Hemingway and Scott Fitzgerald also travelled south, while other literary figures, Somerset Maugham for example, found the experience so compelling they never returned northwards.

This route to the sun is also inseparable from the social and cultural development of the Mediterranean. Nice, Cannes and other

Côte d'Azur resorts owe their existence to two largely British activities, wintering in the sun and gambling at casinos, habits that took root in the late 19th century. The Mediterranean remained smart, elegant and exclusive until the late 1930s and it was not until after World War II that the emphasis switched to popular tourism. The only thing the two types of visitor had in common were the trains that carried them southwards.

In the 19th centruy the route was laid out by the Paris, Lyons and Mediterranean Railway, generally known as the PLM, a company not noted for fast running. In the 1880s it could take up to 25 hours to travel the 537 miles (864km) between Paris and Marseilles, but journey times rapidly improved in the years preceding World War I.

The other ghosts who haunt the line are

■ The historical appeal of a journey southwards to the Mediterranean sun is considerable, and the Paris-to-Marseilles route carries the stamp of many famous figures from the worlds of art, literature, film and theatre, and politics. Many travelled in the 1920s and 1930s on the famous Train Bleu, one of the world's great luxury trains.
South from Paris the line crosses a flat agricultural plain before entering the hilly country of Morvan, the Nivernais and the Saône Valley. This is the high speed section and so detailed study of the passing landscape is not practical. Instead, there is pleasure in the rapidly changing nature of the countryside, from fields to woods and hills. There are no towns of any size on this section, and the villages are passed too quickly to leave any

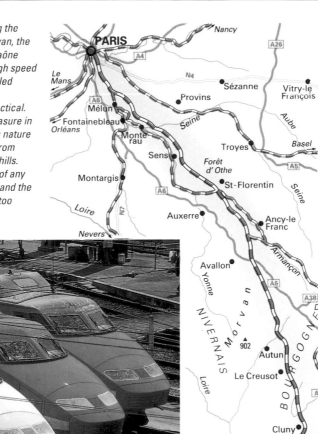

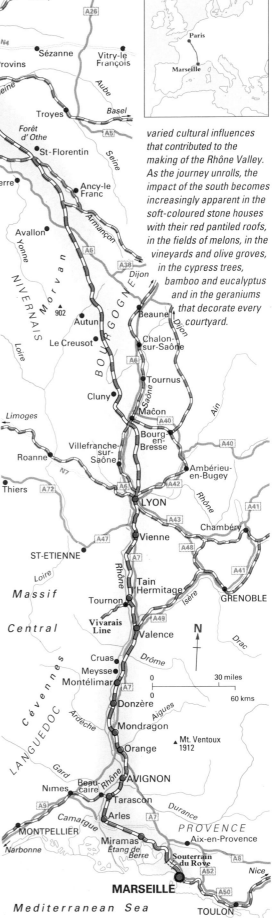

varied cultural influences that contributed to the making of the Rhône Valley. As the journey unrolls, the impact of the south becomes increasingly apparent in the soft-coloured stone houses with their red pantiled roofs, in the fields of melons, in the vineyards and olive groves, in the cypress trees, bamboo and eucalyptus and in the geraniums that decorate every courtyard.

the fashionable socialites of the 1920s and 1930s, the aristocrats, politicians and rich industrialists with their entourages of actors and actresses, writers, artists and musicians, film stars, entertainers and sporting heroes. These were the people who really brought the Côte d'Azur to life, and inseparable from their memory are the trains that carried them there. The most famous is the Train Bleu, an all-Pullman luxury service introduced in 1922. With its richly ornamental art deco carriages and its litany of famous passengers, this quickly became one of the great trains of the world. It even inspired a Diaghilev ballet, with sets designed by Picasso.

Paris is blessed with a series of splendid railway stations, not the least of which is the Gare de Lyon. This was the starting point for all the great journeys to the Mediterranean, and its concourse must have been a highly decorative place during the great days of the Train Bleu. Today it is a very different kind of place, devoted to travel in the modern frenetic style. However, there is still a tangible link with the Train Bleu, and this is the restaurant of the same name. Set high above the concourse, with a fine view of the trains arriving and departing, it is

impression. The emphasis rather is on the experience of high speed travel and the remarkable smoothness of the train.
At Lyon the TGV joins the Rhône Valley route south, and follows the twists and turns of the great river. Dramatic rocky hills frame the valley to east and west, foothills of distant mountains. The Rhône itself, tamed by navigation locks and hydroelectric schemes, irrigates a fertile valley filled with vineyards and fruit orchards.
An artery of development at least since the Roman period, the Rhône links together a series of famous towns and cities whose buildings echo the growth of France since the Middle Ages. Among these are Valence, Montélimar, Orange, Avignon, Beaucaire and Tarascon and Arles. Their castles, palaces and churches reflect the

ABOVE, *pulling away from the station – the yellow engine leads the mail train*

BELOW, *shark-nosed TGV engines represent high speed and high performance, a symbol of the modern world*

chocolates, I all but missed the train. Only a frantic dash for the platform, scattering passengers to left and right, averted this disaster, and I reached the train with seconds to spare.

ALL ABOARD...

French trains tend to leave on time and this TGV was no exception. The doors closed and with that silent, almost imperceptible shift into motion the train pulled out. It is a characteristic of many French trains, and notably the TGV, that they make no fuss about leaving. There is no whistling or shouting, no jerking or banging. They just very quietly start to move, and the platform slips away. The Gare de Lyon may be full of the memories of the past, but the TGV is a direct step into the future. First introduced over ten years ago, these high speed trains, which are capable of travelling at up to 320 miles an hour (515kph), have given railways a place in the 21st century. Alone among the nations of Europe, the French have spent money to create a truly modern intercity network. When the TGV was first developed, the concept was completely unproved, and no one knew whether such trains would be a great success or a wildly expensive white elephant. The expense lay not so much in the trains themselves as in the fact that modern high speed trains cannot operate properly on tracks laid down in the 19th century to carry a mixture of fast, slow and freight traffic. Despite intensive campaigning by road and air lobbies, the French grasped the nettle and built a completely new high speed railway between Paris and Lyon. The costs were huge, the engineering complex and the politics risky. However, the TGV proved to be an immediate success and the network has steadily expanded, radiating out from Paris to cover the west, the south-west, the south and the east of France. Other routes are under construction, notably the link north-wards from Paris to the new Channel Tunnel. In terms of speed, comfort, economy and city centre-to-city centre convenience, the TGV-style train clearly represents the future, and other countries, with the notable exception of Britain, have been quick to learn the lesson.

one of the best restaurants in Paris, probably without equal among the station restaurants of the world. The Train Bleu is an experience deeply satisfying for all the senses.

Visually, the interior is a delight, a rich compilation of murals, stained glass, cast iron and carved woodwork in the extravagant fin de siècle style. There is the sound of other people enjoying so splendid a setting, and as for touch, it is sufficient to be in contact with a place so filled with memories of a glorious past. The smells are a delight, lacking only those delicate smoky aromas of the steam age, but the major sensation is, inevitably, the taste. As my train was to leave by mid-morning, eating in the Train Bleu was not a realistic option and so I spent some time reading the menu to imagine the meal I might have had. Having, metaphorically speaking, sampled every course, I moved on to the souvenir stall. Spending too much time examining the extensive range of Eiffel towers and the very smart TGV

ABOVE, *red-roofed Fleuri, surrounded by extensive vineyards*

The usual TGV is a nine-car unit, with the characteristic electric powered, shark-nosed locomotives at each end. Each unit has First and Second Class cars, a café, telephones, and sometimes a restaurant, and at busy times two units will be joined together. The First Class cars, with three seats across and a central aisle, are extremely comfortable. Second Class have four seats abreast and more of them, no carpet on the floor and no curtains, but are still far more comfortable than most aircraft. There are facilities for disabled passengers, and on some trains SNCF operates a hostess system to look after unaccompanied children aged 4 to 14.

On my train, children were very much to the fore, as they are in many aspects of French life. The First Class car was full of families with small children and plenty of luggage, underlining the point that the distinction between First and Second Class today is to do with comfort more than social structure. It was all very domestic as the children got to know one another and sorted out their pecking order, the mothers quick to contain any unruly elements and the conductor always willing to lend a hand. In the Second Class there was a more democratic mix of elderly couples, students and the business people.

HIGH SPEED COMFORT

What sets the TGV apart from other trains is its speed. Leaving the Gare de Lyon, it winds its way out past the sidings, maintenance yards and freight depots and out into the green and leafy suburbs that seem to stretch for miles between the hypermarkets and parking lots. Paris is a far bigger city than its familiar, historical centre suggests. Thus far, the TGV is just like any other train, but after 18 miles (29km) it reaches the special high speed track and then becomes something completely different. With no noise or fuss it accelerates rapidly to its 168mph (270kph) cruising speed, and the sensation is akin to that of an aircraft climbing away after take-off.

The TGV appears to float along and is very quiet, with none of the clatter and thumping of a conventional train at speed. And it doesn't do anything quirky or unexpected, like leaning into corners or stopping suddenly. The only clue to the speed is the blurred view from the window, with clarity of detail only at a distance. As a result, you can be aware of the passing landscape only in general terms, as a patchwork of changing shapes and colours, sometimes flat, sometimes undulating. The high speed routes deliberately avoid towns and so orienteering has to be by the clock rather than the consistently rural view from the window. The speed of the train makes changes in weather more marked, sun giving way to rain, rain to broken cloud, and cloud to sun again. The noise of the rain hitting the windows was louder than the train itself.

The café car, to which everyone seemed to gravitate from time to time, was a relaxed and social place, full of easy chatter, and remarkable for having neither microwave nor junk food. The food was convenience-based pizzas, sandwiches, excellent fresh salads, yoghurts, biscuits, and assorted drinks, alcoholic and otherwise – but it reflected a concern for quality and price that is typically French. In the restaurant cars, full meals can be served at all First Class seats. The tea, not un-expectedly, was not memorable, but truly remarkable was the availability of British-style railway cake, served in slabs and full of cherries and sultanas. It was even called cake on the packet and, although made in France, the taste was exactly right.

As the train flew on, there was a definite feeling of going south. The landscape became more exciting as the flat farmland gave way to hills and forests, and there were tantalizing glimpses of rivers and twisting valleys as the sun brought the colours alive. Seen so quickly it lost any sense of reality and only the lines of distant hills and mountains had any permanence. Sometimes a scene stuck in the mind as it flashed past – a little château on a hill, a winding river among the trees and an old farm with animals grazing, all in bright jewel-like colours, almost a page from a medieval Book of Hours – but generally it was just the blur of speed, hypnotic and sleep-inducing. Heads were nodding all over the place and even some of the children were stretched out.

At midday I saw my first vineyard and a few minutes later we were out of the hills and rejoining the old main line for the descent into Lyon. We crawled through the station and then picked up speed again. From here onwards the TGV followed the old PLM route south, and it became a more conventional journey. We passed other trains, we sped through stations with names that could be located on the map, and even some of the ordinary noises and move-ments of train travel began to intrude. We were still a high speed train, flying south, but gone was that special quality, that sensation of gliding effortlessly through the landscape.

From Lyon south to the Mediterranean the line follows the Rhône, and it is an exciting journey with the great river never far away. Vineyards spread over the steep hillsides to the west, and in the fields by the river were fruit trees and melons. One by one the tell-tale signs of the south began to appear, wisteria and lilac in flower, the dusty yellow houses with their pantiled roofs, the shaded courtyards filled with geraniums, the ruined châteaux and churches set high on rocky pinnacles overlooking the water. And always there was the Rhône, a huge expanse of glittering water tamed by its locks and hydroelectric stations, with a few barges plodding north against the current. The train sped on, sometimes running right beside the river and following closely its great bends, and sometimes away among the fields of the valley.

The views were continuously enjoyable, the details now clearer. Vineyards came thick and

■ There are about nine TGV trains daily, each way, between Gare de Lyon in Paris and Marseilles. The 537-mile (864km) journey takes 5 hours. The Paris-to-Lyon section is along special high speed track, where the cruising speed is 168mph (270kph), while from Lyon south the train runs along the upgraded conventional track. Conventional, but much slower trains also cover the route, with sleepers and couchettes.

■ All seats have to be booked in advance. Many trains are full, so advance planning is recommended. Business and holiday peak times are best avoided. A supplement is payable for all TGV journeys, cost varying according to day and time of travel.

■ The Paris-to-Marseilles journey is attractive at all times of year, but spring is a good time to see the Rhône Valley and Provence.

■ The TGV network is operated by SNCF, the French national railway system. In France bookings can be made at stations or travel agents, or by telephoning one of about 100 major stations. Abroad, tickets can be bought and seats reserved at international rail offices. In Britain contact International Rail Office, Victoria Station, London SW1V 1JY. Tel: (0171) 834 2345 (enquiries); (0171) 828 0892 (credit card bookings). Fax: (0171) 922 9874. For further information in the US, contact French National Railroads, 610 5th Avenue, Rockafeller Center, New York, NY 10020. Tel: 212 582 2816.

fast; at Tain l'Hermitage the steep slopes to the east carried all the region's famous names. Across the suspension bridge on the other side was Tournon, the starting point for a very different rail journey, a climb into the hills behind the panting steam engines of the Vivarais line.

Valence was the first stop since leaving Paris, a brief pause barely long enough to draw breath, and then we galloped on southwards, past the huge nuclear power station at Cruas-Meysse, past the great quarries inexorably eating away the hills to the west, and past Montélimar without so much as a whiff of nougat. In fact, the air conditioning ensures that there are no whiffs of any kind, and so you miss all those distinctive smells that mark the start of the Midi, the real south – the pines, the eucalyptus, the heat. But the light is there, with the quality that drew the painters southwards. The landscape now is all in the colours of Cézanne, greys, browns and greens, and so it is no surprise to see on the eastern horizon the towering peak of Mount Ventoux, the shape familiar from so many of his paintings. Criss-crossing the Rhône's long navigation canal that takes boats away from the river between Donzère and

Mondragon, the train races on through Orange, well away from the town centre and then slows for a short pause at Avignon, with brief views of the ramparts that still ring the city. Leaving the city, the train crosses the Durance and then runs through a typically wild Provençal landscape of irregular hills broken by twisted rocks and dotted with olive groves. The hills are then left behind, replaced by the vast agricultural plain that covers the Bouches du Rhône region. Tarascon and Arles flash by, and then the huge freight yards of Miramas mark a return to a much hillier landscape, with villages clustered on rocky peaks. Stretching away to the south is the Etang de Berre, a vast landlocked lake that at first sight looks like the sea. The line curves round the lake against a background of dramatic rocky crags, and all around are vineyards divided by rows of cypress trees and acres of greenhouses.

As the fields yield increasingly to industry, the train enters the long Nerthe tunnel which burrows through the ring of rocky hills that surround Marseilles. The train leaves the tunnel and there, at last, is the Mediterranean. The line curves round the bay, with a good view of the docks and the coming and going of the ships, and on to Marseilles and its famous offshore islands. Journey's end is St Charles Station, and here the TGV drifts to a halt, half beneath the glazed canopy of the old train shed and half in the bright sunlight. It is a fine arrival, for the station is magnificent, set high above the old city. From the handsome stone façade, full of PLM echoes, a broad staircase decorated with classical sculpture in the grand imperial tradition leads down to the streets, streets full of noise, colour and chaos that in turn lead down towards the Vieux Port, a few minutes' walk away.

Through Southern Italy from Rome to Palermo

TIMOTHY JEPSON

❖

The Peloritano leaves Rome in the morning, winds through Naples a couple of hours later, and follows the Italian peninsula south before crossing the Straits of Messina to Sicily. It then shadows the island's northern coastline, arriving in Palermo in the early hours of evening. During the journey the train touches some of the Mediterranean's most beautiful coastline and skirts Italy's wildest mountains, including Europe's greatest active volcanoes, Vesuvius and Mount Etna. It also crosses the threshold between Italy's prosperous north and the poorer regions of the south where peasant ways of life have remained unchanged for centuries. In Sicily it encounters not only the home of the Mafia, but also a world apart whose position on the edge of Europe often makes it more reminiscent of Africa than Italy.

———

ABOVE, *the Peloritano travels south through the changing landscape of Italy, crossing to Sicily and finally reaching Palermo*

RIGHT, *the old and the new – the train is seen to great advantage from the ancient hill village of Centalo*

MOST ITALIAN train journeys start with pandemonium. The Peloritano was no exception. Chaos reigned in the corridor as the train lurched out of Rome on a clear blue morning to start its 569-mile (915km) journey south. A similar confusion had prevailed earlier, as I battled through a throng of nuns, locals, soldiers and lowlife – anything from ravaged drug addicts to Brazilian transsexuals – to win a hearing at one of the station's teeming ticket desks. In the corridor boxes, bags, mysterious sacks and briefcases were being manhandled and jammed into bodies coming the other way. A tight wedge of backpackers, tetchy businessmen and elegant Roman matrons seemed to have descended on the train at the last minute. Limbs flailed in all directions and oaths, shouts and an irritated air of impatience filled the carriage.

The luckier souls with seats had been ensconced for an hour or more, and now sat torn between these Dantesque goings-on and the view of Rome's southern suburbs unfolding through the train's windows. Few of the city's ancient glories, sadly, are on show; just the odd spire, a glimpse of St Peter's and the weather-beaten stone of Porta Maggiore, a magnificent three-portalled gateway in the city's 4th-century walls. Much of the view instead is dominated by traffic-clogged streets, modern apartment blocks and a huge, tangled forest of television aerials.

Within minutes, though, the train begins to nudge into countryside and the worst is behind us. Drawn by a smooth electric locomotive we cross the Roman *campagna*, a flat, fertile plain that reached right up to the old walls as late as the 1950s. For a while the railway parallels the Via Appia Antica, one of ancient Rome's most important consular roads, still covered by its original cobbles and lined by the ivy-clad remains of ancient tombs and sarcophagi. Thousands of early Christians were buried in labyrinthine catacombs near by, and it was along this road that Spartacus and 6000 of his followers were crucified, following an uprising against the Empire. Here, too, close to where the train crosses the old road, is the spot where St Peter is said to have met Christ as he was fleeing Rome, in an encounter which prompted Peter to return to Rome and Christ's eventual crucifixion.

PAST GLORIES

The train then shadows the wonderfully preserved remains of an old imperial-era aqueduct which strides arrow-straight towards the distant Colli Albani. Hundreds upon

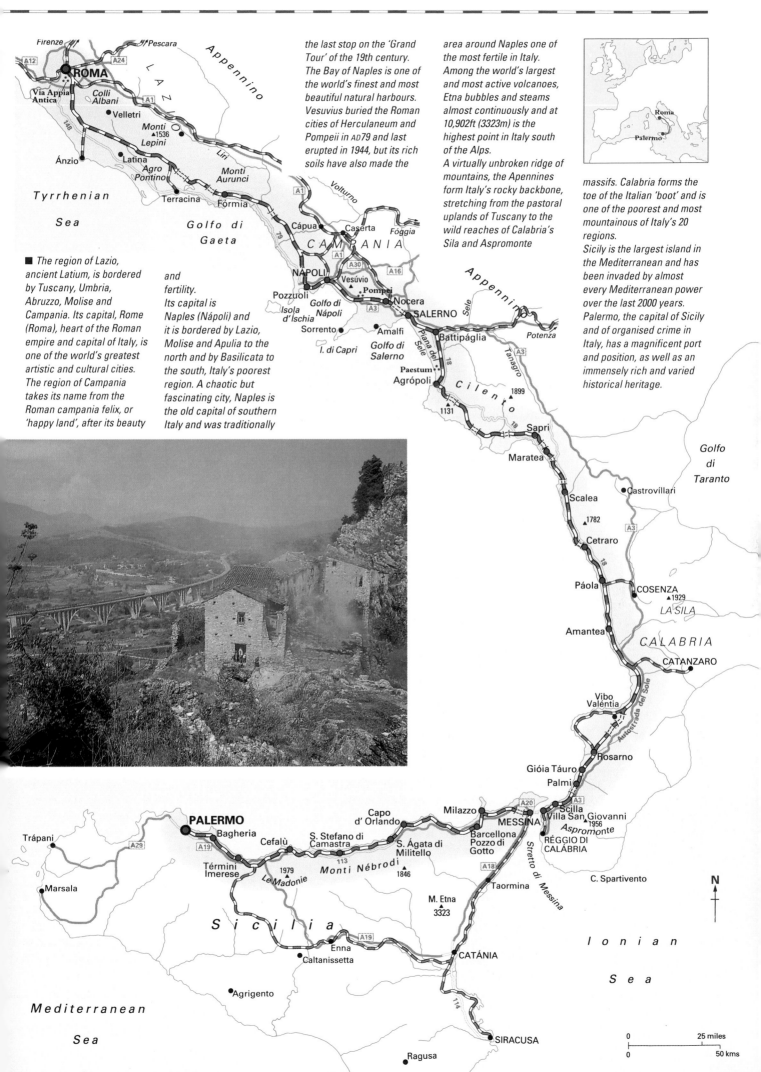

the last stop on the 'Grand Tour' of the 19th century. The Bay of Naples is one of the world's finest and most beautiful natural harbours. Vesuvius buried the Roman cities of Herculaneum and Pompeii in AD79 and last erupted in 1944, but its rich soils have also made the

area around Naples one of the most fertile in Italy. Among the world's largest and most active volcanoes, Etna bubbles and steams almost continuously and at 10,902ft (3323m) is the highest point in Italy south of the Alps.

A virtually unbroken ridge of mountains, the Apennines form Italy's rocky backbone, stretching from the pastoral uplands of Tuscany to the wild reaches of Calabria's Sila and Aspromonte

massifs. Calabria forms the toe of the Italian 'boot' and is one of the poorest and most mountainous of Italy's 20 regions.

Sicily is the largest island in the Mediterranean and has been invaded by almost every Mediterranean power over the last 2000 years. Palermo, the capital of Sicily and of organised crime in Italy, has a magnificent port and position, as well as an immensely rich and varied historical heritage.

■ The region of Lazio, ancient Latium, is bordered by Tuscany, Umbria, Abruzzo, Molise and Campania. Its capital, Rome (Roma), heart of the Roman empire and capital of Italy, is one of the world's greatest artistic and cultural cities. The region of Campania takes its name from the Roman campania felix, or 'happy land', after its beauty

and fertility.

Its capital is Naples (Nápoli) and it is bordered by Lazio, Molise and Apulia to the north and by Basilicata to the south, Italy's poorest region. A chaotic but fascinating city, Naples is the old capital of southern Italy and was traditionally

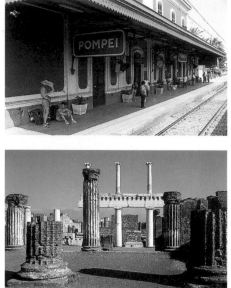

ABOVE, *built in the shadow of Vesuvius, the once busy commercial city of Pompeii was destroyed in the erruption of AD47, buried – and preserved – in a thick layer of volcanic mud*

hundreds of arches carry the old causeway across the *campagna*, wonderfully silhouetted against the morning sky. This is one of several aqueducts built by the emperors and restored by the Renaissance popes: some still feed icy clear water to much of the city, or empty into great monumental fountains like the Fontana di Trevi. Off to the north the Alban hills are already wreathed in haze, their faintly etched pyramid profiles, a legacy of their volcanic origins, draped in olive groves and vivid sun-dappled vineyards. Here is produced Frascati, one of Italy's most famous white wines.

In the carriage a sort of calm has descended. People appear to be reading newspapers and magazines but most are secretly more interested in their fellow passengers. The six-seat compart-ments, decorated with pictures of Italy, might almost be designed for intimacy and sure enough conversations are gradually struck – unleashing the great flood of chatter, anecdote and opinion that accompanies any Italian rail journey. I could bide my time as a foreigner, but sooner or later I will be drawn willy-nilly into the compartment's collective confessional. Outside the Pontine Marshes are rolling by, the vast coastal swathe south of Rome drained first by the Romans and then by Mussolini – about his most famous achievement after making the trains run on time. In the corridor brooding Italians are smoking their first cigarettes. These silent smokers, capable of staring out of windows for hours, are another feature of all Italian trains. They are especially prevalent at night, gazing out into the darkness, or staring with vain and lugubrious fixation at their own reflections.

Many are still there as we approach Naples two hours later. It has always been a moot point where the *mezzogiorno* starts, the so-called 'land of the midday sun'. The Milanese say Florence, the Florentines argue for Rome, but Naples is as good a place as any. Beyond it, manners are different, the people poorer, and the landscape more uncompromising. For an hour or so the train has cut through the *Terra di Lavoro*, an agricultural region known for its buffalo and the mozzarella cheese from their milk. Soon, however, the countryside is left behind and we are on the unprepossessing outskirts of Naples, looking out over interminable industrial landscapes and one of the world's most densely and dismally populated areas. It is a horror at first glance – filthy, chaotic and jammed with traffic – but it is also the quintessence of the vibrant and peculiarly Latin world that outsiders usually associate with Italy.

This is the home of the pizza, of fanatical devotion to football, of washing strung across the streets, and of sentimental Neapol-itan songs like 'O Sole Mio'. Sophia Loren's birthplace is also close by. It would be wrong to romanticize the place too much, though, and the safety of the train is perhaps the best place to enjoy what Henry James described as the 'picturesqueness of large poverty'. We stop at a couple of the city's big stations, and at both nimble children sweep down the corridors hawking baskets of food and drink. 'Panini, coca, birra' – 'sandwiches, coca-cola, beer' – resounds through the train in the half-intelligible babble of the Neapolitan accent.

Napoli-Campo Flegrei is the first stop, a stone's throw from the Campo Flegrei, the 'flaming' or Elysian Fields believed by the ancients to be the entrance to the underworld. Homer and Virgil both chose the spot for their heroes' descent into hell, prompted by its volcanic rumblings and sulphurous hot springs, and by its eerie landscape of extinct craters, dark hills and deep, mysterious woods.

IN THE SHADOW OF VESUVIUS

Still unblighted by the city's spread, these fiery environs lie on one of Europe's most dangerous lines of seismic and volcanic activity, a fault that parallels the Italian coast and culminates in the smouldering bulk of Mount Etna on Sicily. The railway follows the line almost exactly, passing another volcano, Vesuvius, Goethe's 'peak of hell rising out of paradise' and a mountainous Sword of Damocles that looms over Naples and threatens to bury the city as it did Herculaneum and Pompeii in AD79. It erupted most recently in 1944 when the travel writer Norman Lewis was on hand to record the event:

It was the most majestic and terrible sight I have ever seen, or ever expect to see . . . Fiery symbols were scrawled across the water of the bay, and periodically the crater discharged mines of serpents into a sky which was the deepest of blood reds and pulsating everywhere with lightning reflections.

Vesuvius erupts about every 30 years, so it's running late, yet Naples has no emergency plans should an eruption threaten its southern suburbs with oblivion.

The train pushes on, the volcano's bulk to the east, the Bay of Naples to the west, running past Herculaneum and Pompeii, neither visible through the blanket of roads and houses that smothers this part of the coast. The concrete tide turns a few minutes later, opening up sweeping views across the Sorrento peninsula and its coronet of famous islands, Capri, Ischia and Procidia. This idyllic enclave forms one of Europe's most beautiful coastlines, blessed with plunging cliffs and flower-strewn uplands cast against an aquamarine sea. The ensemble has lured the rich and the famous since the days of Tiberius, who came here to indulge his strange sexual appetites in 12 specially built villas on Capri.

Dusty Salerno passes, site of the Allied landing in 1944, and with it the last fleeting glimpses of cliff-backed villages clinging to the peninsula's southern flanks. Thereafter the train arcs inland across the Sele plain, spotted with palms and milky-white buffalo, before the Cilento mountains push it back towards the coast. The honey-coloured temples of Paestum pass in a flash, among the best preserved Greek temples in the world. There is little time for culture on the train, however, as attention increasingly turns to food. During previous trips on this line I have looked in vain for restaurant cars, being told by homeward bound Sicilians that the train is known colloquially as the *treno dei poveri* – 'the train of the poor'. Following the migrations of southerners to Italy's northern factories in the 1950s, when the Palermo run first became popular, so many people brought their own food in order to save money that it apparently was not worth the railway company's trouble to hitch up a buffet car.

The Peloritano is an Intercity train, however, the super-fast élite of the Italian railways, and its special status brings with it the bonus of a buffet car. Few people in the compartment – most of whom are elderly Sicilians – are ready to indulge, though, and huge spreads of wine, olives, hams, cheese and fruit are laid out on laps. Titbits are offered round, as they invariably are on Italian trains, but especially on trains in the south where

ABOVE LEFT, *a colourful jumble of houses and boats on the Amalfi shoreline at Cetera*

ABOVE RIGHT, *villas ancient and modern cling to the steep, rugged coastline of Amalfi, south of Naples*

ABOVE LEFT, *the Peloritano leans into the graceful curve of a viaduct*

ABOVE RIGHT, *part of the rail ramp which allows the train to roll on and off the ferry for Sicily at Villa San Giovanni*

FAR RIGHT, *roses flourish below pink domes in the sun-baked cloisters of the church of San Giovanni degli Eremeti, at Palermo*

the old-world Mediterranean habits of honour and hospitality die hard. After sharing hunks of cheese and rough red wine I wander down to the buffet, easing past the sullen ranks of smoking, staring men, and buffeted by the booming breeze which blows hot through the open windows.

The *ristorante*, by contrast, is air conditioned, and doubles as an observation car, with a counter and line of stools on each side and picture windows along the length of the carriage. Reheated and plastic-looking pasta is on offer (perhaps poverty is not the only reason people bring their own food) but the thimble-sized cups of coffee are as excellent as you would expect in Italy. By now the train is in Calabria and will stay wedded to the coast all the way to Palermo. A string of small fishing villages pass by: splashes of white houses against a turquoise sea. Out of the other window the grey, haze-veiled mountains of the Apennines stretch into the far distance.

It has now become very hot. Summer temperatures in the south reach 40°C, often bolstered by the scorching sirocco winds that blow hot from the Sahara. By the time we stop at Páola, a junction for trains headed for the interior, a heavy sun-stifled calm has settled on the countryside. The silent station appears much the same as stations throughout Italy, its name picked out in white on huge blue signs and with the hard lines and travertine marble that lend it a faintly Fascistic look. It is the middle of the afternoon siesta and there's hardly a soul about: all down the long platforms the heat is shimmering, and the only sound is the whirring of the cicadas. People are dozing in the carriage, and through the open window the smell of coffee mingles with diesel and warm creosote. Palms and orange trees at the edge of the station shade banks of oleanders, rich red and white blossoms basking in the Mediterranean sun.

Slowly the train cranks out of the station, bringing the temporary relief of a warm breeze before the old women, neurotic as only Italians can be about the danger of chills, close the window to the smallest crack. Down come the shutters, too, to keep out the sun, and people are soon squirming uncomfortably as clothes stick to clammy limbs on the plastic seats. By now views have opened across the sea to Sicily and Etna, and up to the Autostrada del Sole, Italy's main motorway, as it teeters along huge viaducts hugging the cliffs of the southern Calabrian coast. The railway's own engineering is almost as impressive, built, like much of Italy's west coast route, by gangs of British navvies who came to Italy once Britain's (and then France's) railways were more or less finished. Peasants supplemented the labour force, drifting back to their villages once the line had moved on.

ALL AT SEA

After whisking in and out of tunnels, the train passes Scilla, ancient *Scylla*, home to one of the dreaded monsters mentioned as a danger to sailors in Homer's *Odyssey*. The other, Charybdis, corresponds to Cariddi about 4 miles (6km) away across the Straits of Messina (in real life they were probably whirlpools). A few minutes later the train clanks into Villa San Giovanni, ready to embark on one of the journey's more fascinating episodes. Unlike many railways confronted with sea crossings the train does not duck the issue; it is simply broken up and shunted on to the ferry. On night crossings most people try to sleep through the clunking and grinding, but in daylight the train empties for a breath of sea air and coffee on deck.

Sicily is a strange and exotic place, and though the crossing takes only a matter of minutes, the sense of entering a world stranded on the edge of Europe, almost a stepping stone to Africa, is overwhelming. It is a place heady with history and antiquity, once among the most beautiful places on earth. Today, blessed with a superb climate and fertile soils, it can still be a paradise of swaying wheatfields (this was the 'bread basket of the Roman empire'), lemon groves, vineyards and silver-grey olive trees. On much of the coast, though, it can also be a nightmare of unplanned speculative building and, in the summer heat, a forbidding collection of sun-baked mountains and primal landscapes. And of course there is always the Mafia.

Progress is plodding over the last few hours to Palermo: Sicily's railways are single-track and there is a good deal of waiting for the *coincidenza*, the 'connecting' trains coming in from the branch lines of the interior. The Peloritano's intercity status now counts for little, and it is an ill-tempered and impatient train that finally arrives in Palermo, a bustling, sometimes eerily sinister place of Arab bazaars, shanty towns and run-down baroque splendour. People have jammed themselves in the corridor in a re-run of this morning's departure. Out on the platform there is a huge crowd looking as if they are ready to greet soldiers back from a war or travellers from some foreign land. But then Sicily, which has known emigration for centuries, is used to farewells and homecomings: they are a part of the island's psyche. Looking out at the dark faces, half Greek, half Arab, and listening to the guttural slur of the Sicilian dialect, it is as if we have left Italy. Only the emptying train, for the moment, belongs to that other country.

PRACTICAL INFORMATION

■ About 12 trains daily run directly between Rome (Roma) and Palermo, including five given over to sleeping cars and couchettes. The Peloritano covers the 569 miles (915km) in 11½ hours; sleepers take 90 minutes longer. Night trains are usually busy, and all services are likely to be full around Easter and Christmas, and at the start of July and end of August. It is usually not a good idea to accept offers from hotel agents who hover around the stations.

■ Temperatures in the south of Italy can be very high in mid-summer; it is probably more comfortable to travel either in spring/early summer, or in late summer/ autumn.

■ For information on this journey and details of all train travel in Italy contact any Citalia office. In Britain Citalia is at: Marco Polo House, 3–5 Lansdowne Road, Croydon, CR9 1Il. Tel: (0181) 686 0677. Fax: (0181) 686 0323. In the US contact CIT New York, 342 Maddison Avenue, Suite 207, New York, NY 10173. Tel: 212 697 2497. Tlx: 023 224927.

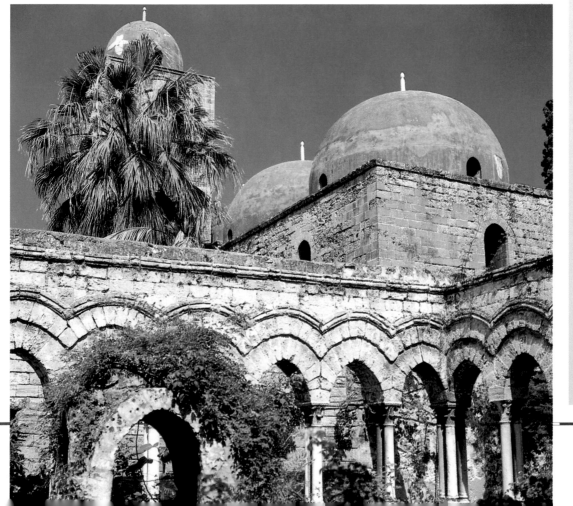

Around the Aegean from Athens to Istanbul

PIERS LETCHER

The main railway line from Athens runs north, up the eastern coast of Greece to Thessaloníki, and then east through Macedonia and Thrace to reach Istanbul, 846 miles (1353km) away. The start and end points of the journey are two of the world's most culturally and historically interesting cities, and the train journey takes you slowly past Parnassós and Olympos, along the Aegean coast, and through the endless emptiness of ancient Thrace. The journey is not a comfortable one, with at least one sleep-free night guaranteed on or near the Turkish border, but the rewards far outweigh the discomfort.

ABOVE, *waiting for the train on platform 1 at Athens' Lárisa Station*

RIGHT, *the Acropolis stands proud above Athens, capital of modern Greece and the starting point of this journey around the Aegean*

THE ARGENTINIAN gynaecologist sitting next to me on the flight down to Athens wants to know how long the train to Istanbul takes. I tell him I don't know, but the guidebooks reckon on anything between 30 and 40 hours, or, worryingly, that it is no longer possible. There is, however, a tentative connection in the Thomas Cook timetable which would make it in 24. Much seems to depend on the number of hours the through carriages spend on the border, abandoned.

Arriving at Athens' main railway station shortly before midnight is not a great idea; the few remaining staff seem to think my request for a reservation on the 07.20hrs to Istanbul is pretty amusing. Don't I mean

Constantinópolis? Probably. Well, there is no through train to Constantinópolis; change at Thessaloníki. Thanks. Can I have a ticket? No, you have to get that at the International desk, in the next building. The next building looks long deserted, but by repeated knockings at a grimy window I manage to rouse a bellicose-looking man who turns out to be capable not only of selling me a ticket but also of making me reservations 'from Thessaloníki'. I wonder half-heartedly where to, and pocket the ticket.

Athens' Lárisa Station is endearingly small-time – three platforms for the principal railway station of a capital city with a population rapidly approaching five million. But even at night it is surprisingly busy; people milling around, old suitcases packed to bursting, badly wrapped parcels littering the floor, the café tables crowded.

By the time dawn comes around, late, there are huge crowds on Platform One waiting for the northbound train, and I am glad of my reservation. It is a good moment to stock up from the stalls with essentials for the journey – bottled water, bread, biscuits, orange juice, cake, cheese pie, nuts, and a small bottle of Ouzo for emergencies.

As the train comes slowly into sight old women swathed in multi-layered cotton dresses and headscarves are still drifting across the tracks from Platforms Two and Three. Carrying picnic baskets and shopping bags full of fresh food, they are followed by their menfolk gripping string-tied bundles and cardboard cartons under their arms, their weatherbeaten faces shadowed by flat caps.

Even before the train comes to a complete

summit (a long but not difficult walk) is incomparable. There are also great views of the whole range from the train. In Thessaly (Thessalía) the railway winds through a series of spectacular tunnels and over bridges as it comes out of the mountains and down on to the plain; on several occasions there is a clear view straight across the valley to the next section of track.

Mount Olympos (Ólimbos), at 9570 feet (2917m), is Greece's highest peak (eight peaks, in fact) and a tough but rewarding hike. There are fine beaches near by which are easily accessible from the railway (stop at Kateríni or Lárisa and catch a local train).

Thessaloníki, port and Byzantine crossroads, is home to another brilliant archaeological museum, this time housing the treasure from Vergina.

Thrace is a sparsely populated and unspoiled area of countryside that is partly in Greece, partly in Turkey. There are practically no tourist facilities, but friendly locals more than compensate.

Alexandroúpolis may look tempting on the map, but is not a place to stop.

The Evros River marks the present day border between Greek and Turkish Thrace; the train follows the river all the way from the coast to the frontier post at Pithion/Uzunköprü.

Istanbul (Byzantium, Constantinople and now Istanbul): mosques, minarets, the Bosporus dividing the world's only city to span two continents, seat of influential empires – there is enough here to keep visitors occupied for weeks. If you have time, you should at least see the main sights on the south side of the Golden Horn – the Sultanahmet (Blue) Mosque, Ayasofya, and the embarrassment of riches in the Topkapi Palace.

■ *Athens (Athínai), capital of Greece, is enormous and hugely polluted now, but is the birthplace of Western civilization and home to the Acropolis, the Agora, the (first class) National Archaeological museum, and many ancient Greek, Roman and Byzantine ruins.*

Mount Parnassós is the centre of Greece's largest skiing area, but the view from the 8060ft (2457m)

TOP, *wrapped in a layer of cloud, Mount Olympos looks broodingly out over the bay*

ABOVE, *the uncompromising nose of the Athens Express*

halt, there are passengers clambering on board. But I am lucky; the reservation yields a comfortable seat in an otherwise full carriage. The platform clock ticks off another minute and we are off, exactly on time. And for the next six and a quarter hours this is to be the pattern: the train glides punctually into each station, and arrives in Thessaloníki five minutes early and in plenty of time for the connecting train to Constantinópolis. The 320-mile (515km) line from Athens is newly electrified and the train is a wonder; previous journeys on this line took upwards of ten hours.

HOME OF THE GODS

The winding journey up towards Parnassós, its lower slopes ablaze with late lilac blossom, is delightful. Pastel beehives clustered at the tops of small pastures and whitewashed orthodox shrines flash by close to the train. Today is a holiday, as much celebrated in Greece for being Flower Day as Labour Day, and I keep catching glimpses of people setting out picnic tables in the shade of olive trees and alongside streams.

Coming slowly out of the mountains and on to the plain of Thessaly, we catch our first sight of the Aegean, and soon afterwards we skirt Mount Olympos, towering above us to the west. The extended family that surrounds me seem almost as awed by the mountain as their ancestors (who made it the home of the Gods), and I get looks of disbelief from two of the older men when I mention climbing it two years earlier. Now there is snow capping the whole upper half, and it gleams white against the watery blue sky.

There is just time between trains in Thessaloníki for a beer at the station's giant bar, where half a dozen customers sit dwarfed by a room the size of a small concert hall. I am slightly jittery because the last time I was on this train every single seat, eight to a compartment and no hint of a couchette, was full. The water ran out in Thessaloníki, and the toilets ceased to function soon afterwards. But this time major hygiene improvements have been made – the toilet works all the way to Istanbul, and is cleaned regularly, and the washbasins provide water almost to the end of the journey.

Two slightly older carriages with chalked numbers matching my 'from Thessaloníki' reservation have been attached to the long train to Alexandroúpolis. These are the through carriages to Istanbul, although it does not say so anywhere.

Needless to say, those of us with reservations have all been crammed into two adjoining compartments. It takes us a while to realize this, after leaving Thessaloníki, but here we are, all the foreigners grouped together; three Americans, two Mexicans and one Australian to accompany me to Istanbul.

Every so often one of us makes a foray into the all-Greek carriages, but this is a risky enterprise because it is not exactly clear when the train splits; although both parts of the train do eventually go through Alexandroúpolis they do not appear to do so at the same time. The guards I ask seem as unsure as the passengers. One of the Mexicans comes back to the compartment with Dimitri, a young well-travelled, multilingual Greek, and he stays with us until Xánthi.

Greece for the most part is rural and underpopulated. With over half of its people now living in the capital, and most of the mainland being mountainous, this should not be surprising, but the train

winds on through the endless fields of Macedonia and Thrace, and the tiny stations at which we stop never seem to yield or exchange more than half a dozen passengers, practically all of them middle-aged or older; the young have abandoned the countryside forever, here as in so many other places, for the lure of the big cities.

Dimitri disappears for a few minutes and returns with a loaf of bread, some pungent feta cheese and olives – a gift from his family, several carriages down the train. We are busy picnicking when we pull into the small town of Dráma. I am nearest the door and after a little while I am sure I can smell burning. I go out into the corridor, and sure enough smoke is billowing out of one of the light fittings. The train is on fire. I would not mind, but this is the second time this has happened to me in Greece, and last time we were stranded for half a night in the Peloponnese.

An engineer arrives and makes short work of the light with a hatchet, waving away all offers of screwdrivers and spanners from a party of helpful locals who have climbed on board to enjoy the spectacle. Molten plastic runs out and the smoke clears. He points up happily at

the now severed electrical cables, and we resume our journey. The wires hang accusingly from the ceiling thereafter, and still have not been repaired three days later when I make the return trip.

The train arrives in Xánthi only an hour or so behind schedule, and we wave off Dimitri and his family, but it is not long before we discover that the driver and engineer have disappeared too, along with our friendly cleaning woman. The engine is ticking quietly to itself as it cools down, and the station master just looks at us blankly when we ask what time we are leaving. We wait and we wait, and it begins to get dark. A wash of scent comes drifting towards the open windows from a sweet-smelling rose-garden beside the tracks.

WEST MEETS EAST

Night falls, and it seems much later still that our lighthearted crew return, looking as if they have ingested a fine meal and much Retsina while they have been gone. Meanwhile the Turkish train, some 100 miles away, has arrived at the border, found us not there and has gone away again, shrugging its shoulders.

We rumble on, painfully and patently late. At Pithion, the Greek border post, the station master lifts his hands to heaven and is cheerfully apologetic: there may be another train tomorrow morning, at around 6 o'clock. A man in uniform gathers up our passports and disappears with them into the night. His sidekick waves his torch vaguely towards our bags in an all-encompassing customs inspection. The Greek engine wheezes off into the night, leaving us without heat or light, and we settle down to sleep on our individual bench seats.

Some time during the night, paralysed with the cold (it has dropped to near freezing after a long hot day) I wander around the station buildings looking for warmth. The two solitary carriages of our train look rueful with the Greek engine gone and the Turkish one nowhere to be seen. I share a coffee with the bleary-eyed station master who explains that my misconception about the timetables is best explained by the fact that I do not realize that there is not only a right way and a wrong way of doing things here, but a Greek way. He also swears to me that the delay was caused by an engine breakdown. I am sceptical; nobody tampered with our locomotive during the long and silent stop at Xánthi.

Things improve as dawn breaks and a burly unshaven man with his tunic buttons undone comes bustling noisily along the carriage, wrenching open the doors and proffering a variety of passports at me. The change of

LEFT, *Thessaloníki was badly damaged by fire in 1917 – but careful reconstruction and a wealth of historic buildings have helped to confirm the city's status as the capital of northern Greece*

identity offered by, say, a Mexican passport, is momentarily tempting, but I settle for my own. A Turkish engine appears to one side in the dawn light and tantalizingly sweeps past, only to reappear a short while later on the other side, with carriages attached. It takes a good deal of shunting and lurching before our two carriages are picked up, and as we are flagged away by the guard we have the frustrating sight of the station's coffee bar being opened up, just too late.

It is only a 20-minute ride to Uzunköprü, the Turkish frontier post, and here things are a good deal more businesslike. Herded off the train by men with guns, we stand in a huddle in the biting wind on the grassy tracks outside the border post. Inside, a darkly bearded man bearing an alarming resemblance to Bluto, Popeye's arch-enemy, calls us in one by one and stamps our passports by bringing down his huge forearm with all the force he can on to a tired and barely moistened rubber stamp.

Back on the train, as hunger overtakes us, one of the Americans delves deep into a holdall and comes up triumphantly with his last two slices of singularly greasy spinach pie. We break it up between us, and it is delicious, washed down with the last of the Ouzo.

And we are on our way again, travelling through the fertile fields of the tiny part of Turkey that is in Europe – just three per cent of the whole country; it feels like more. We pick up fresh passengers at each of the many hundreds of stops, but while the other carriages become ever more crowded, ours remains mysteriously empty.

The morning passes, the day warms up quickly, and lunch is just a sign of hunger which we try to avoid discussing, silently promising ourselves huge feasts in Istanbul.

Standing in the corridor, with our heads out of the window, blithely ignoring the quatrilingual signs advising us against this, we watch the countryside crawling past. The train is going so slowly that small children beside the track can run alongside and clamber on board. But there are other distractions: an old man wearing a tatty skullcap ushers a herd of geese across the level crossing, bescarved women walk in groups with, but separate from, men in suits cut to fashions from the forties and fifties, barefoot urchins run in circles, hair cropped to the last quarter inch. Gravestones, unmarked and forgotten, keel over in ramshackle cemeteries in the Islamic way, in startling contrast to the ornate and well-kept Orthodox graveyards to be seen in Greece

New housing developments herald our

narrows. At the last minute there are suddenly tremendous views of the Blue Mosque and Ayasofya from underneath, and then the train pulls around the corner inside the old Topkapi Palace walls with a long view across the untended gardens. This was the heart of such vital empires, of intrigues and despotism and power turned corrupt, and even now, inside the harem, there are hundreds of dusty rooms, closed up and abandoned at the turn of the century, intricate carvings, acres of priceless carpets and tapestries and cedarwood inlaid with mother of pearl crumbling to dust.

A last flashing view across the deep blue waters of the Golden Horn to the crush of buildings on the other side and the train slides around the final corner into Sirkeci Station, 32 hours out of Athens, and half a continent away.

Back in Athens, after a 40-hour return journey, I stop in a narrow marble-paved street to marvel at the Parthenon. An old woman dressed in black shuffles up the street towards me, stops, looks me straight in the eye, crosses herself and hurries on. I stare at her, startled. A few moments later the same thing happens again, this time with the added benefit of muttered imprecations. I wonder what I must look like. After it happens a third time I shoulder my bag – and only then do I see the tiny Byzantine church behind me.

impending arrival in Istanbul, and although this turns out to be still an hour away there is a tangible air of excitement throughout the train. Istanbul is exciting, and is attracting something like half a million new residents a year from the arid, impoverished eastern half of the country. It looks all set to grow into one of the world's largest cities.

The views from the train coming into Istanbul are unparalleled. We catch our first glimpses of the Sea of Marmara, resplendent in the midday sun. On the horizon great tankers and ships are massing for the plunge through the narrow straits of the Bosporus into the Black Sea.

The train comes in on the most attractive side of town, breaking first through the oldest wall, just a few stones and fragments now, before running along the shore as the Sea of Marmara

PRACTICAL INFORMATION

■ One train sets off each day from both Thessaloniki and Istanbul, and arrives at the other end 14–24 hours later (there is no sleeping accommodation or buffet car). Nine trains a day run from Athens to Thessaloniki and vice versa (night trains have sleepers and couchettes). The shortest total theoretical journey time from Athens to Istanbul is 24 hours 15 minutes, with the return journey 19 minutes shorter.

■ Reservations are compulsory and must be bought before the day of travel, although being caught without one is disciplined only by a small fine.

■ The best time to travel is early summer or autumn – July and August can be scorching and busy with Eurailers. Take warm clothing or a sleeping bag from September to June for the overnight wait on the border. Bring food and drink.

■ A visa is needed for Turkey. They are available on the border, depending on the time of day you cross; you may be asked to walk the mile and a bit (2km) to the local post office to buy one. Visas are difficult to obtain in advance. Currency exchange between the two countries fluctuates, and rates should be checked in advancve.

■ Abroad, tickets can be purchased through International Rail offices. Thomas Cook publishes the best and most reliable timetables, and these can be used for advance planning (though actual arrival and departure times are subject to 'local variations').

Across the length of Austria from Bregenz to Vienna

COLIN AND FLEUR SPEAKMAN

Variety is the keynote of this journey through Austria from Lake Constance in the west to the Danube in the east – from the high Alps to the Danube plain. If the most celebrated landscapes and most spectacular section of railway lie in the Vorarlberg and Tyrol to the west, further east in Upper and Lower Austria is to be found a less familiar, but equally charming countryside of old farms, quiet villages, vineyards, churches and monasteries. This is a railway journey which links some of Austria's most famous cities – Bregenz, Feldkirch, Innsbruck and, after a short excursion through Germany, Salzburg and Linz, before reaching Vienna itself.

RIGHT, *the journey of discovery across Austria begins at Bregenz, on the shores of Lake Constance*

ABOVE, *a visual warning that the tracks are for the trains!*

I T IS POSSIBLE to arrive in Austria by boat – if not exactly across open sea, at least across Lake Constance (or the Bodensee), of the Alpine lakes second only to Lake Geneva in size. We had taken a train to Konstanz, a charming lakeside resort on the Swiss–German border, and stayed overnight in order to take the morning boat to Bregenz.

It was a dull, wet day as our handsome, refurbished 1930s boat moved quietly away from the tree-lined quayside. The Bodensee fleets are operated jointly by German, Swiss and Austrian Federal Railways and provide public

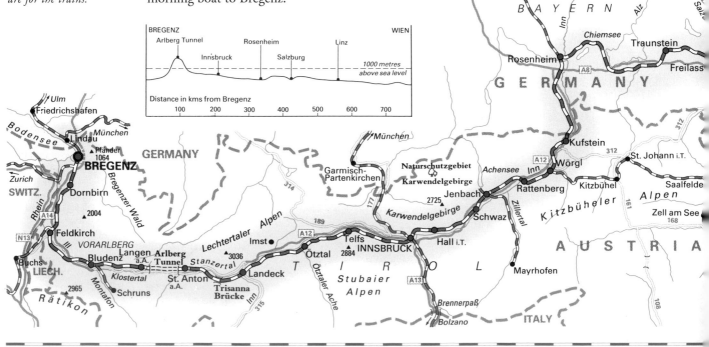

transport between lakeside communities, as well as pleasure cruises on the lake. Our route lay along the German shore to the north and while we devoured *Kaffee* and *Kuchen* in the elegant salon, the boat called at landing stages and harbours serving attractive, often medieval, townships that nestle among the steep vineyards. By the time we had reached the island town of Lindau, our last halt in Germany, the rain had finally petered out and straight ahead, shimmering in the sunlight, lay Austria and the town of Bregenz. Beyond, the summit of the Pfänder at around 4250 feet (1064m) was capped by low cloud and swirling mists, forming a dark and mysterious backcloth. Our boat slipped almost silently into the little landing stage and, improbably as it seemed, we were rustling for passports at the one-man customs and passport check on Bregenz quayside to permit our entry into Austria.

Bregenz is the capital of the state of Vorarlberg, the first of six Austrian Länder, or regional states, through which we would be travelling. Originally a Celtic settlement, in Roman times it proved to be a useful strategic site on the eastern

shores of Lake Constance. Now an elegant lakeside resort, it retains a medieval heart away from the bustling, modern town centre. It is dominated by the Martin's Tower, a large dark onion shaped dome (reputedly the largest of its kind in central Europe) within a network of charming little streets, alleyways and churches.

Though many services operate through from Lindau in Germany, our train started its journey in Bregenz, allowing us plenty of time to select seats in one of the comfortable bright red and dark grey InterCity carriages. It was a chilly day, and this would be a mountain run; the guard's

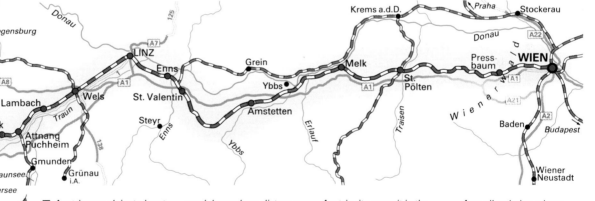

■ Austria can claim to be at the road and railway crossroads of Europe, between East and West. Soon to join the EEC herself, she lies directly in between two major EEC states, Germany and Italy, and there is real fear that a vast increase in heavy lorries between the two countries as EEC trade expands will cause immense environmental damage to the Alpine republic. For this reason there has been considerable development and investment in the rail network, aimed at getting as

much heavy long-distance freight as possible off roads and on to the railways. Passenger services have also benefited as lines are upgraded. In this way, several single track Alpine main lines, including that over the Arlberg, are being progressively doubled, for faster transport.

By far the most dramatic section of the route across Austria is the Arlberg line, between Bludenz and Innsbruck. The line crosses the high mountain ridge which divides Vorarlberg from Tyrol and the rest of

Austria, its summit in the Arlberg tunnel between Langen and St Anton, at 4400 feet (1340) above sea level. The line ascends 2500 feet (781m) from Bludenz over a mere 24 miles (39km), the steepest gradient being 32 per 1000 (about 1:32). The Arlberg tunnel is about 6 miles (10.25km) long. Completed in 1884, the line was only electrified in 1925. In steam locomotive days three powerful locomotives would be required to take a heavy train over the summit; even now, two engines are needed.

As well as being a busy railway junction, Linz has an important place in railway history. Mainland Europe's oldest railway, between Linz and Budweis, in Czechoslovakia, opened as a horse-drawn line in 1832. On the summit of the Pöstlingberg, to the north of the city centre, is a beautiful baroque pilgrimage church. It is served by the steepest unassisted (adhesion) railway in the world, built in 1898, with a gradient of 10.5 per cent (about 1:9.5) rising 840 feet (256m) over a distance of 2 miles (3km).

BELOW, *pink geraniums brighten a station sign*

BOTTOM, *heading towards the Arlberg pass, the train travels through narrow, high-sided valleys*

advice was to sit in the open saloon coach where it would be a little warmer. In charge of our train was a powerful 5300kw Class 1044 electric locomotive, the kind used for most high speed InterCity expresses in Austria.

Austrian Railways succeed in combining efficiency with a touch of good old-fashioned charm. EuroCity and InterCity expresses are invariably named. Where else in the world can you travel on trains named after a flower – the *Blauer Enzian* (the 'Blue Gentian'), an opera – *Der Rosenkavalier*, operetta composers such as Strauss and Lehar, an orchestra – the *Wiener Symphoniker*, or even a dance – the *Wiener Walzer*? Where else in Europe when your express train passes a small, local station deep in the countryside do you see the stationmaster, in full uniform, standing outside his office door, as if to salute the passing train, to ensure all is well with locomotive, coaches and passengers?

In the event it was on the *Niederösterreichische Tonkünstler*, or the 'Lower-Austrian Composer', that we travelled. We left precisely on time, the train of some 13 coaches

easing its way forward past the lakeside promenades before turning south and inland towards the market, textile and commercial centre of Dornbirn. To our right lay the upper part of the River Rhine (or Rhein) which flows into Lake Constance, here forming the boundary with Switzerland. To our left rose the thickly wooded mountain slopes of the Bregenzer Wald.

Just before Feldkirch, the line from Buchs in Switzerland, which carries the Orient-Express, joined our route. At Feldkirch, an ancient town dominated by the Schattenberg Castle with its Katzenturm (cat's tower), we were surprised to see skiers joining the train but were later to discover why. From here the railway follows the Illtal, the valley of the River Ill, heading south-eastwards. The hills are steeper and higher, the massive ridge to the south, known as the Ratikon, forming a natural frontier between Austria and Switzerland.

We were soon at the old town of Bludenz, which lies at the junction of two valleys, the Montafon and the Klostertal. Montafon is a particularly beautiful, narrow Alpine valley, containing the resort of Schruns, which is linked to Blundenz by a private railway, the Montaferbahn. Buses continue to the head of the valley and to the summit of the Silvretta Pass into Tyrol. Our route, however, lay due east through the Klostertal, and over one of the most spectacular railway passes in central Europe, the

Arlberg, named after the high, rocky ridge which separates Austria's most westerly state or Land from the rest of the country – hence its name Vorarlberg.

At Bludenz an additional Class 1044 locomotive came to bank our heavy train, pushing from the rear; even so, as the railway began to climb away from the valley sides, soon drawing level with the roof-tops and the typically Austrian onion-domed church steeples, the locomotives, for all their power, were struggling against the gradients, their progress not helped by greasy, wet rails. Our train was soon down to a walking speed which only gradually increased to a steady trot as the machines warmed to their task.

TACKLING THE ARLBERG PASS

The 85-mile (173km) Arlberg line between Bludenz and Innsbruck is an engineering marvel. It was built between 1880 and 1884, the strategic importance of its linking Vorarlberg with the rest of Austria highlighted by the fact that it was opened by Emperor Franz Joseph himself on 6 September 1884. Even after well over a century, it is difficult to appreciate the astonishing feat of the line's construction, following narrow rocky shelves carved into and along the mountainside, spanning great ravines with delicate bridges and viaducts, some, like the celebrated (and much rebuilt) Trisanna bridge between Pians and Strengen, features of great architectural beauty in their own right. The building of the line cost a great deal in both financial terms and human lives – no fewer than 135 men lost their lives in the construction, 37 in the building of the Arlberg tunnel alone.

Problems of both construction and subsequent operation were compounded by almost impossibly wild Alpine terrain and a hostile climate, with avalanches and landslides frequently sweeping away whole sections of tracks and even trains, with tragic loss of life. Trains were regularly trapped not only by blizzards but by rockfalls on the line. Nowadays a complex system of avalanche shelters over the tracks protects the line on the most exposed sections, but in severe weather the Arlberg is still a formidable barrier to both men and machines.

These thoughts were very much in our minds as we climbed through an increasingly wintry landscape towards Langen, soon passing the snow-line with dark forest now silhouetted against the snowy upland pastures, the mountain summits lost in mist. As our cheerful guard had prophesied, the chill of the air was evident, even through a double-glazed window. Though it was April, outside was bleak mid-winter, with

villages in the valley, already far below, looking vulnerable and isolated, the snow piled in thick, layered drifts by the trackside and the two locomotives at either end of the long train still working flat out. We finally passed the little mountain station of Langen and were plunged into the long, black abyss of the Arlberg tunnel, our speed quickening and the two locomotives almost heaving an audible sigh of relief as we passed the summit and emerged into the bright daylight of St Anton and the Tyrol.

Now we understood what we had seen at Feldkirch Station; we had entered a skiers' paradise, and the slopes were dotted with tiny black figures ascending by ski lifts or weaving down the *pistes*. But we had to begin our long descent through Stanzertal, the landscape typically Alpine – high peaks, steep snowy pastures, farms with deep, high roofs. Near Landeck we had to pause, first for a passenger train approaching in the passing loop, and then

ABOVE, *the line curves to accommodate villages on the valley floor, heading for St Anton*

BELOW, *the Achenseebahn is a summertime steam rack railway, linking Jenbach with the beautiful Karwendel Mountains Nature Reserve*

FAR RIGHT, *the crazy, colourful shapes of Vienna's Hundertwasser Haus contrast with the more formal – but no less striking – Classical architecture of the city*

to pass a freight train with one of the old-timer Class 1020 'Little Crocodile' locomotives, dating back to World War II, banking in the rear.

By the time we reached Landeck, an Alpine resort where the Arlberg line enters the Inn Valley, we were below the snow-line, the greener, softer landscape with crocuses and daffodils in bloom seeming like a gentler, more civilized world. Our rear locomotive had departed, and our train could now gather speed, as if just reminded of its InterCity status, through the ever widening, flat-bottomed and glacial valley of the River Inn. Brief stops at Ötztal and Telfs, and we were hurrying towards Innsbruck Hauptbahnhof.

Innsbruck is capital of the Tyrol Land, and its legacy of beautiful buildings, which include the Royal Palace and St James's Cathedral, recalls the influence of the Habsburg monarchs. For most people, however, it is the city's majestic backcloth of the snow-covered Karwendel mountains which makes the greatest impression.

After the thrills of the Arlberg line, the main line between Innsbruck and Salzburg was a much more relaxed affair. True, the landscape was still impressive, but the high and spectacular mountains were now a safe distance away from our train as we moved swiftly along the broad, flat-bottomed valley shared by motorway, farms and a scattering of industry.

Jenbach, our next stop, is of interest to all railway lovers. Not only is it the home of the Jenbacher works, one of Europe's leading manufacturers of railway equipment and locomotives, it is also the starting point of two delightful and contrasting narrow gauge railways. South of the main station the Zillertalbahn heads 20 miles (32km) up a particularly beautiful Alpine valley, Zillertal, to the ski and summer resort of Mayrhofen. In contrast, the Achenseebahn, to the north, operates between May and the end of October up the steep hillside to the Achensee, a narrow mountain lake from where there are superb walks into the Karwendel Mountains Nature Reserve (Naturschutzgebiet Karwendelgebirge).

SHORTCUT TO SALZBURG

At Wörgel, our next stop, we could have changed trains to link into the route to Salzburg which lies purely within Austria, via Kitzbühel, Zell am See and Bischofshofen, a marvellously scenic route, but as time was not on our side, we remained with our InterCity express. At

Kufstein our train became a 'Korridorzug', in effect a customs-sealed train which goes non-stop through the south-east corner of Germany, re-entering Austria at Salzburg. It is an attractive stretch, through the undulating countryside of scattered farms and woods of southern Bavaria (Bayern), close to the lovely Chiemsee. The train does not stop until it has crossed the bridge into Salzburg, with that thrilling panoramic view from the carriage window of river, castle, spires and domes.

It is difficult to believe that the wealth that produced this city of glorious architecture originally came from that humble commodity, salt. But it was the royalties from their salt mines that enabled the powerful Archbishop Princes of Salzburg to rebuild the city's earlier medieval core with magnificent baroque palaces. It also enabled them to become patron of a certain local musician – Wolfgang Amadeus Mozart, whose reputation helps to perpetuate Salzburg's glittering International Festival.

Too soon we were heading north-eastwards, away from Salzburg, climbing through quite steeply rolling countryside, past lakes, woods, farms and scattered villages, across the northern tip of Salzburger Land and into Upper Austria, a softer, gentler landscape than Alpine Tyrol.

Not that upper Austria has not got its share of mountains. The railway actually curves around one of the most spectacular lake and mountain regions of Austria, the Salzkammergut, where for centuries the emperors' soldiers and excisemen guarded the 'white gold' produced by the area's deep salt mines, so essential for food preservation in the days before refrigeration. The best introduction to the Salzkammergut is to leave the main line at Attnang Puchheim and take the scenic Salzkammergut line to Gmunden, Bad Ischl and Hallstatt. The railway follows lake shores past the limestone peaks and glaciers of the Dachstein Alps, a landscape of haunting beauty.

After a short pause at Wels, another attractive old Upper Austrian town and a junction for the main line into Germany and the little branch railway to the resort of Grünau in Amtal, we were soon curving into the Danube (Donau) Valley to Linz, the capital of the Upper Austria Land. After eight hours' travel from Bregenz, and an astonishing variety of landscape, it was a good place to break our journey and take a tram from outside the station to explore this much underrated city.

Linz, an important trading centre in the Danube on ancient amber and salt trade routes, boasts Austria's oldest church, the Martinuskirche, built 1200 years ago. A regional capital since 1490, it is both a thriving industrial centre and a city with great style and charm, whose elegant 18th-century façades in the main square conceal medieval and even Roman architectural features, with a strong Mediterranean influence.

From Linz, we took the morning InterCity express, called appropriately enough *Der Rosenkavalier*, to Vienna. This was a German train, hauled by a streamlined DB Class 103 express passenger locomotive, reflecting increasing cross-frontier co-operation between the two railway undertakings. It was running a few minutes late, but soon made up time across an open countryside of sleepy farms and scattered villages, each with its little onion-domed baroque church. St Valentin, though our express did not stop there, is the junction with the Wachau Line, a delightfully scenic railway along the north banks of the Danube.

Der Rosenkavalier crossed the River Enns into the Lower Austria Land, curving its way across the Danube plain into the Danube Valley itself, with tantalizing glimpses across the great river to the left, castles dotted along the skyline. At Melk we were able to enjoy breathtaking views of the great 18th-century baroque abbey before our train turned south-eastwards away from the river, stoping at St Pölten, a regional centre noted for its fine architecture, and an important railway junction feeding a network of local lines to Krems and deep into Lower Austria.

Soon after St Pölten, and for the first time since we entered Upper Austria, the train had to slow to cope with unexpected curves and steeper gradients. Thicker areas of forest gave the clue – we were entering the Wienerwald, those wooded hills which provide such an impressive backcloth to the city of Vienna, or Wien. The influence of the metropolis was already being felt – local

stations ringed with car parks for commuters, and villages with urban-style villas, some of them in typical, elaborate Biedermeier styles.

A short pause at Hütteldorf Station for links to the Stadtbahn, Vienna's underground railway network, and we were cruising through crowded suburbs of tall houses, terraces and shops. Almost to time, *Der Rosenkavalier* eased into the busy platforms of Wien Westbahnhof. Within moments, we had crossed the great entrance forecourt to catch a tram into the city centre. One of Europe's most fascinating and enchanting cities awaited our pleasure.

PRACTICAL INFORMATION

■ Hourly InterCity trains link Bregenz with Vienna (Wien), the full 480-mile (771km) journey taking about ten hours. There is not normally any need to book ahead.
As the train passes through the corner of Germany it becomes a customs-sealed 'Korridorzug' and there are no border controls.

■ Austria is beautiful at any time of the year, but those who wish to start the trip by crossing Lake Constance (the Bodensee) to Bregenz should note that steamers operate only from early April to the end of October. Supplements (Zuschlag) are payable on all InterCity and EuroCity trains, even for a short journey.

■ Within Austria a variety of rail passes is available, including the 'Rabbit' Card (under and over 26), valid on all Federal Railways (including supplements) and most private railways, and giving half-price on Lake Constance boats. The cards are valid for four days in any ten and within Austria are available at major stations. Outside Austria, passes and tickets are available from International Rail Offices.

kingdom, but broke away in 1814, drawing up its own constitution. However, to the disgust of many, Norway was forced into the kingdom of Sweden, from which it only escaped – after a national referendum – in 1905. This struggle to achieve recognition has made the Norwegians proud of their country, and its symbol. They are also proud of the fact that theirs is one of the oldest formal constitutions in Europe, signed in Eidsvoll in 1814. Not surprisingly, flags were fluttering at Eidsvoll as the train moved quietly through, about 50 minutes after leaving Oslo. By then the last of Oslo's sprawl was half an hour behind, the backyards replaced by a beautiful country studded with small lakes, stands of pines and low hills. This is a clean, clear and beautiful land.

Beyond Eidsvoll is Lake Mjøsa, the largest of Norway's many lakes, covering over 140 square miles (360sq km). Duck and grebes, startled by the train, scooted out across the water and a number of them took off in fright. The line then edged away from the lake shore, becoming somewhat twisty. It is single track here, with the odd 'lay-by' passing place.

We arrived at Hamar, where, on the outskirts of the station, there is a turntable that feeds a semi-circular engine house, a working marvel to add to the exhibits of the town's open-air Railway Museum. Also in the town are the superb remains of a 12th-century late Viking cathedral and endless reminders of Hamar's convenience as a base for the 1994 Lillehammer Winter Olympics.

WINTER HAVEN

Lillehammer looks beautiful on its tourist posters, a darling collection of snowbound wooden chalets grouped around a pretty church with a charming pyramidal spire. But it is actually bigger than that, around 20,000 people, and now, when stripped of its warming white blanket, it looked tired and worn. Many of the noisy downhillers got off the train, with much adjusting of bumbags and re-arranging of sun glasses on to expensive hair styles. A few cross-country skiers got on and sat quietly. One group were loading *pulks* (small sleds pulled by skiers to carry provisions for several days), while a single skier was bringing a smaller *pulk* along with a dog, complete with harness, that would tow it for him.

A few minutes north of Lillehammer the train crosses a tight gorge, with a stunning waterfall, on a bridge under which any self-respecting Troll would want to live, and soon we passed the main downhill skiing area, with its lifts and drags. The cross-country skiers looked the other

way, brooding quietly on a generation gone wrong.

The conductor appeared, a large, jovial man keen to talk to us. Our tickets had not been checked when we got on in Oslo, it being standard Norwegian practice to check them on the train. The conductor was a lifetime NSB employee, a man in love with railways. He asked where we were going, and when we told him of our plan to spend a few days on the Kungsleden (King's Way) trail in Sweden's Abisko National Park, a far-away look came into his eyes. He told

LEFT, *a tumbling waterfall in the beautiful Gudbrandsdal*

TOP, *a little wooden house in Meløyfjord is dwarfed by the mountains*

ABOVE, *modern offices in Trondheim echo an older building style*

ABOVE, *Bodø lies some 50 miles (80km) north of the Arctic Circle – it is seen here bathed in the golden half-light of the midnight sun*

RIGHT, *the distinctive sharp, black peaks of the Lofoten Islands, a haven for birdlife*

us of the pleasure that cross-country skiing in winter and walking in summer gave him. He was typically Norwegian, helpful and cheerful but a lover of solitude, and a man to whom the physical effort of achieving it is a pleasure rather than a daunting prospect. As he spoke a child crashed into him. Ever since we left Oslo there had been children rushing up and down the carriages, oblivious to everyone. An American teacher, on an exchange visit, told us later that Norwegian parents do not believe in disciplining children other than by reasoned argument, and so they are, she says with obvious despair, an unruly bunch. But no one seemed to mind.

HIGH PEAKS AND GLACIERS

We had now reached Gudbrandsdalen, said by many to be the most beautiful valley in Norway, and usually called the 'Valley of Valleys'. It is a wonderful landscape, the more so for being sprinkled with centuries-old wooden farmhouses, scrupulously maintained in original condition. At Ringebu the view broadens out and the first high peaks and glaciers come into view. Here there is another working turntable, necessitated by the single track line.

The view continued to dominate the trip as

the train passed through the little village of Dovre, at the foot of the mountains which give this railway its name – the Dovrebanen, or Dovre Line. The village lies just to the south of Dombås, where the track divides. The western spur is the Rauma Line, leading to Åndalsnes in Romsdal, one of Norway's most beautiful areas.

But we were heading north, the line climbing over a pass and descending through country that was now more tundra-like, with stunted birch trees and mountain huts dotted across the snow. Occasionally we passed a lone skier, and once we saw a man ice-fishing (fishing through a hole drilled in the ice of a frozen lake). That made us think of food and we made our way to the café bar. The train has a reasonable trolley service for drinks and snacks, while the bar, which has a sizeable lounge area, sells more substantial food – the open sandwiches that are a national speciality and microwaved cheeseburgers that are not. The tundra floated by, the snow sometimes broken by the tracks of elk or reindeer. The animals are often seen, we were told, but we were not lucky, though we did see a pair of arctic hares later on. A refill of coffee and we had reached Trondheim.

The train arrived mid-afternoon, giving us

time to look around the town. The Nidaros Cathedral was begun in the 11th century, though the oldest surviving sections are 12th-century. The coronation of Norwegian kings takes place here, and the Crown Jewels are a popular attraction. There are several fine museums, while the Ringve Botanical Gardens are the most northerly in the world. The old quayside areas, close to the cathedral and at the old fish market, are very picturesque. It was cold and getting much colder as we made our way to the hotel and it was no surprise to find the snow hard and sparkling next day as we headed back to the station. The new train, pulled by a Bo-Bo diesel engine that was built by the same company that built the previous day's electric engine, left on time, hauling its quiet way along the side of the Trondheimsfjord to reach the point where the line divides, one branch heading east into Sweden and ours going north through Stjørdal and on to Levanger. The countryside was looking pretty again, with snowy peaks beyond the long lake of Snåsavatnet.

At Grong we met an old friend, Magne Raum. Almost 60 years ago Magne spent time in north-east Greenland trapping arctic fox, and a while ago we had been back to Greenland with him. His eyes sparkled now as we talked of that trip and of mutual friends. Too soon we had to be on our way again and he waved us off, his smiling face set below a tea-cosy bobble hat.

Outside a sudden snow flurry obscures the view as we recall some of Magne's stories. To spend several months alone in one of the world's harshest spots, living by hunting, is beyond the comprehension of many of us today. Magne survived encounters with polar

bears and a fall into the sea through thin ice. Norway breeds a tough character, we were thinking, as we watched the arctic landscape go by from the luxury of our heated carriage.

We turned to reading or dozing, and came to just as the train was crawling up to Støndi and the Arctic Circle. The Circle is marked on the track's east side by a strange pyramid of pebbles that holds a metal globe-frame aloft. Behind the cairn stands the Polar Museum. Both the cairn and the museum can be reached by bus from Bolna or Lønsdal, but that does mean having to wait for another train.

ABOVE LEFT, *this sign-board in the centre of Narvik puts the town in its place*

ABOVE RIGHT, *the monument to Svarte Bjørn in Narvik*

TOP RIGHT, *the Swedish mining town of Kiruna, its spoil heaps rising from the snowy landscape like a great ocean liner*

RIGHT, *drill in hand, a fisherman prepares to go out on the Arctic ice*

North now, the landscape is genuinely arctic, the train more frequently travelling in snow galleries and tunnels built to avoid the line being blocked by drifts. We were sitting and drinking some coffee in silence when a longish sentence in Norwegian came over the speakers. Not speaking the language we assumed it was another station announcement. Wrong: we should have noted the man opposite taking a hold of his bottle. Suddenly the train lurched as it hit a snowdrift – the same snowdrift that the voice had just warned us about. All the engines have snowploughs below their buffers, and blind bends and tunnels mean that trains occasionally drive into drifts at high speed. In future we would take heed, but in the meantime we set about mopping up our spilt coffee.

LEAVING THE LINE

We got off at Fauske, a stop before the line's end at Bodø. Outside the station the Togbus was waiting to take us to Narvik where the railway line restarts. As it was late we were not looking forward to another five hours on the move, but the bus drive was magnificent, a magical journey through rugged mountains on a road cut with great skill and enthusiasm. The bus stopped twice for refreshments, and the ride also included a 20-minute ferry crossing of Tysfjorden. We leant on the rail and watched the sun falling towards the Lofoten Islands. This must be one of the most beautiful places on earth. And one of the coldest too.

The Narvik-to-Kiruna railway was built to transport Swedish iron ore to the sea, Sweden's Baltic ports being frozen in winter while the Norwegian ports remain ice-free. Construction started in 1898, the 100-mile (160km) track, through some of Europe's most hostile country, taking four years to complete, with work virtually impossible in winter because of the snow, the cold and the long arctic night. The navvies who built the line are remembered each year in a week-long festival in February and March. In Narvik there is also a statue to Svarte Bjørn ('Black Bear'), the workers' female cook who was legendary for her commitment to feeding the hundreds of men in all weather conditions. It is said that without the Black Bear, a dark-haired local girl named Anna Hofstad, there would have been no railway.

PRACTICAL INFORMATION

■ There are several trains a day covering the seven-hour journey from Oslo to Trondheim. Trains also run daily from Trondheim to Fauske and Bodø (approximately ten hours), and from Narvik to Kiruna (approximately three hours), but not quite so frequently.

■ There are no border formalities as the train crosses the Norwegian–Swedish border.

■ The train is heavily booked at all times of year, carrying skiers in winter and tourists in summer. Bookings are especially heavy over Easter, the most popular of Norwegian holidays. It is, therefore, always advisable to book. Travelling in summer has the advantage of moving north to the Midnight Sun, while winter offers a fairy-tale landscape of ice-bound mountains and snow-loaded trees.

■ The train is operated by Norges Statsbaner (NSB), the Norwegian state railway. Details of the Togbus from Fauske to Narvik are given in the train timetable.
In Norway tickets for the trains and the Togbus can be bought (and seats reserved) at any station or travel agent. Tickets for the catamaran *Hurtingbåt* and steamer *Hurtigruta*, operating between Bodø, Svolvær and Narvik, are best booked through a travel agent (reisebyrå). Abroad, all bookings can be made through a travel agent or any office of the Norwegian State Railways.
In Britain the NSR is at 21–4 Cockspur Street, London SW1Y 5DA. Tel: (0171) 930 6666. Fax: (0171) 321 0624.

Kiruna and its iron ore fields have seen a decline, but multi-truck trains still passed ours as we made the phenomenal climb out of Narvik and up to the Swedish border. There were no border formalities, nor any mark at the trackside to note our passage into Sweden. That morning at Narvik the train had filled with cross-country skiers. Many set down at Bjørnfjell, the last stop in Norway, though many more stayed on for a further ten minutes to reach Vassijaure in Sweden. There were no formalities at either station, and none at Abisko 30 minutes later.

Abisko was where we would be staying but first we wanted to see Kiruna, so we stayed aboard and enjoyed the Lapland scenery for 60 minutes more. Kiruna is a sad place: once a rich mining town, now depressed and with high unemployment. It is trying to become a centre for cross-country skiing and deserves to succeed, if only to please the cheerful waitresses in the café where we drank coffee and waited for the train back to Abisko. We had a refill, and then another. You see, the Narvik-to-Kiruna train is the only one without a bar or coffee trolley.

Federal capital, it is to some extent relinquishing this role. Bonn is also celebrated as the birthplace of Ludwig van Beethoven in 1770, and every third year is marked by an international festival. The city, with its splendid view of the Siebengebirge or Seven Mountains, remains a delightful mixture of charming baroque façades and palaces and a modern thrusting, bustling area of skyscrapers and high-rise apartments. Because we wanted to see the Siebengebirge, we left our train at Bonn to take

a tram across the Rhine to the resort of Königswinter. From here we took a little electric train up the Drachenfelsbahn to the summit of the Drachenfels (the Dragon's Rock), one of the seven peaks and a famous landmark. There are breathtaking views from the top, downstream towards Bonn and Cologne and to the east towards the dense woods of the Siebengebirge Nature Reserve (Naturpark), while away up the valley much of our journey stretched out before us, with the broad, silver-grey ribbon of the

spectacular crags, extensive Roman remains and medieval legends.

Back in Königswinter, we were faced with a choice. We could go back to Bonn by tram and take the ferry across the river to Bonn Mehlem Station in order to rejoin the Left Bank train for Koblenz, or, as we in fact chose to do, take the railway up the Right Bank, passing the spa resort of Bad Honnef, Unkel with its orchards, Linz and Bad Hönningen, all attractive small wine resorts on the banks of the river. To our left lay the densely wooded slopes of the Nature Park Rhein-Westerwald, a popular area for walking, and then we worked our way past the larger, more industrialized town of Neuwied before crossing the 650 yards (600m) long bridge over the Rhine at Engers, to rejoin the main line a little downstream from Koblenz.

THE CARGO ROUTE INTO EUROPE

The direct, fast line on the Left Bank passes through the suburbs to the resort of Bad Godesberg and joins the riverside at Rolandswerth, with grand views across the river to the Siebengebirge. Sharing the bank with the main road and the Rhine cycleway, it passes the little harbour of Oberwinter, where Rhine barges can usually be seen unloading their cargo. The Rhine is a major European freight artery and there is always a seemingly never-ending procession of single or sometimes tandem or even quadrupled barges making their way along the river, laden with oil, coal, building materials, chemicals and containers. Boat owners live on board their barges, and often not only bicycles but even the family car can be seen on deck.

This constant flow of river traffic reflects an ancient tradition of river transport. Until the early part of this century, gigantic rafts were used to transport huge quantities of timber from the forests of the Upper Rhine to the Low Countries. These were mentioned by Julius Caesar in his writings, and a 13th-century customs roll at Koblenz stresses their importance since they paid as much toll as the largest ships of their day. Later these rafts became enormous floating wooden islands, made of thousands of logs fastened together, often as big as a small village. An 18th-century writer describes one of these as 1000 feet (300m) wide and 90 feet (27m) across with a dozen roomy huts in the middle, complete with a crew of 400–500. Gargantuan supplies to feed the crew were required, including meat on the hoof for consumption during the voyage. The rafts also carried a series of anchors to negotiate the difficult curves and currents on the Rhine and to

ABOVE, *the Drachenfelsbahn is a pleasant diversion from Königswinter – built in 1883, it is Germany's oldest rack railway*

LEFT, *travelling below the extraordinary Rhine Castle of Stolzenfels, almost too Gothick to be true*

river, its parallel roads and its two twin-track railways along either bank. It is an awe-inspiring river, 820 miles (1320km) long, yet accessible in every sense. The writer Heinrich von Kleist called it 'Nature's pleasure grounds', and it does indeed offer an astonishing variety of features: romantic castles and dramatic hilltop fortresses, vineyards looking in spring like patches of green corduroy, riverside towns and villages colour-washed in whites, creams and pinks, elegant spa towns offering curative mineral waters,

Scotland's Scenic West Highland Line

PAUL ATTERBURY

The West Highland line from Glasgow to Mallaig was opened in two stages, from Glasgow to Fort William in 1894, and from Fort William to the port of Mallaig in 1901. Built initially to serve the west of Scotland fish trade, the line was, from its early days, popular with tourists, and it is tourism that keeps the trains running today. The route is through spectacular Highland scenery, ranging from the Clyde and Loch Lomond to mountains and wild moorland, lochs and rivers. The magnificent views throughout, as well as the dramatic selection of viaducts, tunnels, cuttings and steep climbs, make this one of the best railway journeys in Britain.

WITH A SCREAM from its whistle the black locomotive, wheels skidding slightly on the wet rails, eased the long train out of the platform. As we cleared the station rain poured on to the windows, flattening the smoke and steam that drifted past. Gathering speed, the locomotive settled into that particular panting rhythm so evocative of the steam age, hauling its train into the heavy mist. It was a typical Highland morning in Fort William, where we had broken our journey with an overnight stay. You can always take a day return on the Glasgow-to-Mallaig West Highland line, but it is better to take more time to enjoy the route and its magnificent scenery.

RIGHT, *steam excursions are a summertime feature of this beautiful route through some of Scotland's finest scenery*

FAR RIGHT, *heading westwards along the shore of tranquil Loch Eilt*

We had left Glasgow the previous day, the sun shining as the train ran along beside the Clyde. The line follows the river for some time, with views of Dumbarton, Newark Castle, the old resort of Dunoon and Holy Loch, and then swings north along the shores of Gare Loch to Garelochhead and the Faslane submarine base before crossing inland to Loch Long, climbing

steadily high above the water. At the head of Loch Long is the pretty resort of Arrochar, with one of the decorative timber stations characteristic of the line. From Arrochar the train leaves the salt waters of the sea lochs for the fresh water of Loch Lomond, and for the next few miles there are wonderful views out across the loch to the woods and sheer rock walls of its eastern shore. Plenty of boats were out making the most of the fine day, and the waterfalls crashing down towards the loch were a reminder of recent heavy rain.

It is a steady climb up towards Crianlarich, the junction with the line westwards to Oban, and with each mile the scenery becomes more exciting. Scotland is all about light, and when the sun comes out, at any time of year, the range of colours in the landscape is breathtaking. When the sun goes, that particular magic disappears, hidden by the dominant greys and browns. In the late afternoon sun the richly varied landscape was looking its best.

Dwarfed by Beinn Odhar and Beinn Dorain,

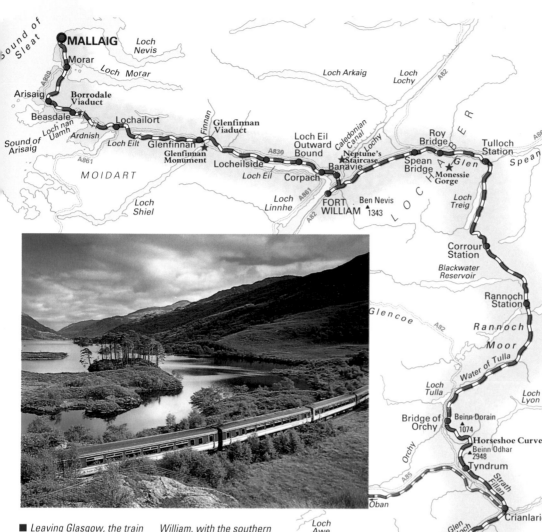

remote region of peat bogs, heather, secret streams and lochs, caused great problems to the builders of the West Highland line. In the event, they floated the line on a bed of brushwood, which then supported tons of ash and earth. Nearly a century later, trains are still crossing the moor on its floating tracks.

Famous for its heavy engineering, the Mallaig line was expensive and slow to build. To save costs the contractor in charge, Robert MacAlpine, pioneered the use of concrete as a structural material on a grand scale, earning himself the nickname 'Concrete Bob'. His first major challenge was the Glenfinnan viaduct, a curving series of 21 arches that carry the railway high above the rocky Finnan valley. This was the first time concrete had been used for such a structure anywhere in the world, and the viaduct's scale and lasting elegance have long underlined MacAlpine's foresight. Other impressive viaducts are those at Loch nan Uamh and Morar, while the castellated façade of Borrodale viaduct, added to please the local landowner, conceals what was at the time of its building the largest single-span concrete arch in the world.

■ Leaving Glasgow, the train runs beside the Clyde and then follows the shores of Gare Loch, Loch Long and Loch Lomond. It then makes its way up Glen Falloch, crossing wild mountain streams against a backdrop of mighty hills, to Crianlarich. Clinging to the steep valley sides, it rounds the Horseshoe Curve before leaving the mountains to cross Rannoch Moor. Cutting through rocky gorges and narrow valleys, the line winds its way down to Fort William, with the southern horizon increasingly dominated by Ben Nevis. With towering hills and mountains all around, the train runs along Loch Eil and the route is then a continuing series of dramatic tunnels, cuttings and viaducts through a spectacular landscape. From Lochailort, the line winds high above the rocky coast, with fine views out to the Atlantic, before dropping down to Mallaig. The huge plateau of Rannoch Moor, a wild and

the Fort William line clings to the rocky mountainside high above the river valley as it rounds a dramatic horseshoe curve, with great viaducts at each end. To the west a wild area of woods and moorland is framed by distant hills and mountains. After Bridge of Orchy the line runs high above Loch Tulla and then turns east to enter Rannoch Moor. Covering some 60 square miles (50sq km) and surrounded by a ring of distant hills, Rannoch is a wide expanse of heather moorland, broken by hillocks, boulders and peat-coloured streams. This is wild

PREVIOUS PAGE, *this spectacular scenic line links populous Glasgow with some of the most wild and remote regions of the western Highlands*

PREVIOUS PAGE INSET, *the Auch Gleann viaduct on the horseshoe curve, near Bridge of Orchy*

RIGHT, *a closer view of the statue on the imposing Jacobite monument at the head of Loch Shiel*

BELOW, *a steam excursion train rounds the curve of the famous Glenfinnan viaduct*

FAR RIGHT, *the fishing harbour of Mallaig is the end of the line – but the gateway to the Western Isles, including Skye*

and desolate country, the landscape of Robert Louis Stevenson's famous novel *Kidnapped.*

AN EERIE LANDSCAPE

At the heart of the moor, and completely isolated, is Rannoch Station, not a place to miss the train. The empty landscape continues to Corrour, where the line climbs to its highest point, 1350 feet (411m) above sea level. The descent begins alongside Loch Treig. As the waters narrow, the train enters the rocky Glen Spean, and soon after leaving Tulloch it thunders along a narrow ledge cut through the vertical walls of the Monessie Gorge. Far below, the white water crashes among the rocks. From here the landscape opens out again and Ben Nevis increasingly dominates the horizon during the approach to Fort William via Roy Bridge and Spean Bridge, the latter famous for the memorial to the Commando forces, many of whom trained in the surrounding Highland countryside.

The next morning in Fort William looked unpromising. The rain fell steadily and the mountains had vanished under layers of grey mist as we set out to explore the town. Set up as a military base in 1654 by Cromwell's General Monck, Fort William was originally called Inverlochy. Renamed in honour of William of Orange, it remained little more than a garrison until the completion of Telford's Caledonian Canal in 1822. The emphasis then switched to trade and tourism, with the latter gradually

gaining the upper hand thanks largely to the presence of Ben Nevis, whose towering walls appealed greatly to the Victorian sense of the picturesque. Despite its tendency to attract rain and mist, Ben Nevis still brings the tourists to Fort William.

The dripping rain quickly dispelled whatever slight appeal the souvenir and craft shops may have had, and we made our way early to the station, a very unpicturesque modern building. The train stood ready in the platform and at its head, surrounded by photographers and clouds of damp steam, stood *Black Five* locomotive number 44871, one of the few survivors of a famous pre-war design by the chief engineer of the London, Midland and Scottish Railway, William Stannier. We did our share of staring at the highly polished hissing beast, and then took our places and sat back to enjoy the drama of the departure, and the noises and smells of the steam age.

THE WHEELS OF INDUSTRY

The difficult and expensive task of building railway lines across the western Highlands during the last years of the 19th century was a reflection of the fierce competition that then existed for the fish and tourist trades between Scotland's leading railway companies, the Caledonian and the North British. The West Highland line had reached Fort William in 1894 but it took another six years, vast sums of shareholders' money and government subsidy to complete the 40-mile (64km) section to the coastal port of Mallaig. Heavily engineered throughout, the route included 11 tunnels,

several major viaducts and steep gradients. At last, on 2 April 1901, the *Glasgow Herald* was able to write: 'Now the shrill sound of the railway whistle breaks the stillness of Morar and Mallaig, new glories of West Highland scenery are opened up for the insatiable tourist'.

Packed with the equally insatiable descendants of these Edwardian tourists, the train puffed and clanked out of Fort William and then rattled over the antique swing bridge that carries the line over the Caledonian Canal at Banavie. To the right is Telford's famous staircase of locks that marks the start of the canal's long journey across Scotland to Inverness. Next comes the aluminium smelter and paper mill at Corpach – industries that in their time saved both Fort William and the railway from terminal decline – and then the train sets off along the shore of Loch Eil. The mist lay heavily on the water, hiding the famous views of Ben Nevis. The locomotive galloped along, pausing only briefly, making the most of

the 12-mile (19km) level beside the loch. At the head of Loch Eil the line climbs sharply before crossing the River Finnan at the head of Loch Shiel on the famous curving Glenfinnan viaduct, over 1000 feet (300m) long. It was from here onwards that the 3000 navvies who toiled to build the line with their picks and shovels earned their keep. Sometimes the track was floated across peat bog, sometimes blasted through solid rock in a series of dramatic cuttings and tunnels. On a good day Bonnie Prince Charlie's monument can clearly be seen down in the valley at the marshy head of Loch Shiel, the tall column crowned with its 1831 statue of the prince, a memorial to all those who took part in the 1745 rising.

With the locomotive's rhythmic bark echoing through the hills, the train continued upwards to Glenfinnan Station and then, crossing the watershed, it wound through rocky cuttings and past Loch Eilt to Lochailort, following the river that runs down to the sea in the Sound of Arisaig. With the Atlantic far below, the line crosses the dramatic landscape by a series of tunnels and viaducts, some of which follow directly one upon the other. The most spectacular is at Borrodale, high above the point where Bonnie Prince Charlie first landed on the Scottish mainland, a viaduct enriched with battlements. Yet this decorative stonework is merely a façade concealing a single-span concrete arch.

FROM THE MOUNTAINS TO THE SEA

As the train wound its way down towards Arisaig the mist began to lift, allowing us a glimpse of the islands of Eigg, Rhum and Skye, a tantalizing hint of the wonderful view on a clear day. Leaving behind the remote mountains, inhabited at the time of the line's building by fewer than ten people per square mile, we made our way across an attractive landscape of green hills, clumps of trees, white cottages and, far below, sandy bays. Turning north, the line now runs beside the sandy Morar Estuary, with Loch Morar to the east. This, the deepest loch in Scotland, is said to be the home of Morag, a close relative of the monster that lurks in Loch Ness. A few more rocky cuttings followed and then the locomotive eased back, steam hissing from the safety valve, for the last stretch into Mallaig along the shore of the Sound of Sleat, with seagulls echoing the scream of the whistle.

Mallaig, its harbour still busy with fishing boats, was created by the railway, and although it is many years since the trains carried the herring catches southwards to market, it is still dependent upon the railway and the visitors it brings. Many take the ferry to Skye, whose rounded peaks face the quay.

After its brief respite, the rain was now redoubling its efforts but undaunted we set off to explore the streets of whitewashed houses.

PRACTICAL INFORMATION

■ Scotrail, a division of British Rail, runs about five trains each way between Glasgow and Mallaig on weekdays, three on Sunday. The 164-mile (264km) journey takes at least 5¼ hours. All trains have a trolley buffet service.

■ Seats should be booked in advance during the peak holiday season or to guarantee a window seat, which is essential. It is better to sit on the left as you travel from Glasgow to Mallaig.

■ Highland colours look good at any time of year, so long as the sun shines, but the line is probably at its best in spring and autumn, and in the winter snow.

■ The special steam-hauled service on the Fort William to Mallaig section operates four days a week from June to September. This train, the *Lochaber*, requires a reservation and the payment of a supplement. Bookings can be made at any British Rail station or through a travel agent.

■ Alternatively, this line can be explored in Pullman-style comfort on a 'West Highlander' luxury cruise. Details of these weekend excursions can be obtained from Waterman Railways, PO Box 4472, Lichfield, Staffordshire WS13 6RU. Tel: (01543) 254076. Fax: (01543) 250817.

■ In the US, contact the British Tourist Authority at 40 West 57th Street, New York, NY 10019. Tel: 212 581 4700. Fax: 212 265 0649.

Around Southern Spain on the Andalusian Express

DAVID SCOTT

The Al Andalus or Andalusian Express is a luxury train, a 'five-star hotel on wheels' in an elegant style recalling the heyday of Continental train journeys, and offers what is possibly the most expensive rail travel in the world. The train is best known for its journeys around southern Spain to the historic and romantic cities of Andalucía. The circular tour described here began with a trip from Madrid to Seville aboard the highspeed AVE Express train before joining the Al Andalus itself in Seville and moving on to visit Córdoba in the heart of Moorish Spain. From here the train travelled through the fertile vineyards, olive groves and white villages of Andalucía to stop in Granada, home of the famous Alhambra, and then returned to Seville.

MY AL ANDALUS Southern Journey began at Atocha Station, Madrid, terminus of the high speed rail link with Seville. Atocha is a large, bright and airy station with a cool, marble concourse, part of which is given over to an oasis of palm trees and

FAR RIGHT, *Al Andalus offers a most luxurious way to see southern Spain – this is one of the double suites*

RIGHT, *travel on this train is a gastronomic delight, and the excellent food and wine are very much part of the fun*

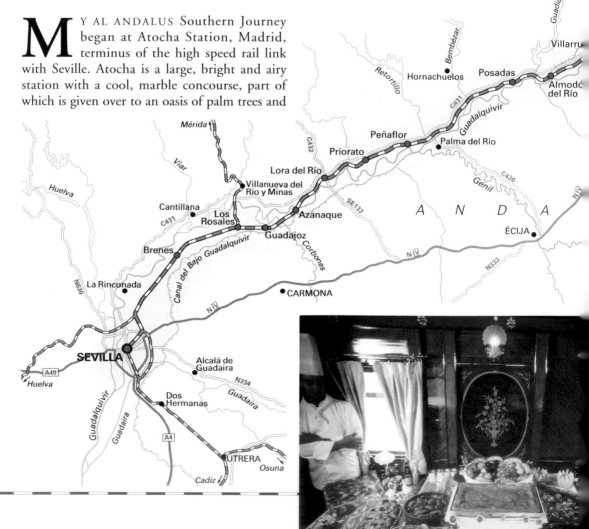

other sub-tropical plants. I waited there for my train, enjoying the greenery and that mild but distinctive smell of Spain that is reminiscent of freshly ground coffee and Turkish cigarettes.

Passengers join the Al Andalus train in Seville, but those arriving in Spain at Madrid are booked to travel Club Class on the AVE Madrid-to-Seville express. I met my fellow travellers for the first time in the AVE club departure lounge, where, airport style, we booked in our luggage before boarding the train. The front of the clinical white-coloured AVE (Alta Velocidad Espanola) electric train has a bullet nose sloping to a duck's beak wedge. It pulls narrow, streamlined carriages fitted with aircraft-style seats. Tray meals and drinks are served from a trolley pushed down the aisle by a hostess, and an 'in flight' film is shown on video screens in each carriage. The 292-mile (470km) journey is completed in 2 hours 45 minutes. A fellow (Spanish) passenger told me that with this rail link, Andalucía's future was no longer to be that of an undiscovered region known only to the middle-class, independent traveller. It was to

become the Los Angeles of Europe!

The train pulled out of the station, smooth and quiet on the rails. The surprisingly low skyline of Madrid quickly passed us by and we started out across the hot, sparsely cropped plain on which the city stands. Occasionally villages of white and sand-brown houses roofed with faded red tiles silently came and went from view. The earth grew redder as we sped south towards Seville. We passed a seemingly endless stretch of olive trees standing in rows that extended to the horizon, a potential ocean of olive oil.

The train slowed through Córdoba. On a patch of grass in a park near the railway I saw a couple lying on the ground, kissing passionately. Near by two men, one leaning on a moped and the other a sweating jogger getting his breath back, ignored them

■ The Al Andalus Southern Journey travels through the heart of Moorish Spain, the homeland of much that we think of as quintessentially Spanish. Flamenco singing and dancing, bullfighting, sherry bodegas and extravagant religious festivals are all native to this region. The food and wine enjoyed on board, the urban and rural landscape beyond the window, and the excursions taken off the train, all part of the Al Andalus journey, give an authentic flavour of definitively Spanish Andalucía.

Andalucía remained a feudal, agricultural society long after anywhere else in Europe and it is a region that retains much of its original natural beauty. There are landscapes of yellow ochre earth lined with ranks of olive trees, fields of wheat with horsemen on the horizon, dazzlingly white hilltop villages and historic cities. Orange and lemon trees, jasmine bushes, palms and other semi-tropical shrubs thrive beneath the bright blue sky.

The Southern Journey is punctuated by a triangle of stops at the three dramatic and solitary cities of Seville, Córdoba and Granada. Seville is home of the biggest Gothic church in the world. Simultaneously gloomy and spectacular, its spires act as useful landmarks if you get lost in the cobbled alleyways and squares of the old part of the city.

Córdoba, visited on the second day and the northernmost city of the journey, is more compact and, although built originally by the Romans, more Arabic in style than Seville. The Christian-Muslim history of Córdoba is echoed in its Mezquita-Catedral (mosque-cathedral). This is an enormous building with a bleak exterior but an inspiring mystical interior of marbled pillars and exquisitely decorated arches and ceilings.

Granada is the last stop before the return of Al Andalus to Seville. It lies at the foot of the Sierra Nevada mountains, snow-capped even in the heat of June. Granada is justly famous for the Alhambra Palace and the beautiful Generalife Islamic gardens which sit high on a promontory overlooking the city.

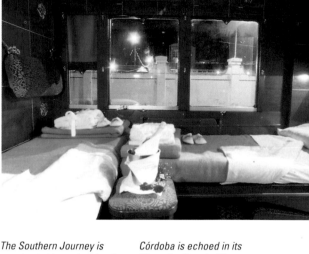

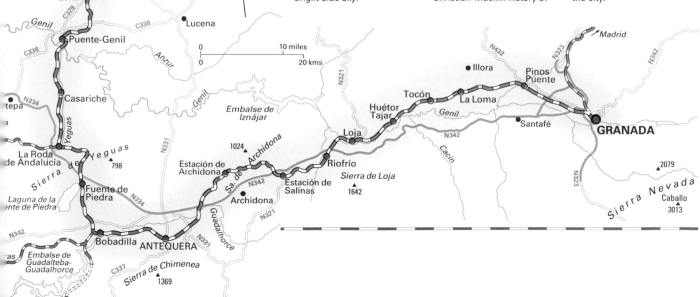

RIGHT, *Seville, starting point of the Al Andalus journey and home of Expo 92, is no stranger to world fairs – the splendid Plaza de España is a legacy of the 1929 Ibero-Américana Exhibition*

completely. Public displays of affection are a common sight in new Spain. For me it was embarrassing, but perhaps this behaviour is a reaction to the moral strictures of the Franco era. I had earlier read in a British newspaper that during the 36 years of dictatorship under the late General Franco, intolerance unquestionably became a characteristic of Spanish society. Nowadays, however, Spaniards are almost obsessively determined to avoid censure of anything – other perhaps than racism, terrorism and corruption.

The AVE express pulled into one of the pale concrete platforms of Santa Justa Estación, Sevilla. Above us the steel-framed, curved glass roof let in shafts of dazzling sunlight. The Al Andalus couriers guided our party across the station to a quiet, shaded siding where the Al Andalus awaited and where we were to spend our first night aboard.

OF ROYAL DESCENT

The square-shaped brown and cream carriages are the widest of any train in Europe, and Medina Azahara, the club and reception car in which we were welcomed and given our compartment keys, was spacious as well as ornate. Built in Spain in 1930, its plushly fitted interior was resplendent with leather upholstered chairs, veneer inlaid, polished wood tables, bevelled glass and walnut panelling.

The five sleeping cars began life in France in the 1920s, bearing royalty and the nobility of Europe on their Continental travels. Restored in Spain in the late 1960s to the original *belle époque* style, the carriages each hold two spacious double suites with private shower and toilet, and six smaller two-berth compartments with shower/dressing rooms in a separate carriage.

The upper bunk in my two-berth cabin was folded flush to the wall and the bottom bed (a daytime seat) had been made up with crisp white sheets and soft woollen blankets. There was good air conditioning, but to get some fresh air – and finding it hard to resist the temptation to try out the large, old fashioned brass

handle that operated the mechanism – I lowered the window.

The cream, domed roof of the cabin was fitted with four art deco flower-shaped lampshades. The walls were panelled in walnut. Two fitted, outward curving doors opened to reveal a wash basin and mirror, a well-equipped wash bag, towels and a bath robe. There were drawers for underwear and a zipped, hanging canvas wardrobe for suits and dresses. During the day dress can be casual, but more formal attire is encouraged for the evenings and men are requested to wear a jacket and tie for dinner. So I changed.

We ate in the Alhambra restaurant, one of two sumptuously furnished dining-cars built in 1929 in France and transferred to Spain in 1941. I sat with Dave, a photo-journalist from San Diego and Will, a retired but prosperous and well-travelled computer and telephone cable salesman from Los Angeles. Most of our 25-strong party were American, with a sprinkling of English, Belgian and Spanish guests. Many were retired or rich enough not to need to work.

Dinner was served formally and with style by the Spanish staff. A selection of prawns deep fried in batter, smoked salmon, chicken croquettes, *terrine de foie* and tiny mushroom tarts was offered as a first course. Crayfish with vinaigrette sauce and a main dish of fillet of steak with baby stuffed tomatoes followed. To accompany the meal we chose a Rioja Tinto from the extensive, well-chosen but slightly expensive wine list. Baked Alaska, fresh fruit, coffee and *petits fours* ended the meal. After dinner some people prolonged the evening drinking and dancing in the Giralda bar carriage, originally a Wagons-Lits restaurant car, built in 1928 for luxury European trains. I went to bed, however, pleased to enjoy the quiet and luxury of my own compartment.

ECHOES OF AN EMPIRE

In the morning, after breakfast, we were taken on a short guided tour of Seville. The bus drove us alongside the Guadalquivir River, past one end of the dramatic Seville Expo 92 site – the first world fair since Osaka in 1970 – past the 18th-century bullring, the new opera house and on to the entrance of the dauntingly huge Seville Cathedral. It was begun in 1402 when the city Fathers, who paid for its construction, declared their intention of creating a structure so large that men would look at it and think them mad. The immensity of the interior certainly rendered in me a keen sense of my own insignificance.

The 322 feet (98m) high Giralda, originally built as a minaret but later turned into a bell tower; the Alcazar, the remains of an extensive royal palace built by Peter the Cruel; the Alcazar Gardens, a quiet hideaway behind high crenellated brick walls; and the 18th-century university building that was once a cigar factory and the setting of Bizet's *Carmen*, 'Seville's most famous woman', were our next stops before a rest in the gardens of the Plaza de America.

Several pairs of snow white doves were introduced into the Plaza in 1929 to celebrate the opening of Seville's first world fair. Nowadays their many descendants flock, whirl, bunch and fight for the corn sold by local vendors to tourists who wish to feed the birds. I found the sight quite menacing but for others it was obviously a great 'photo opportunity'.

The last stop on our tour of Seville was at the Casa de Pilato on calle Aquilas in the centre of the city. It is an inspiring two-storey Renaissance palace, built in 1480 by Pedro Enriques de Ribera ostensibly in the style of the Roman villa of Pontius Pilate. Happily, one of the architects, a Muslim, introduced a degree of Islamic symmetry and spaciousness which lifts the heaviness of the elaborate ceilings and stucco walls designed by the Mudéjars (Moorish artisans working under Christian control). The combination of Moorish and European sensibilities is appealing and could well act as a metaphor for Seville itself.

We returned to the train for lunch. The seven-course repast occupied most of the afternoon, while the train carried us up the Guadalquivir Valley to Córdoba. It was a surreal experience to be eating a gourmet meal in such gracious surroundings while outside the window were passing fields of corn, sunflowers and wheat, grasslands speckled with red poppies and groves of olive, orange and lemon trees, with mules standing motionless in patches of shade or plodding wearily along stony tracks.

Slowly I ate my way through cream of asparagus soup, shellfish mousse, fresh salmon and endive salad, hake in wine sauce, cheese, pastries and fruit. The meal reminded me that the Arabs, through the gateway of Andalucía, introduced to Europe foods such as almonds, sweet oranges, banana plants, date palms and sugar cane (originally from the Nile Valley but well suited to the semi-tropical regions of the lower Guadalquivir Valley). Meanwhile outside, the pastoral scenes that we were rolling past saw some of the bloodiest battles between El Cid and the Muslim infidels during the Moorish occupation of Spain.

A LAND OF CONTRASTS

While I digested my lunch I read an article about Spain and the Spanish in which the writer concluded that it is hard for an outsider to know what they are really like. For, although the different regions that we know as Spain have been governed by the same rulers for five centuries and during that time the various people have inter-married and swopped cultural and social ideas, Spain is too diverse a country to be susceptible to generalization. Thus 'Ethnic and linguistic differences, poor communications, a varied climate, a geography divided by mountains and a history fractured by religion have all combined to produce immense regional disparities in temp-erament and custom. What separates

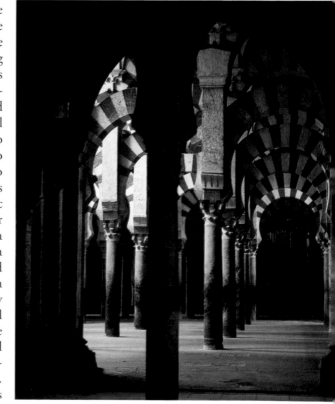

BELOW, *the massive, exotic double-arches of the Mezquita-Catedral (mosque-cathedral) in Córdoba*

FAR RIGHT, TOP, *the elegant 'Alhambra' dining car, glowing with polished, inlaid wood and gleaming brass*

FAR RIGHT, BELOW, *the remarkable Alhambra Palace stands high above Granada*

BELOW, *shady cloisters in the Generalife, Granada, once the sultans' summer palace*

Galicians, Asturians, Basques, Catalans, Castilians, Valencians, Andalusians and Canarians is arguably as great as what unites them. Indeed, there are times when one feels that Spain is a sort of Western Europe in miniature, with a dash of Latin American thrown in.' Certainly Andalucía feels very different from other parts of Spain.

MOORS AND MOSQUES

The Mezquita-Catedral (mosque-cathedral) in Córdoba is one of the few tourist destinations that really live up to the expectations often engendered by overly enthusiastic guidebooks. It is a massive and awe inspiring structure, built in stages by successive caliphs from AD785 onwards. Enter the mosque from the exterior Court of Orange Trees, and one is presented with a kaleidoscopic vision of row upon row of marble, jasper and porphyry pillars supporting two tiers of arches of white stone and red brick, under ceilings decorated with myriad mathematically designed patterns. The effect is dreamlike and mystical. Sadly this feeling is lost when one comes upon the 16th-century Roman Catholic cathedral actually constructed in the middle of the mosque (after the removal of 63 central columns). The Gothic church, black-hearted and gloomy, sits very uneasily amid the quiet meditative air of the Moorish colonnades. Fortunately the mosque is huge enough to allow a visitor to ignore even the intrusion of an ugly cathedral.

After the cathedral our guide took us around the Jewish quarter, the castle and gardens and several private courtyards, well-known locally for their exotic displays of potted plants and shrubs. We then returned by bus to the train, which had been shunted into a siding outside the village of

Villafranca, 11 miles (18km) from Córdoba. Immediately we had boarded, the train set off for Granada. I showered and changed for dinner.

Don Juan, Andalucía's original Latin lover, was a 17th-century nobleman who in later life repented of his sins and founded a charity hospital. It occurred to me that this combination of Dionysian living and religious practice had a parallel in our lives aboard the sybaritic Al Andalus and our pilgrimage-like visits to the famous mosques and churches of Seville, Córdoba and later Granada.

The train continued travelling through dinner and into the night, heading south through an increasingly mountainous landscape.

I awoke to the sound of a whistle blowing, and the noise of a train leaving a station. I lifted the blind on my window and looked out. The Al Andalus was standing at a platform in Granada Station and opposite a commuter train was pulling away. To the south-east, from the corridor window, I could see the snow-capped mountains of the Sierra Nevada.

I had enjoyed breakfast aboard the train the previous day but today I had the extra treat of a view of the mountains from my window seat, as well as the pleasure of freshly squeezed orange juice, hot croissants and coffee. There was cooked food available – but after the previous night's dinner, a light breakfast was quite sufficient.

I sat with Dave again and he told me that, in the course of his photographic assignments, he had been to over 100 countries. Such was

the widespread ecological damage and poverty he had seen that he felt only a technological miracle could save the world from great suffering. The thought was an uncomfortable one in our opulent surroundings and I felt very aware of the privilege I was fortunate enough to be enjoying.

The Alhambra and Generalife Gardens occupy a promontory which hangs over the flat plain on which Granada stands. It is a haven of calm and beauty above the seething traffic of the city below. We spent the morning on a guided tour, firstly of the Renaissance palace that is part of the Alhambra complex of buildings and then of the fountains, pools and blooming plants of the Arabic designed gardens. We then returned to the train for lunch and a final afternoon on board while we travelled westwards back to Seville, through the mountains and down on to the plain.

The powerful smell of olive oil as we passed the stainless steel storage tanks of a local co-operative; solitary, white farmsteads sitting on the green horizon; an occasional man riding his mule; a billowing sea of black plastic crop covers and the life-size, white-painted statues of two men in shirt and trousers, like cricket umpires, standing guard as gateposts to the entrance of an

estate – these are just some of the memories and images of that last afternoon, window viewing from the Al Andalus.

In the evening we left the train and went to a restaurant in the medieval town of Carmona in the hills above Seville, for a special Andalusian dinner. The food was excellent and afterwards a Flamenco group composed of young people from Carmona sang and danced for us. Quite unpretentious, they performed with an innocent passion. It was a touching and memorable end to the journey.

PRACTICAL INFORMATION

■ The Al Andalus Southern Journey described here is a trip of four days and three nights, covering a total of approximately 440 miles (705km). In 1993 the journey is to be extended to five days and four nights, with additional stops between Granada and Seville at Málaga, Ronda and Jerez.

■ The Al Andalus makes four separate main tours and it is also called into service for special occasions. It follows the 'Southern Journey' in May/June and September/October. In August it travels to cooler northern Spain for the pilgrimage route known as the Camino de Santiago. July finds it touring the wine producing areas around Pamplona, and in the winter months on the 'Monumental Towns Journey' through Madrid, El Escorial, Avilia, Segovia and Toledo.

■ The Southern Journey is the most popular itinerary, and as accommodation is limited, early booking is advisable. Bookings are made with the Al Andalus agency or through a travel agent in your own country, or from Al Andalus Expresso, Calle Alcalá 44, 28014 Madrid.
Tel: 521 4827/4764.
Fax: 521 4877.
In Britain an agent is Excalibur Holidays, Austin House, 43 Poole Road, Bournemouth, Dorset BH4 9DN.
Tel: 01202 766650.
Fax 01202 767759 .
In the US contact Abercrombie & Kent, 1520 Kensington Road, Oak Brook, Illinois 60521.
Tel: 708 954 2944.
Fax: 708 954 3324.

enjoy the final 21 miles (33km) to Mettuppalaiyam. It is worth moving to a non air-conditioned first class coach, where the windows can be opened to enjoy the morning air and sights.

The sun begins to gild the earth and brighten the white rendering of the small, neat, red-tiled houses, often almost hidden by the trees that provide shade when the sun grows fierce. Boys heave on well pumps as their fathers disappear to squat among bushes on the edge of the village, their privacy rudely broken by the passing train. Pigs begin their search for scraps while dogs stretch and shake off sleep. Bicycles and buses taking people to work or school cluster round the level crossings.

As the ground to the north begins to rise, the first view of the Nilgiris lives up to the expectations raised by their name, Blue Mountains; around dawn the jumbled ranges of hills receding out of sight are a palette of pastel blues. Within ten minutes of sighting the hills, the train is rolling into the island platform at Mettuppalaiyam. It is advisable to be ready to alight the moment the train stops, to cross the platform to the waiting metre-gauge train for Ooty; it has only two First Class compartments, right at the front, and the best seats are the four on the far side from the platform. The front is the opposite end from the locomotive, which remains at the back of the train, propelling its carriages on both adhesion and rack sections.

The railway reached Mettuppalaiyam in 1873, but construction of the line to Ooty by an independent company did not begin until August 1891. Financial difficulties delayed progress, and it was not until 15 June 1899 that the line between Mettuppalaiyam and Coonoor opened under a new company based in London.

At 07.45hrs the Nilagiri Passenger, as the board at the front of the train proclaims, departs from Mettuppalaiyam. Whistling frequently, the train shuffles through the outskirts of the town before crossing the Bhavani River on an impressive girder bridge. Buffaloes and women

ABOVE, *passing high above the road to Coonor, the train pushes its way slowly uphill on the rack*

freshly washed clothes are laid out on the grass to dry.

Diesel traction replaces electric at Jalarpet (Jolarpettai), though no tell-tale sounds permeate the sealed coaches. At Coimbatore, however, the reversal of the train and shunting operations open most eyes to the grey light of early dawn. A drink of tea or coffee from a platform vendor will arouse the senses enough to

washing clothes share the riverbank that forms the boundary of the town, a creation of the railway but now a producer of synthetic gems.

For much of the 4½ miles (7.4km) to the first station, at Kallar, the line carves a straight route through plantations of coconut and areca nut. It is the fomented nut of these tall slender trees that is wrapped in betel vine leaves and placed between the gum and upper lip as an aid to digestion. The residue is spat out, leaving blood-like splashes on the ground.

LEFT, *rack teeth allow the train to tackle the steepest gradients*

BELOW, *the coal-stained crew of engine 37391; this is one of the few all-steam, regular, working routes left in the world*

ON THE RACK

The train's progress over the barely rising ground to Kallar is rapid, but that comes to an end as the rack is engaged soon after the train leaves the station. The fireman descends to watch the pinion engage the rack correctly and has to scramble aboard the ascending locomotive. From here up to the home signal at the approach to Coonoor Station, the rack is continuous except for short sections at the level intermediate stations. It is only just over 12miles (19km) to Coonoor, in which the railway climbs 4363 feet (1330m) on gradients of up to 1:12.5, though the slow pace of about 8mph (13kph) makes it seem much further.

But most passengers would not wish to lose a minute of the journey. From Kallar to Ooty the scenery is of constant interest and delight. It is as though the surveyors who laid out the route were determined that every one of the 208 curves should open up a different view. The thin scrub beyond Kallar soon thickens to become dense forest, which is home to abundant wildlife. Fearless monkeys like the Nilgiri Langur and the bonnet macaques are a frequent sight, but elephants are rarely seen though they do come down on to the line in search of jack fruit.

The mountain slopes become steadily more precipitate as the valley narrows, until passengers are looking across the valley to the left at an almost vertical wall of rock rising up from the jungle floor.

Soon the train stops for water at one of several stopping places *en route*; some are termed stations though there is not even a village remotely near. The British ancestry of the railway can be in no doubt, with names for the halts like Hillgrove, Runneymede and Glendale. At Hillgrove the tiny station boasts a 'Combined Fruit and Vegetarian Light Refreshment Stall' which does a roaring trade for 15 minutes once a day as the entire train descends to savour the view and the cooler air. For those with a mechanical bent, it is an opportunity to examine the locomotive at ground level.

Appropriately the 12 rack locomotives (eight of them in use) were built at Winterthur in Switzerland between 1920 and 1952. Unusually the two central low pressure cylinders that drive the rack pinions can be cut out, allowing the outside high pressure cylinders to power the locomotive by adhesion only. This was necessary as the section beyond Coonoor is not steep enough to warrant the use of a rack.

A whistle ushers everyone back into the train, which on departure plunges straight into one of the 16 tunnels on the line. Its black crown testifies to decades of locomotives slogging up the hills with trains of tired expatriate civil servants or convalescent soldiers, equally eager for a respite from the heat of the plains. They travelled to Ooty not just because of the climate, but for the way it evoked memories of landscapes at home in Britain.

But there is nothing very reminiscent of Britain about the scenery here; the scale alone dwarfs anything that the English Lake District or Scottish Grampians can offer. And between Hillgrove and Runneymede the first tea bushes appear, sometimes on slopes that look steep enough for the pickers to need crampons. It was a Frenchman, M Perrotett, who introduced the first tea bushes in the Nilgiris and his success led to tea becoming the staple crop in the hills.

The climb towards the white-painted tea factory at Glendale and the nearby viaduct provides some of the most spectacular views, enlivened by jacaranda trees ablaze with purple flowers and the delicate pink lantana that grows with abundance beside the line. On the summit of the hills on the opposite side of the valley was one of Tipu Sultan's outposts, to warn of threats to his palace fort at Srirangapatna which was finally overrun in 1799.

Glendale viaduct takes the line across the head of the valley and into a tunnel, in which the locomotive's distinct exhaust beats become a muffled roar. The line negotiates a series of sinuous ledges and cuttings before drawing into the station at Coonoor. Alongside for the first time is the road from Mettuppalaiyam that has twisted and turned through endless hairpin bends beneath the railway; the belching buses and trucks make it a disagreeable way to ascend the Nilgiris; and being at a much lower level, road users naturally enjoy views inferior to those from the railway.

The locomotive barks its way up towards the level crossing, at which point the gradient has eased and the rack ended. The hills around Coonoor provide a fine background to the Victorian station buildings and single terminal platform. The locomotive's supply of coal is all but exhausted, so a fresh engine comes on for the final 12 miles (19km) to Ooty. This allows passengers time to patronize the station tea stall, or to inspect the railway's principal engine shed.

The departure from Coonoor is a theatrical event, with the curtain call provided by the vigorous ringing of the hybrid station bell – a toothed pinion wheel which is hammered with an iron bar. The guards who stand on the front of each coach are the star performers; while the train is on the move their function is to relay warnings or 'all clear' messages from the guard on the front coach to the driver – the curvature of much of the line makes this vital for safety.

Here they indulge in pure histrionics, simultaneously waving their green flags as the train reverses out of the terminal platform. A little history is necessary to explain this procedure. The line to Ooty was opened in 1908, nine years after the first public train reached Coonoor; it proved impossible to extend the level line into the station, so trains have to back out before charging up a 1:25 gradient past the signal box. The noise of the departure from Coonoor can be heard all over the town and surrounding hills. From here to Ooty the engine works on the two outside high-pressure cylinders alone, the inside rack mechanism and cylinders being disengaged.

Between Coonoor and Ooty the scenery is softer than the rack section, the upland plateau providing much more distant views than the

PRACTICAL INFORMATION

■ The Madras-to-
Ootacamund service
operates once daily,
throughout the year.
The 400-mile (640km)
journey takes 16 hours,
with a change at
Mettuppalaiyam, and
advance booking is
advisable.

■ The train from Madras
to Mettuppalaiyam is
divided into First Class AC
(air-conditioned) with
sleeping compartments
providing basin and
bedding, AC 2 Tier 'open'
coaches which have no
compartments but are
inevitably a good way to
meet people (bedding
available for hire at a
nominal cost), and Second
Class. Non air-conditioned
First Class coaches are
also available.

■ The best time of year to
make this journey is either
February to March or
September to October,
when temperatures are
most comfortable.

■ Contact travel agents in
your own country who will
arrange tickets, including
the IndRail passes, and
reservations through the
local Indian Railways
agent.
In Britain the agent for
Indian Railways is
SD Enterprises Ltd,
103 Wembley Park Drive,
Wembley, Middlesex
HA9 8HG.
Tel: (0181) 903 3411.
Fax: (0181) 903 0392.
In the US the agent is
Messrs Hari World
Travels Inc, 30 Rockafeller
Plaza, Shop 21, North
Mezzanine, NY 10112.
Tel: 212 957 3000.

steep valleys further down. Wellington is soon reached, home of the Madras Regiment (the oldest in the Indian army), and the train passes a firing range on the right. Part of the bullets used may have originated in the next town, Aravankadu, where a huge cordite factory fills the valley on the right beneath the railway.

The gentler slopes around Wellington and Aravankadu allow terracing for agriculture, and full advantage is taken of the climate to grow all kinds of vegetables. Much of the line between Aravankadu and Lovedale passes through plantations of eucalyptus, from which oil is extracted in Ooty. Recent disturbance of the soil reveals earth the colour of curry powder until the sun bleaches it to sienna.

The approach to Ooty is marked by a great curve around the boating lake, originally built in the 1820s as an irrigation tank, and the imposing cream tower of St Thomas's Church standing proud above the line, surrounded by a century of memorials to those who came here and stayed, many of them tea planters.

Much has changed with the coming of factories during the last few decades, among them a large plant producing Hindustan film for photographic and scientific use, but there remains much to see and enjoy in Ooty and the surrounding hills and smaller stations like Kotagiri. The churches, government offices, botanical gardens and the former palaces all survive to give the visitor an inkling of the life that attracted so many servants of the Raj to retire here rather than return to Britain.

A pleasure not to be missed – and a good way to savour something of the atmosphere of Ooty – is afternoon tea on the lawn of the Savoy Hotel, surrounded by trees and flowers, while the distant whistles of the afternoon local train from Coonoor rise up from the valley below.

Taking the Mandalay Express from Yangon

BEN DAVIES

❖

From the dilapidated old capital of Yangon, formerly known as Rangoon, the Mandalay Express chugs its way through the rice fields of Myanmar (formerly Burma) and through a land of 10,000 golden spires to the town of Mandalay, perched on the banks of the Irrawaddy River. Fourteen hours of crowds, chaos and sheer unutterable local colour – surely no other train in Asia has so much to offer.

RIGHT, *the bureaucracy involved in catching the train proved almost impossible – but it was worth the difficulties*

FAR RIGHT, *the Mandalay Express, waiting for the 'off' at Yangon Station; formerly Rangoon, the city was renamed in 1989*

HOURS BEFORE DAWN reared its head over the deserted streets of Yangon, the platforms were already filled with figures, camped and silent, queues of humanity awaiting the departure of the grandiose institution that they call the Mandalay Express. Like some demi-god, it lay beyond a fence of barbed wire, a line of 13 orange, white and brown carriages that would carry us along the road to Mandalay, city of palaces and promise that lay just 385 miles (616km) to the north.

'Tickets,' said the man dressed in spotless beige flannels who stood between me and the rapidly filling train. 'You must have a special ticket. All tourists must go with Tourist Burma.'

'Writer,' I explained. 'Special permission. No need,' I said, thrusting forward a well-fingered letter given to me by the Minister of Transport.

The man grew nervous and discussed the unlikely situation with a colleague, who talked to a third colleague. 'Train full,' they said in unison. 'Talk to Tourist Burma.' Were it not for a former naval officer who bought me a local ticket costing less than one US dollar and herded me on to a carriage more crowded than the platform, I should no doubt still be waiting.

And so at 06.00hrs precisely, to the sound of an electric bell and the long drawn out whistle of the guard, I find myself lurched forward, propelled along rusty metal lines towards Mandalay.

Dawn has already come and I can make out glimpses of a world already wide awake, children washing under torrents of brackish water and pariah dogs wandering along the lines used by locals as walkways. 'Yangon,' sighs my next-door neighbour, 'too many people'.

As if we don't have enough on board – people on trunks, under seats, on top of carriages. According to the little handbook on the Burmese Railway proudly presented to me by a railway official, more than 50 million passengers travel on the local railways every year, carrying more than 1.74 tonnes of goods. Looking around, I cannot help feeling that we appear to have more than our fair share of them, and specifically in this carriage.

■ From Yangon, the train heads north, passing the towns of Pegu, Daik-u, Penwegon, Pyu, Toungoo, Yeni, Pyinmana, Yamethin, Thazi, Myittha and Mandalay.
Construction of the railway line began in 1877 under the Irrawaddy State Railway, subsequently renamed Burma Railways. The first leg between Yangon and Toungoo was officially opened on 1 July 1885, and the second leg from Toungoo to Mandalay was opened on 1 March 1889. On 1 April 1989

the corporation was renamed Myanmar Railways. Yangon (formerly Rangoon) is the beautiful old capital whose dilapidated buildings speak of days gone by. Do not miss the golden Shwedagon Pagoda, the most famous temple in Myanmar.
Pegu, a former capital of the Mon people, is dotted with temples. Most famous are the Shwemawdaw Pagoda, the Mahazedi Pagoda and the Shwethalyaung Buddha. Explore them by hiring a horse and cart.

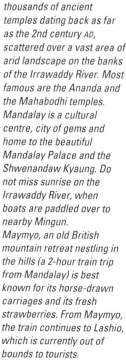

Fairy-tale Inle Lake, reached from Thazi, has floating gardens made from weed and mud and anchored to the lake floor. It is best seen in early morning when the floating market is at its most active.
Pagan, the greatest relic of Burma's former glory, has

To some extent this reflects hierarchy. Burmese trains have two classes, Upper Class and Ordinary Class. Upper Class carriages have nice, cushioned reclining seats, where government officials and businessmen travel. Ordinary Class has only wooden seats, where the less prosperous members of society travel. Even Ordinary Class carriages, however, are divided into the 'haves' and the 'have nots'. The 'haves' bought tickets three days prior to departure and are in possession of seats. The 'have nots' purchased tickets before the train left by queueing before dawn on the platform and have only the floor to sit on. I am of the latter unfortunate category.

Still, I am in good company, with a monk, a cripple carrying two live chickens, and a soldier brandishing something that resembles a double-bore shotgun.

By the time I find myself an unoccupied space of floor, we have left the wide open city with its faded, grandiose buildings and somnolent air of decay. Concrete buildings give way to wooden shacks as we thread our way through the suburbs and enter a rural world, a world where the majority of people work the land as they have done for centuries.

As the train settles into a gentle, unhurried rhythm, the countryside unrolls before us, a flat pan of rice fields broken here and there by small hillocks, each bearing its own white pagoda tipped with a cone of solid gold. For much of the year the land is a sea of green. Now, in March, it is dry and arid, almost desolate looking.

We pass the once great city of Pegu, former capital of the Mon people, several glistening temples rising up from the plain. On one side is the white marble outline of Mahezedi Pagoda and on the other the golden spire of the famous Shwemawdaw (great golden god) Pagoda, 374ft (114m) high and containing two hairs of the Buddha along with one of his sacred teeth.

thousands of ancient temples dating back as far as the 2nd century AD, scattered over a vast area of arid landscape on the banks of the Irrawaddy River. Most famous are the Ananda and the Mahabodhi temples.
Mandalay is a cultural centre, city of gems and home to the beautiful Mandalay Palace and the Shwenandaw Kyaung. Do not miss sunrise on the Irrawaddy River, when boats are paddled over to nearby Mingun.
Maymyo, an old British mountain retreat nestling in the hills (a 2-hour train trip from Mandalay) is best known for its horse-drawn carriages and its fresh strawberries. From Maymyo, the train continues to Lashio, which is currently out of bounds to tourists.

A SEA OF PEOPLE

ABOVE, *in 1889
Kipling repeated an
account of the lovely
Schwedagon temple: 'It's a
famous shrine o' sorts...
and now the Tounghoo–
Mandalay line is open,
pilgrims are flocking
down by the thousand
to see it.'*

Along the platform, just a short distance from the Schwemawdaw, crowds of people have gathered to meet the train, selling ducks' eggs, onion *bhaji*, and the 'wackin' great cheroots' that Rudyard Kipling would instantly have recognised. Children rush by, brandishing great pots of water on their heads and on we go.

By the time we pass Daik-u, my fellow passengers are sprawled in all directions, sitting on seats, under seats, and along the passageways, propped up head to head. They include several traders, a young well-to-do family travelling to see their aged mother in Maymyo, two soldiers and a *shaan* from one of the states in rebellion against the government. One young lady especially intrigues me. Her face is painted with large white sweet-smelling splotches of eucalyptus paste known as *Thanadkhar* and she wears a pink T-shirt with 'Porn' written in big letters over it. Most passengers wear the *longyi*, a silk wrap-around material, knotted at the front for men and at the side for women. 'Porn' wears a pair of jeans.

The train locomotive is equally distinctive. 'French,' the driver proudly tells me, pointing to the Alsthom label. It is a diesel. Until ten years ago, steam engines used to huff and puff along the route, but now they are used on goods trains and the odd passenger train in Upper Burma.

'Progress,' says the driver. I reflect sadly on how 'progress' in Burma has meant the removal of great institutions like the steam train, but the preservation of even more outmoded ones like Tourist Burma and the state bureaucracy.

After an hour or so, a little Burman carrying a great plastic sack fights his way through the corridor, stopping at each wooden seat and handing out bundles of paper to the enthusiastic passengers. These are Burmese magazines, romantic novelettes and cartoons, hired out by the hour and the main reason why passengers hardly move for the entire journey.

AGAINST ALL ODDS

Of course there's trains and there's trains. Some are renowned for great engineering feats, others for their history or for the countryside through which they pass. In fact, probably the greatest feat about the line between Yangon and Mandalay has been the ability of the authorities to keep it open despite countless attempts to blow it up (although not recently). When writer Norman Lewis made the journey in the mid-1950s, he did not get much beyond 150 miles (241km) before the White Flag communists or one of the countless other groups of insurgents mined the front of the train and then the back of it, only to disappear rapidly into the jungle.

Burmese nonchalance in the face of disaster has been a hallmark of the railroad in other ways too. At one stage it was going to link Singapore, Malaysia and Thailand, part of a grand design dreamed up by the Japanese during the 1940s and recalled with tragedy in the events of the River Kwai. These days the train simply chuffs up and down a strip of line 385 miles (616km) long, theoretically taking 14 hours and averaging some 27mph (43kph), but generally taking several hours longer and spending a considerable period of time at a standstill.

One reason for this is the number of unscheduled stops called for by a uniquely Burmese method of travel. Rather than taking an expensive horse and cart from the main station to their home or sitting on the crowded roof rack of a truck, the pragmatic locals have come up with an alternative: bribe the train driver to stop at a prearranged spot (pricier) or to slow down near their home so that they can rapidly leap off (cheap).

Nor is the driver the only one on the make. Upper Class carriage conductors are more than happy to sell you their seat and will spend the rest of the journey spread-eagled on the floor. In time of extreme overcrowding, I am reliably informed, it is even possible to pay for standing room in the locomotive.

By the time we reach Penwegon and Pyu, the whole train is beginning to resemble a restaurant car. At every stop, more vendors spring on board. One sells an assortment of bottled Coca Cola, sugar cane juice, a ghastly sweet lemon brew called Sparkling Lemonade, and Mandalay Beer. Another sells fried kebabs, another stewed birds.

Already the monk who shares my carriage is lunching on pieces of chicken, vegetables and rice donated by fellow passengers in the hope of gaining merit and paving the way for a better life hereafter. Even the delightfully beautiful girl with 'Porn' written on her shirt indulges in a plate of *sarga-lay-gyaw*, a sort of fried sparrow which she eats bones and all. For those in search of other delicacies, fried crickets, doves and glutinous rice served in bamboo or packed in banana leaf are all on offer.

Outside, beyond the crowd of feasting passengers, the train cuts alongside great dried riverbanks, breaking into a landscape that is vast and surreal. A cart moves slowly across the horizon, a lone figure carrying sugar cane pulled by a pair of bullocks, heads held high to the world. Ponies, trishaws and trucks bursting with workers kick up the dust along the winding dirt tracks. Occasionally the people catch glimpses of me, and laugh and wave at the sight of a strange-looking foreigner, sitting on the floor of the carriage, feet dangling out of the train.

At Yeni, the train again slows sufficiently for another drone of vendors to clamber up the sides, juggling trays of fried grass-hoppers and a huge dented teapot, green cheroots sticking out

ABOVE, a pause along the route allows time for refreshment

of their mouths. Those that have sold all their goods hurl themselves off at various points or merely wander up on the roof.

By now it is fiercesomely hot. Most of the Burmese passengers are fast asleep, gentle features and painted faces stacked up on and under the wooden seats. Outside, even the water buffalo take shelter in the shade or wallow in vast mud baths formed by irrigation channels.

The further north we go, the more mountainous it becomes, with fields of sunflowers splashing colour over a landscape still dry and arid. Small towns pass us by, nameless places framed against the distant outline of the Shaan Hills stretching towards the Salween River.

At every station, small children rush up balancing clay pots on their heads filled with water, covered by a tray and bearing three tin drinking cups. When the train arrives, they run from carriage to carriage selling their precious liquid (supposedly boiled water). But when the train leaves, the remaining water is ceremoniously thrown at the passengers through the open windows as the carriage gathers speed.

PREVIOUS PAGE, *the dreaming spires of a Mandalay palace, pointing high above the telegraph wires* INSETS, *scenes on the route to Mandalay*

ABOVE, *as the afternoon wears on, there is little to do on the crowded train but doze in the heat*

RIGHT, *a watermellon seller outside Pyu Station*

FAR RIGHT, *a striking golden Buddha in the ancient city of Pagan*

By the late afternoon, the interior of the Ordinary carriages resembles an Egyptian camel market, piled high with watermelon skins, empty plastic bottles and betelnut juice. One old man even clutches a ferocious and faintly senile-looking chicken, its feet tied with string, its eyes glazed with vicious stupefaction.

As we pass the town of Thazi, the main junction to Myingyan and Taung-gyi, the first kerosene lamps come to life, smoke drifting muffled through the air. Outside their homes, fishermen waist-deep in water cast for fish, their nets cut by the golden rays of the setting sun.

The carriage conductor celebrates our departure from Thazi by opening a bottle of local whisky or *Ahyetphu*. He is joined by the security guard, who has changed out of his uniform into a T-shirt and *longyi*. Both talk in the local dialect.

A HUMBLE LANGUAGE

Burmese is a strange nasal language, generally spoken in a soft tone with no apparent emphasis whatsoever. If you imagine some simpleton talking to himself you would probably find a number of similarities. Many Burmese do not speak English. Those that do, use it with a mixture of charm and gregariousness.

'Where do you come from?' asks the conductor, dolloping out a large glass of extremely potent liquor and handing me the most prized piece of food he has in his possession – the inner cheeks of a curried fish-head. On hearing I come from England he becomes extremely excited. 'England war. Myanmar very strong. Bang, bang. Myanmar win,' he says, referring to the events of World War II. In fact it was the Japanese whom the Burmese beat, but the British off whom they gained independence. I cannot help admiring the forthrightness of a people who for more than 40 years have been mired in various armed struggles.

As if that is not enough, the conductor coughs, lights a cheroot and as final proof of Burmese superiority adds 'Myanmar girl very good looking. Number one beautiful.' By now we have been joined by a crowd of onlookers, adding bits of advice, offering me cigarettes, commenting on Margaret Thatcher, Liverpool football team and other worldly matters.

'Where you go to school?' says the conductor. 'I went to university,' I reply. 'Oh, very clever, Mr Ben, very clever,' he announces to his friends, who look suitably impressed.

By the time we reach Singaingmyo, the carriage attendant is drunk, along with the plain clothes security guard. I am sitting in a reclining

seat in an air conditioned carriage (despite having only an Ordinary Class ticket) and I have been presented with gifts ranging from a bamboo container of sticky rice to a map and a hunk of sweetcorn. If the train went any further, I suspect I would end up being offered a sleeping compartment.

Half an hour before we arrive in Mandalay, there is a commotion outside. Figures from above leap down from the roof or jump out of the doors, carrying bags stuffed with illegal cigarettes and liquor smuggled from over the border. Their accomplices grab the sacks and are swallowed into the darkness, part of a black market that controls almost every aspect of the Burmese economy and which keeps locals and government officials in ready supply of their favourite whisky (Johnnie Walker) and cigarettes (555).

Within moments of the last one jumping off, we enter the outskirts of Mandalay, home to the famous Mahamuni image, and to the great Irrawaddy River of which Rudyard Kipling once wrote. The conductor is laughing uncontrollably, the security guard is asleep and it is 10 o'clock, an hour before curfew begins and eight hours before my return trip to Yangon.

PRACTICAL INFORMATION

■ The Mandalay Express leaves Yangon twice daily, taking anything from 12 to 18 hours to cover the 385 miles (616km). All tickets must be bought through Tourist Burma, preferably two or three days in advance, and should be paid for in US dollars. The night train has sleepers.

■ All visitors to Myanmar must have a visa which can be arranged at embassies or through local tour agents. The maximum length of stay is two weeks.

■ The best time to travel is November to February, when the countryside is lush and the weather cool. Between the months of March and May temperatures reach well above 100°F (40°C).

■ Independent travel by tourists is not allowed without special permission, and you should contact a Myanmar Embassy for further information. In the US, the Myanmar Embassy is at 2300 South Street NW, Washington DC 20008. Tel: 202 332 9044. Or you can contact the Permanent Mission of Myanmar, 10 East 77th Street, New York, NY 10021. Tel: 212 535 1310.

Down the Malay Peninsula from Bangkok to Singapore

BEN DAVIES

The Bangkok to Singapore International Express leads 1026 miles (1650km) south from Thailand through the lush heartlands of Malaysia to Singapore, home to one of Asia's most vibrant economies. It is a journey from the old chaos of Asia to the sparkling new that takes in three worlds joined by a span of railway line. Even the great Raffles would not have wanted to miss it.

ABOVE, *there are over 400 temple-monasteries in Bangkok; this is part of the famous Wat Phra Kaeo, or Temple of the Emerald Buddha, which adjoins the Grand Palace*

BELOW, *life beside the railway lines, Bangkok*

AT 15.15HRS PRECISELY, to the sound of a whistle and the wave of a green flag, the southern bound International Express lurched forward, stopped and started again. A sudden rush of people erupted in the corridors, people waaing, hawkers jumping off selling legs of chicken and bottles of Fanta, and a young girl cradling a baby. By the time the last carriage had cleared the end of Hualamphong's Platform 5 and the old windowless trains parked on the sidings, the vendors were gone and the inside of the carriage regained an air of respectability, cleanliness and second-world order.

Outside our thread of modernity lay drab Bangkok – not the temples one hears about, but the poor areas, the rubbish tips and traffic jams of a city of split personalities, a cacophony of sounds and existences with little in common. A handful of people waved, solitary figures framed against corrugated huts. A few others were drying their washing on the ashen-coloured ground alongside the track.

From Hualamphong Railway Station, the International Express steams west across the city, past the murky *klongs*, the king's residence and the giant billboards, and finally, after what seems an age, into the countryside, a landscape of rice fields that unrolls like a tapestry woven with the promise of the Orient.

Of course, trains are not the first things that come to mind when you think of Bangkok. Nor exactly are temples or, for that matter, monks. It is bars and brothels for which the place is renowned and which among other things have given it the name 'City of Angels'. Passengers expecting such things on the International Express to Hat Yai and Butterworth may be disappointed. A bar and restaurant, yes. A brothel, no.

Indeed, probably the first thing that you notice about Thai trains is not the shower in the lavatory, nor the Buddha statue in the

locomotive, but the people themselves, with their diminutive smiles and infectious enjoyment of life. Thais do not think in terms of tomorrow. They believe in the now, and this gives them an air of liberation of which the *farang* or foreigner can only dream.

Besides a large and portly monk, who according to Buddhist rules must abstain from alcohol, women, and food before midday, the other Thai passengers in my carriage appear gracefully close to heaven or, in the case of Buddhists, 'nirvana'. They play cards, chat, drink whisky, eat kebabs and sleep propped up against one another, a pile of gentle features and clothes smelling of lotus blossom and jasmine.

Foreign passengers, on the other hand, look self-conscious and dirty. Those within my second class, non-air-conditioned carriage range from the semi-respectable beachcomber with knock knees and a large paunch to the veritable savage, covered in earrings, with pierced nostrils, a shaved head and a faded T-shirt saying 'Gotcha'.

This version fits in pretty well with how the Thai have always viewed anyone of Western complexion. One early chronicle, the *Thai Nya Phuum*, sums up the *farang* or foreigner as follows: 'They are exceedingly tall, hairy and evil smelling'. Looking at some of my neighbours, I cannot help agreeing occasionally.

Shortly after leaving the town of Nakhon Pathom, three railway officials wander through the train. The first is a ticket officer, spotlessly dressed in blue flannels, a light blue shirt and an official-looking cap. He checks my ticket, nods and passes it to the second officer who ticks an important-looking list, before passing my ticket to the third officer who checks that the first two have done their job.

What's more, they smile. One possible reason is that like many Thais they are inherently

■ From Bangkok, the train heads south passing the major towns of Phetchaburi, Hua Hin, Hat Yai, Butterworth, Kuala Lumpur, Johor Baharu and Singapore. Bangkok is Thailand's chaotic capital of temples, factories and sheer unutterable calm and chaos. Do not miss the glittering spires of the Grand Palace, the murky canals, the bustling markets and, last but not least, Patpong, the most famous red light district in the world.
Phetchaburi, ancient town of temples and caves, is famed above all for its Phra Nakhon

Kiri Palace complex, best seen at sunset.
Hua Hin was the old royal capital, now popular for weekend breaks. It has beaches, fishing boats and, further afield, waterfalls, temples and the Kaeng Krachan National Park.
Surat Thani is, after Phuket, the most famous beach area in Thailand. From Surat Thani boats leave to the paradise islands of Ko Samui, Ko Phangan and Ko Tao.
Hat Yai, southern Thailand's fastest growing city, is popular above all as a centre for smuggled goods and for Thai masseurs. Malaysians

come over by the thousands, to do all the things they are not allowed to back home. Pinang is the oldest British settlement on the Malay Peninsula. Visit the fine old Chinese city of George Town. Further afield is a sprinkling of good beaches and international hotels. Cameron Highlands, a popular hill station dotted with tea plantations and butterflies, is best reached from Tapah.
Kuala Lumpur, once famous for its deposits of tin, is now the Malaysian capital and a bristling economic hub, with high rises, hotels and an air

of prosperity.
The modern city state of Singapore is a shopper's paradise, clean, easy, the extreme of Western values in an Asian world, and the very antithesis of Bangkok.

happy. The other is that they are doing as they have been told. Instructions to railway staff pinned up on the wall of most Thai stations include these directives: 'Smile at all times, speak clearly, pleasantly and courteously, be nice, charming, gentle and graceful, try your best to avoid saying no, keep your temper to keep your job – and the customer is always right'.

From the small town of Ban Pong, to the south-west of Bangkok, the International Express steams on past Ratchaburi and Pak Tho through vast areas of cleared land, rice paddies and distant hills. Dotted here and there are new factories and condominiums, harbingers of the

Thai and English, these include seaweed soup with shrimp, smoked chicken breast with gravy served with buttered vegetables, and the *pièce de résistance*, 'roast pog's head neck sliced'. In one corner, under a poster of a semi-naked girl drinking Guinness, sit several jovial Thais listening to rock music played over loudspeakers. Around them, seated at other tables, are workers returning home, fishermen, businessmen, foreigners with their paid-for Thai 'girl friends', and two policemen who are playing a game of cards and drinking substantial quantities of local whiskeys.

Passengers wishing to forgo the exercise but not the food do not have to come as far as the

RIGHT, *a combination of patience and impatience as passengers wait for the train to move on*

growing economic power that will one day turn this into one of the most prosperous nations in the east.

At Phetchaburi the train slows, sounds its siren and then lurches to a halt. From a little temple on the hill, King Mongkhut, famed from *The King and I*, had once searched for stars and was able to foretell a famous eclipse in the mid-19th century. He eventually died after visiting the nearby marshes at Sam Roi Yot to witness the great event, but not before he had sired 83 children from 35 different wives.

Dusk is falling as the train leaves Phetchaburi. Already, the searing light of the day gives way to the shadows of late afternoon through which the train steadily chugs, a line of carriages pushing through the gentle glow of the setting sun.

I wander down to the restaurant car situated in the middle of the train. Its windows are flung open to the world and there is an air of joyous mirth. Waiters dressed in blue rush eagerly around, taking orders and balancing vast trays of steaming gastronomic anomalies in front of them. According to the menu written in both

restaurant car. Instead, the Thai have developed one of the most impressive aisle buffet services in South-East Asia. All you need do is stop one of the blue-uniformed young ladies who circulate continuously around the carriages. You can put in your order, be it fried rice or the famous 'roast pog's neck' and pay for the meal on receipt.

Even the wagons-lits conductors on Thai trains perform their duty with the utmost charm and dexterity, pulling ironed sheets out of polythene bags, uncovering giant pillows and transforming your seat, within seconds, into a perfectly satisfactory bed. This is then equipped with a half-litre bottle of drinking water and covered by a strip of curtain sufficient to conceal even the most modest incumbent from the eye of his or her fellow passengers.

Most of the Thais, having dined and washed, quietly climb up their ladder and disappear into a world of somnolence. A few unruly Westerners can be heard over a card game and a bottle of Mekong whisky, their voices tailing off into the night.

And so the train steams on through an invisible blanket of darkness, the secret gulf of Thailand's heartlands where all one can make out is the thin outline of villages, the producers of 20 million tons of rice a year.

At 2 o'clock in the morning, the gentle rhythm is broken by crashing sounds as crowds of holiday-makers descend at Surat Thani, bound for the promise of the paradise island of Ko Samui three hours off shore. A few hours later, a sprinkling of other passengers descend at Thung Song Junction, bound for Trang.

By dawn, we have reached the town of Phatthalung, set amongst swaying palms on the tip of Songkhla Lake (or Thale Sap Songkhla), and further on we pass small towns, barely dots on the map, once part of the great Sri Vijaya Empire that ruled Sumatra and large parts of southern Thailand until the 13th century.

Most of the Thai passengers are already up and busily involved in another of their great pastimes: washing. Indeed, so seriously do they treat this bodily function that almost uniquely among trains in Asia, there is even a shower in the toilet. After soaping themselves, brushing their teeth and sprinkling water over their face, they breakfast on curry, maybe a little barbecued chicken or a kebab dipped in chilli sauce. A few Westerners emerge from their bunks, gaudy-eyed and puffy, to put in orders for eggs, white toast and butter. The young Thai lady who has spent the night in the bunk below me is by now especially enthusiastic as she tucks into a meal of

sliced durian, the dreaded gladiators' fruit that smells like a mixture of carrion and custard and is renowned amongst the Chinese as an aphrodisiac.

'Pay nai', she says using the term of address which literally means 'where do you go?' but which constitutes the first question that almost any polite Thai will ask. Deng, as she is called, is a nurse from Bangkok and is on her way to Hat Yai to visit her mother who has just been involved in a motor-car accident. Other passengers are travelling as far as Butterworth and Pinang. Few, though, seem to be going the whole way down to Singapore, a further 24 hours away.

The train slows down and stops in the ugly modern town of Hat Yai, best known for its smuggled goods, massage parlours and its monthly bull fights. A crowd of giggling school girls gets off and waves 'choc dee' (good luck), laughing and smiling. Vendors climb on board selling plates of fried chicken and bananas, several locals conceal dubious-looking packages under the seats and the train moves on towards the border.

At Padang Besar, an hour further south, all passengers are obliged to descend from the train, carrying their belongings with them: guards go from carriage to carriage checking that nobody has remained on board. Even the First Class passengers are forced to alight for their comfort.

Fifty minutes later the train has not moved. A queue of foreigners stands in front of two shacks, filling in forms and declarations to appease both the Malaysian authorities, whose

ABOVE, *most carriages on the train are not air-conditioned, so passengers must improvise to keep cool*

LEFT, *the extraordinary Chinese temple at Pinang*

ABOVE, *Kuala Lumpur Station – more like a temple or mosque than a railway building*

FAR RIGHT TOP, *characters from the Chinese opera at Haw Par Villa, Singapore, formerly Tiger Balm Gardens and now the biggest Chinese mythological theme park in the world*

FAR RIGHT BELOW, *the modern city of Singapore*

country they are entering, and the Thais, whose country they are leaving. 'It takes longer to get through Customs here than in China or Vietnam,' mumbles one irate passenger, lugging a huge leather suitcase with a big label saying Hilton Hotel and Cathay Pacific First Class. Here at least, there is no favouritism.

At last though, the Customs officials are through with it, the guard waves a little green flag and a dirty Alsthom 4209 diesel with seven carriages in tow, pulls out of the station, heading south past the towns of Alor Setar, Tokai and Gurun and an increasingly tropical landscape to Butterworth in Malaysia.

ALL CHANGE

Here every passenger must alight since the train goes no further. I buy another ticket, a Second Class single to Kuala Lumpur, eat a Madras curry in the brand new, air-conditioned and plastic-looking restaurant, and climb on to the next train, a grey KTM Bersih engine and seven grey Dingin carriages painted with blue, white and red stripes that give them the look of an upmarket ice-cream van. There is a video in each

carriage showing special rail channel films.

By the early afternoon we are off, cutting through a lush tropical landscape of palm plantations dotted with hills and triangular houses of corrugated roofs. Already the strange gutteral sounds of the Malays have taken over from the gentle sing-song of tonal Thai. The features of the passengers have grown darker, more Indian-looking, elongated and severe. Bukit Mertjaram, Taiping (town of everlasting peace), Ipoh, Tabarot and Kuala Kubu Baharu are the towns we pass through, while further to the east the distant Cameron Highlands are bathed in the soft rays of the setting sun.

Arriving in Kuala Lumpur Station, you sense more than ever that you are in a different country. Gone are the smiles and the easy-going charm of the Thais. The station building itself is beautiful, tidy and mechanical, with arches, spires, towers, minarets, cupolas and red and yellow plastic seats: more like a mosque than a railway station.

Outside the station, a group of Malays hang around, bored, kicking and heading a football. Beyond rises a cluster of high-rise blocks, Prime Minister Datuk Seri Mahathir Mohamad's vision of Malay supremacy, till now stymied by the Malays' own inefficiency and the innate financial flair and hard-working nature of their fellow Chinese.

LAST STRETCH TO SINGAPORE

From Kuala Lumpur another train departs for the final leg to Singapore with a new engine, several grand First Class carriages and the rather distinguished title of the North Star Night Express. By now it is dark, but the heat is still oppressive. Outside you can almost sense the rolling landscape of oil palm plantations which further south will give way to tea plantations that stretch south towards the causeway.

Serdang, Seremban and Keluang – the name of each town has a sleepy twang to it. At each station a few passengers descend and several more join, strangers interchanging, and brought together fleetingly as the train moves on.

Several of them are to be found in the restaurant car with its cheap blue curtains, lurid carpet and air of misery. Most passengers are drinking Coca Cola, or eating cellophaned sandwiches. Many are dressed in sarongs and black hats, or have their faces concealed by veils, symbols of Islam. But these people are not welcoming and the heat is oppressive.

I wander back to the Second Class sleeper. It is filled with sweating bodies and the smell of urine. Through the small wooden block which acts as both an air conditioner and a window, vague shadows pass us by, then a sudden concentration of lights. The gentle rocking sensation pulls one through the night and on into a world of sleep.

I am awakened early by a sudden jolt. The first rays of dawn light up a lush countryside still beautified in the early morning. We are passing Johor Baharu, Malaysia's newest economic hub and a city of modern housing blocks, the boom centre of the region. Immigration officials clamber on board and check our passports.

Directly before us lies the causeway that runs between Malaysia and Singapore, a dividing line of blue sparkling water dotted with boats that takes us from a still largely rural world to a new, progressive and largely mechanical one.

And so at precisely 08.00 hours (one hour later than scheduled) on a Tuesday morning, the North Star Night Express enters Singapura Station, a concrete building that is grey and relatively old, paradoxically owned by the Malaysians and strangely out of character with the clinically concrete city outside. 'No chewing gum. No rubbish, no cigarettes in air-conditioned places, no long hair', are the rules of Singaporean society. Taxis are lined neatly in a queue outside the station. And even the pedestrians are neatly dressed in expensive Western-style clothes. Would the great Raffles have turned in his grave, I reflect, as I rapidly purchase my return ticket to Bangkok.

PRACTICAL INFORMATION

■ The International Express leaves Bangkok's Hualamphong Railway Station every afternoon, arriving at Butterworth in the middle of the following day, in Kuala Lumpur late evening and in Singapore early on the third day. The total distance of 1026 miles (1650km) takes some 40 hours.

■ First and Second Class sleepers and reclining seats are all available, though they should be booked well ahead either at the stations or through a local travel agency.

■ Passengers must change trains at Butterworth and Kuala Lumpur. You must also go through Customs at Padang Besar.

■ The best time to do the trip is from November to February, when the weather is cool and the countryside is lush. The hot season lasts from March to May and the rainy season from June to October.

■ An extremely grand version of the Venice Simplon-Orient-Express, the Eastern & Oriental Express, is scheduled to start operating from Bangkok to Singapore in 1993. Details from travel agents, or from Venice Simplon-Orient-Express Ltd at the address on page 25 of this book.

■ Many big travel agents will be able to arrange trips and obtain the necessary railway tickets. In the US, contact the Thailand Tourist Office at 5 World Trade Center, Suite 3443, New York, NY 10048. Tel: 212 432 0433.

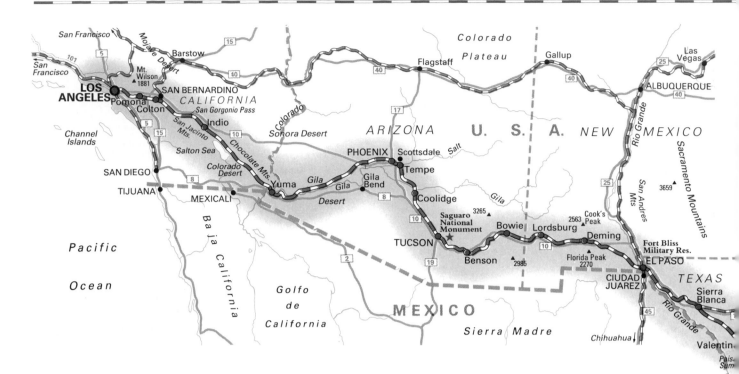

The Sunset Limited from New Orleans to Los Angeles

KEN WESTCOTT JONES

ABOVE, *a Superliner on the Sunset Limited towers above the track*

Operating as one of Amtrak's crack Western trains, the Sunset Limited crosses the southern United States of America from the Gulf of Mexico to the Pacific. It runs over the tracks of the Southern Pacific Railroad on a journey of more than 2000 miles (3200km), starting in New Orleans and ending at Los Angeles Union Station some 43 hours later. Its name, which has been carried by the prime train on the route for nearly a century, is derived from the glorious south-west sunsets enjoyed along the way. At times, the Limited rides a mile (1.5km) high, yet at one stage runs on the lowest railway tracks on earth, more than 200 feet (60m) below sea level.

LINED UP FOR its 14.15hrs departure, the Sunset Limited, with its Superliner roofs more than 18 feet (6m) above the ground, dominates the modern inter-modal transport terminal in the heart of the 'Crescent City's' downtown. There are normally seven Superliner cars, with a single-level baggage and mail car next to the two Amtrak diesel engines heading the train. These locomotives may be a pair of SDP 40s, or a single P–30CH with booster. The head-end Superliner is usually a prototype, possibly dating back to 1963 when the Santa Fe

West of New Orleans the Sunset Limited passes through the Louisiana bayou country, an area of swamps and forests, and into one of the most prolific rice-growing areas of the world, the paddies that produce the famous American long grain rice extending all the way to Houston, Texas.

After mile upon mile of Texan cattle-grazing plains, the climb from Del Rio to the summit of the Texas Rockies comes as something of a contrast. At Paisano summit, 5270 feet (1606m), the railway track is higher than that of one of the crossings of the North Rockies in Montana. From here views extend southwards into the remote Big Bend country, while to the east Mount Livermore, Monarch of Texas, rears up to a height of 8382 feet (2555m).

El Paso, on the Rio Grande River, lies between the Sierra Madre mountains of Mexico and the Franklin Mountains, western outriders of the Texas Rockies.

El Paso itself is 3720 feet (1139m) above sea level, the sunniest place in North America – the sun shines on average 340 days a year. Beyond El Paso, the Sunset Limited passes into New Mexico and the desert that extends into Arizona.

As the train runs along the shores of Arizona's Salton Sea (America's equivalent of the Dead Sea in the Middle East), it is 220 feet (67m) below sea level, the lowest place on earth where railway tracks run. Before journey's end comes the San Jacinto range, the tallest encountered on the journey. The Southern Pacific tracks wind through the middle of the mountains, going over the San Gorgonio Pass at Beaumont Summit, nearly a mile (1.5km) above the Pacific Ocean, before running downhill into Union Station, at the heart of Los Angeles city.

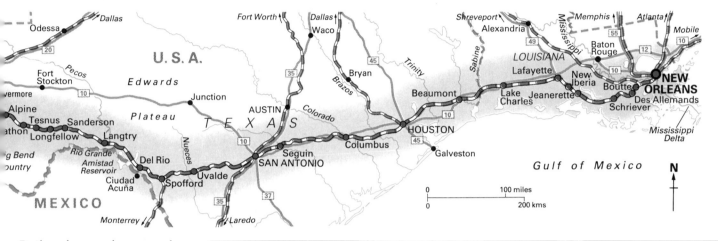

Railroad started to put them into service from its own works. It is the crew's dormitory car, for the porters, cooks, barmen and waiters go all the way across with the train (engineers and conductors change at division points, so do not need on-board accommodation).

The next three cars, built by Pullman Standard between 1978 and 1980 and slightly higher than the prototype, are Coaches, meaning Second or Standard Class, with reclining chairs on the upper levels and various facilities at a lower level such as washrooms and small lounges, the two levels being connected by a curving, well-carpeted staircase. Then comes a Sightseer lounge, a magnificent vehicle with huge glass windows sweeping up into the roof, the modern descendant of the vista-dome observation cars with their glass 'bubbles' that were first introduced by the Burlington Railroad in 1945. Swivel armchairs enable passengers to enjoy an all-round view. After dark, video shows – including full-length movies – are shown in this car. The lower level has a buffet and recreation room complete with musical equipment.

The Superliner standing behind the Sightseer lounge is the dining car, with tables seating four on each side beside picture windows. Some 60

ABOVE, *a traditional jazz band in New Orleans – the home of jazz and start of the Sunset route*

ABOVE, *the dusty Sunset Limited pulls into Jefferson*

RIGHT, *the glittering modern tower blocks of Houston proclaim the US's third busiest port and fifth largest city*

persons can be accommodated in the main part of the diner, and there are a couple more tables slightly higher up at one end. The cooking is done on the lower level and the food is brought up in electric lifts. The last car will be a sleeper – usually only one out of New Orleans, for a second one is attached at San Antonio. This sleep-er will have five de luxe bedrooms on its upper level, each with two beds plus a shower and toilet annexe. By day these large compartments provide a sofa and an armchair, with a fold-down table, the top of which is marked out for chess or chequers. Beyond the top of the stairs there are half a dozen economy bedrooms, each sleeping two persons. The beds are comfortable but there is not much space, and heavy luggage has to be stowed downstairs. There are no private toilets in these modestly priced rooms. On the lower level of the sleeper is a large washroom and a special bedroom for disabled travellers, while next to that, and extending the full width of the car with windows on both sides of the train, is the family bedroom, which can take two adults and two children without a squeeze.

The Sunset Limited suffers from the chronic shortage of rolling stock that is affecting all main line trains in the United States. Pullman went out of business several years ago, but Bombardier of Montréal are now constructing very similar luxury coaches and sleepers, and if all goes to plan these should solve the problem by the end of 1994.

Meanwhile the Sunset is the last remaining Western train to operate only three times a week. It is expected to run daily, with its route being extended eastwards to Florida soon after more equipment is delivered. This will relieve pressure on space for bookings (especially in the sleeping cars), which are heavy for most of the year.

No longer do we hear the time-honoured call of 'All aboard!' when an American train pulls out of a station. The porters take the stepping stools into the coaches, the huge doors are closed a few seconds before scheduled departure time and the whole consist rolls away – slowly and silently

THE MIGHTY MISSISSIPPI

Cantering through the outskirts of New Orleans, the Sunset climbs on to the remarkable Huey Long Bridge which spans the wide Mississippi River. It is named after the notorious governor of Louisiana, Huey P Long, who was involved in heavy controversy from his election in 1928 until his assassination in 1935. Despite all the acrimony surrounding this difficult man

and his reign as State governor, the great bridge which he funded retains his name.

There are 5 miles (8km) of bridge, including the approaches, and its summit is high above the river to allow big ships to pass on their way to Baton Rouge. Before the bridge was finished, in the early 1930s, ferries carried passengers and freight across the Mississippi River and the Sunset Limited began its journey from a riverbank station some 11 miles (18km) west of New Orleans.

Curving away to the right after crossing the bridge, the train enters the Louisiana bayou country, a strange world of alligator swamps and forests and fishing villages largely inhabited by people of French descent called Cajuns. To this day, many speak 'Cajun' French, and indeed the State's civil law is still based on the Code Napoléon. The French came here first as founders of New Orleans and later as refugees from Acadia (part of the Canadian Maritimes), where they had been evicted by British, mainly Scots, settlers.

The Sunset rolls straight through little wayside stations with French names such as Boutte, Des Allemands, Bayou Sale and Jeanerette, and it makes a stop at Lafayette, named after the famous French marquis who came to America to help in the fight for independence. The 145 miles (233km) so far will have taken three hours, including two slowings and perhaps stops at Schriever and New Iberia, the latter name a reminder that Louisiana was once owned by Spain. Lafayette is where the partly French-speaking University of Southwestern Louisiana is located. Local passengers in the Coach seats along this stretch will most probably be Cajuns and there is likely to be some noisy *patois* as check-shirted, bearded men talk across the aisles.

IN SIGHT OF TEXAS

The countryside changes beyond Lafayette as the train begins to pass through the vast rice paddies that will continue as far as the outskirts of Houston. In these same paddies crayfish also are produced, while Lake Charles, where the train stops for a few minutes as dinner gets under way, produces sulphur. The border with Texas is a few miles west at the Sabine River, and from here the Sunset travels through the Lone Star State for no less than 920 miles (1480km) – which surely gives credence to the legendary 'bigness' of Texas, especially as the northern border with Oklahoma, marked by the Red River, is some 450 miles (724km) away.

The view from the diner, then, is rice and more rice, and in keeping with Amtrak's policy

ABOVE, *watching the world roll by from the comfortable Sightseer Lounge*

FAR RIGHT, *San Antonio's most famous landmark is the Alamo – the old mission where Davy Crockett and his Texas volunteers were massacred by Mexican forces in 1836, during the struggle for Texas independence*

of providing local or regional dishes where possible, it is likely that rice with crayfish tails in sauce will be on the modestly priced dinner menu. For First Class passengers (meaning those in sleeper accommodation) there is no charge, for all meals are included in the ticket.

At about eight o'clock in the evening the train stops at Beaumont, and here the rice vistas are interrupted by oil installations. It was here that the Texas oil industry began in 1901, when the Spindletop oil field was developed. Beaumont is 281½ miles (453km) west of New Orleans, and the average speed over the mostly single track line will have been about 50mph (80kph). At this pace the huge Superliners ride very sweetly, even over the bumpy bits. In the wet bayou and rice country, track maintenance is very difficult and these sections are not among America's best – not that their best is of any significantly high standard when compared with Western Europe or Japan.

This far south, there are never any very long, light evenings, so darkness will have fallen, no matter what time of year, soon after Beaumont. The fairly slow, non-stop run to Houston, 82 miles (132km) in two and a half hours (which allows a margin for making up any lost time), can be spent in the Sightseer lounge watching the video, or reading, or having a drink or two in the bars. There is music in the recreation room. Some passengers in sleepers turn in early, for their beds will have been made up during dinner. In the de luxe rooms, the lower bed is a splendidly comfortable wide one.

An agonizingly slow approach through freight yards and past brilliant lights, to the accompaniment of ringing bells and blasts on the locomotive horn, brings the Sunset Limited into Houston at about half past ten in the evening. It is invariably on time, or slightly early, unless some serious delay has been encountered *en route*. The Amtrak station is on Washington Avenue, close to the centre of this great city. Four hundred and fifty square miles (1165sq km), it is the fifth largest city in the United States, an oil and space centre, but also the 'Rice Capital of the World'. It is justifiably famed for its hospitals and medical research.

Despite its size and importance, the city is thinly served by passenger trains, with just the Sunset going west and east, and the Texas Eagle departing for Dallas and Chicago. There are plans, however, for a triangular Texas high speed railway system which will link Houston and Dallas with one new line, and Dallas and San Antonio with another, while the Amtrak Southern Pacific route from Houston to San Antonio will be greatly improved. It is to be hoped that the scheme will actually reach full construction – in the United States many such ideas fail to materialize, defeated by the automobile and airline lobbies.

There is time for a stroll on the low platforms while the train is serviced and incoming passengers are handled, and then the Sunset crawls away into the night, only slowly gathering speed. It is a dull stretch from Houston to San Antonio, with little to see even in daylight but the Texas plains and more and more cattle grazing. There is no intermediate stop and the Limited pulls into San Antonio at 03.10hrs, having covered 210 miles (338km) in a generous 4¼ hours. Only the heaviest of sleepers will escape being woken when another Superliner sleeping car is attached to the rear of the train. This is from the Texas Eagle, whose 1308 mile (2105km) journey from Chicago ended here some four hours earlier.

DUSTY PLAINS

San Antonio gets plenty of sun and for eight months of the year it can be very hot – so hot

Some 805 miles (1295km) west of New Orleans and 231 miles (372km) west of San Antonio, the Sunset dashes straight through a tiny settlement with a small station which no longer handles passenger traffic and only rarely any freight. Its name is Langtry, and this is where the infamous Judge Roy Bean lived, a man who called himself 'The Law West of the Pecos'. In his earlier years he managed to see the actress and singer Lillie Langtry, later mistress of King Edward VII, when she was performing in San Antonio. He fell in love with her, wrote her worshipping letters, and changed the name of his dingy little settlement from Vinegaroon (it had been a construction camp for workers building the Southern Pacific Railroad) to Langtry. After years of intense persuasion, the actress-singer agreed to visit him, arranging for her private railroad car to be detached from the Sunset Limited. But two days before she arrived at the hot, dusty settlement, Judge Bean died of a heart attack.

There is a Judge Roy Bean museum in a large wooden saloon building at Langtry. When I was there on a previous occasion the Sunset roared through the town, raising the dust, and a hunter came in from the Mexican mountain country with packhorses laden with cougar-skins.

To see Langtry, keep a careful watch out on the south side of the train at about eight o'clock while breakfast is being served in the diner. There is a glimpse, too, of the Rio Grande before it loops away to the south as the train heads due west.

At Sanderson there is a divisional stop where conductors change. This is an isolated spot indeed, with crowding mountains and semi-barren tracts of land, exactly 300 miles (482km) from San Antonio and the same distance from El Paso, where Texas finally comes to an end.

that there is an old saying, 'the Devil himself takes a fan when he goes to San Antonio'. This area marks a climatic change, with the humidity and heat of east Texas giving way to even greater heat but dry conditions. Nevertheless, I have visited in January and seen ice on the waters of the Paseo del Rio, the artificial waterway that beautifies San Antonio, with the temperature at 15°F (-11°C).

Travelling through the night the now heavier consist of the Sunset Limited crosses dry, rolling country, reaching Del Rio at dawn. This small town is on the famous Rio Grande, across the water from the Mexican town of Ciudad Acuña. Just beyond is the Amistad Dam, which backs up the river to form a huge reservoir 50 miles (80km) long.

A tributary of the Rio Grande is the Pecos, once upon a time the limit of civilization. A very high bridge carries the rails across the river, and the route continues through wild terrain, with the stark mountains of the Anacacco country over to the south.

ABOVE, *the railroad track stretches into the distance, faint telegraph poles on the left the only other sign of human habitation*

BELOW, *a section of the mighty Rio Grande, which marks the border between Texas and Mexico*

For those who think Texas is mainly flat there is a surprise in store as climbing begins in earnest, through tiny halts at Emerson and Longfellow (both American poets) and on to Tesnus. This dot on the map reads 'sunset' backwards, but it has never handled the famous trans-continental. The train does not even stop at Marathon, a small town at the foot of the Glass and Del Norte Mountains. For 31 miles (50km) the tracks now wind uphill through a pass between 7000 feet (2133km) mountains to a stop at Alpine. The train is almost at the summit of the Texas Rockies, a mile (1.5km) above sea level. From here there are a few more feet yet to climb to the Paisano summit. Near Valentine, a tiny station just over a thousand miles from New Orleans, there is a view to the east of Texas's Mount Livermore, and then it is downhill all the way to El Paso, past Sierra Blanca where the tracks of the freight-only Texas and Pacific Railroad come in from the right. The countryside is dry, with rugged mountains and gulches – just as the golden south-west is expected to look.

FRONTIER CITY

Lunch in the diner will be over as the train runs slowly through the outskirts of El Paso, a big city on the Rio Grande marking the frontier not only with Mexico but with the State of New Mexico. The Sunset Limited spends about half an hour at this major division point, long enough for some leg-stretching in the vicinity of the station. This was an important stop on the Butterfield Stage route on its 28-day journey from the Mississippi to California. In all its years of service the stage coach was never held up, nor was bullion stolen, and all passengers reached their destinations safely. Fort Bliss, which helped to protect the Stage, is now an enormous army establishment, and the major contributor to the region's economy.

Across the Rio Grande is Ciudad Juárez, one of Mexico's larger cities, which can be reached by bus or taxi. From Juárez trains head southwards for Mexico City via Chihuahua 220 miles (354km) away.

Very soon after leaving El Paso the train runs close to the Rio Grande. There are high but largely ineffective wire fences along the bank, erected to prevent illegal immigrants crossing the river into the United States. Hundreds succeed, however, and can be seen from the train windows wading across the river. The meaning of the term 'wet-back' becomes obvious when Mexicans are seen struggling to reach the American shore, almost up to their necks in the water.

We are in New Mexico now, the area closest to El Paso that offers many of the attractions denied to citizens of Texas, where gaming is illegal and spirit drinking in bars is prohibited. Inns, bars and clubs can be seen from the train, and there is a large horse-racing track. But as they fall away the countryside becomes empty and the vistas wide. It is 90 miles (145km) to Deming, where the train makes the lowest crossing of the Continental Divide amid the Florida and Cook mountain ranges. The train may or may not stop; Amtrak declares Deming to be an under-used station and has been threatening to withdraw its service to the town all together.

After 60 miles (96km) of semi-desert, with rugged

rocky outcrops beneath a blazing sun, we come to Lordsburg, a famed stop on the Butterfield Stage route and often featured in Hollywood Westerns. The scheduled time is 16.47hrs Mountain Time, but the clocks are complicated in this region, with Daylight Savings sometimes being used and sometimes not. It is two hours to the next stop, at Benson, by which time the train has crossed into Arizona. To the left of the train the sun will be preparing for the second almost incredibly spectacular setting which gives its name to the train. It depends, of course, on the time of year, but one way or the other, the sun will have set by the time the train reaches Tucson.

Pronounced 'Tewson', this winter resort of Arizona is expanding as a tourist spot and is the home of the University of Arizona. Its low altitude and desert setting make it very hot in summer, with temperatures between 105°F and 110°F (40–44°C) at midday from June to September, but it is also incredibly dry, making the heat quite bearable. Old Tucson seems to blend in as a part of the city but in fact was only built in 1940 as a Hollywood film set and then handed over to the community. 'Shoot-outs' are staged every day!

On both sides of the city, giant cacti can be seen, protected within the Saguaro National Monument that touches the outskirts of Tucson.

BELOW, *an image familiar from numerous old Western movies: the steam engine at Old Tucson, complete with smoke stack, gleaming brass bell and cow-catcher on the front*

This is the second largest city in Arizona, a State which came into being only in 1912. One hundred and twenty miles (193km) further on across the desert and half an hour or so before midnight, the Sunset enters the sprawling mass of lights which is Phoenix and Scottsdale. Over 800,000 people live in this expanding area, eight times as many as in 1950, and more than half the population of Arizona. A great many of them are over 60, enjoying the dry climate and taking refuge in air conditioned houses during the summer.

Only 425 miles (684km) remain of the journey to the Pacific, which the train covers in eight hours, the clocks going back another hour. It is dark, of course, most of the way, but there is a call at Yuma on the Mexican border, a place which, together with nearby Gila Bend, is the hottest region of the United States apart from California's Death Valley.

The scenery is almost all desert, interspersed with scrub and strange-looking trees. It has been downhill all the way from Texas but now the tracks go down even more, until they are 220 feet (67m) below sea level alongside Salton Sea. At about half past three in the morning the train stops at Indio, a station serving the exclusive resort of Palm Springs. At least it is cool at that time of night.

Another 130 miles (209km) remain to Los Angeles and the train is allowed 3¼ hours for this distance. There is some heavy climbing still to be done through the last great obstacle, the San Jacinto range of mountains. The train goes over the San Gorgonio Pass nearly a mile (1.5km) above the Pacific Ocean.

A SEA OF LIGHT

Quite abruptly, it is downhill all the way after that point and, provided the notorious smog of the Los Angeles basin permits, an incredible vista begins to open up. Best observed at night or early dawn, millions of lights sprawl across a hundred square miles (259sq km) as the westbound train rolls through the San Timoteo Canyon, past Colton where enormous Southern Pacific freight yards are located, and comes to a stop at Pomona, California. This is a city in its own right, though dependent upon Los Angeles, and is the site of the annual LA County Fair.

The Sunset Limited passes below Mount Wilson, 6170 feet (1881m) high and famed for its observatory and stellar telescope, and after that the train mixes in with the freeways and meanders towards the busy station at the end of the line. Los Angeles Union Station was the last of the palatial terminals built in the US, completed in 1940 in Mexican-Colonial Spanish style, and standing on Alameda Street.

It is seven o'clock in the morning, if the westbound is on time – and it usually is. Only coffee and juices are available on the train at this hour; for a full breakfast passengers must use the station cafeterias before emerging on to the busy streets of America's third largest city.

FAR RIGHT, *giant cacti stand motionless in the heat of the Saguera National Monument*

BELOW, *Phoenix, a bustling modern city rising from the dust of the Arizona desert*

■ The Sunset Limited departs from New Orleans and from Los Angeles three days a week. The 2033-mile (3272km) journey takes 42 hours, 45 minutes westbound and 42 hours eastbound.

■ A reservation is mandatory, and bookings are heavy for most of the year. Because it travels through the 'sun belt', June, July, August and September are extremely hot (although the train is completely air conditioned). Even in the depths of winter, mid-day temperatures usually reach 61°F (16°C). The periods March to May, and October/November, are the pleasantest for travel.

■ The Amtrak USA RailPass allows unlimited travel all over the system for 45 days.

■ The Sunset Limited is operated by Amtrak USA, America's National Railroad Passenger Corporation. For reservations and information within the United States, call toll free 1 800 USA RAIL, or contact a travel agent.

■ Leisurail, a division of Thomas Cook, are co-agents for Amtrak in Britain. Leisurail, Units 1–3 Coningsby Road, Merlin Business Park, North Bretton, Peterborough PE3 8HY. Tel: (01733) 335599. Fax: (01733) 505451. Destination Marketing, at 2 Cinammon Row, London SW11 3TW, are the other the other.
Tel: (0171) 978 5212.

From New York to Montréal on the Adirondack

PAUL ATTERBURY

A straight line drawn between New York and Montréal follows the Hudson River northwards and then continues along the western shore of Lake Champlain, a vast expanse of water dividing the Adirondacks from the Green Mountains of Vermont. Although built at different times by several independent, and sometimes competing, companies the railway that links the two cities follows the same route. Amtrak's Adirondack makes the journey once a day in each direction, and its leisurely progress through a changing landscape allows ample time for the enjoyment of the Hudson Valley, the rocky lake shore and the woods and farmland that lie between. There is also the added excitement of the frontier crossing as the train passes from the United States into Canada.

ABOVE, *bold numbering on the northbound train*

FAR RIGHT, *preparing to set off – the Adirondack waits panting in the gloom of New York's Penn Station*

IT IS A SCENE familiar from a hundred Hollywood movies. The conductor, smartly dressed in an elegant and surprisingly well-fitting uniform, stands on the platform as the last passengers hurry into the waiting cars. 'All aboard', he shouts, the long-drawn out syllables echoing into the subterranean gloom of the station, and then steps into his compartment as the train begins to move to the accompaniment of a distant wailing from the locomotive.

The reality, at New York's Penn Station on a cold morning in 1992, is still much the same, and that is the problem with travelling by train in North America. Expectations are so conditioned by the cinema that the romance takes over long before you even buy the ticket. Of course, reality constantly breaks in: the passengers, clearly of the 1990s, rarely match the elegance of their screen prototypes, or even the conductor. The station is a confusing and crowded shopping mall with trains hidden away in the basement. The ticket is issued by a computer and the person operating it instructs you to 'have a nice day'. The late 20th century is all around and yet the idea of the journey survives, some-how, all the assaults of modernity, and remains rooted firmly in the

cinematic past. Gleaming silver trains, towering diesel locomotives adorned with hooters, bells and cow-catchers, and the conductors, who all could be out-of-work or retired actors, maintain the illusion.

Despite its modern image and sophisticated marketing, Amtrak, created 1 May 1971 as the National Railroad Passenger Corporation to operate most of the passenger services in the United States, has itself made little effort to play down the romance. The timetable is full of trains with wonderful names, the Yankee Clipper, the Lake Shore Limited, the Silver Meteor, the California Zephyr, the Texas Eagle, the Empire Builder, the Desert Wind and the Broadway Limited, names that are consciously evocative of the great days of train travel.

I had booked a place on the Adirondack, due to leave New York for Montréal at 10.45hrs. Exactly on time, the train moved out of the platform and set off on the slow and rather depressing exploration of tunnels, old industrial sites and derelict waterfronts that mark any train departure from New York. The ambling pace allowed ample time for the appreciation of the graffiti, which included some stylish portraits. After making a series of announcements in a

■ Historically the Adirondack follows an interesting route that spans the heyday of railway building in the United States. Albany, some 140 miles (225km) up the Hudson River from New York, was in at the start of railway building in North America. The Mohawk & Hudson Railroad, incorporated in 1826, opened in 1831 with the locomotive DeWitt Clinton hauling its first train between Albany and Schenectady. From then on lines were pushed out in all directions and Albany became an important railway centre at the meeting point of many independent and often competing lines. The Hudson River Railroad, the Adirondack's route along the eastern shore of the river between New York and Albany, opened in 1851. North from Schenectady the

voice that surely belonged to John Wayne, the conductor began his round of ticket checking. It was a good performance and he played his part to the hilt, setting a standard that his colleagues were unable to match. He looked magnificent, the uniform crisp and immaculate, his every distinguished grey hair in place, and he indulged in plenty of drawling repartee as he sorted out the various little problems that came his way. By comparison the passengers were rather a motley lot: middle-aged and elderly couples in shapeless casual clothes, groups of students, a few families, and only a scattering of sharply dressed professional women in bright suits to maintain the traditional aura of train elegance. Soon after departure they were all reading or eating or both, and then slipping in and out of slumber. Conversations were casual, easily entered and just as easily broken off, and this remained the pattern as the hours unrolled. The train was never more than half full and everyone made the most of the extra space, so the close contacts and surprisingly intimate conversations characteristic of crowded, long distance trains were never on the cards.

A MODERN LOCO

With plenty of space, it was easy to explore the train. Typically Amtrak, it was not grand, but comfortable and well-equipped with air conditioning, adjustable seats, drinking water fountains and plenty of luggage space. At the head, and issuing regular wails in the style associated with American trains, was one of the tall, angular diesel locomotives Amtrak have developed for their passenger services. At their formation, Amtrak inherited a mixed bag of locomotives and rolling stock from a variety of railway companies, but now, 20 years on, they have their own distinct style. Their diesels, silver grey, and marked with blue, white and red horizontal stripes, have replaced the rounded lines of their famous movie ancestors with a chunky, workmanlike quality that looks more suited to hauling freight trains.

history of the route is much more complex, the line from Schenectady to Plattsburgh being built in stages by a series of small companies who were frequently defeated by the combination of difficult terrain and poor finances. In 1832 one company completed a line between Schenectady and the old resort of Saratoga Springs, 21 miles (34km) to the north, and by 1848 other companies had pushed it north to Whitehall. Twenty years later work started on the next section, Whitehall to Plattsburgh, the most expensive and the most demanding section of the route for the railway builders, with the line being carved through the rocks that mark the foothills of the Adirondacks along the shores of Lake Champlain. It was not until 1873, and after several bankruptcies and reorganizations, that all these small companies were

brought together as the New York & Canada Railroad, and the line was then continued to Montréal, opening in 1875. In due time all these companies were absorbed by the grand Delaware & Hudson, and they operated the route until the coming of Amtrak.

RIGHT, *for many people, fall is the time to travel through New England, when the autumn colours glow red and gold*

BELOW, *the spectacular Bear Mountain bridge across the Hudson River*

Behind the locomotive were half a dozen of the modern cars designed originally for the north-east corridor Metroliner trains, with the typical rounded shape that always makes them seem smaller than they actually are. All but one had 'Coach' written on the side, 'Coach' being American for Standard Class. The exception was labelled 'Café', and this proved to be half exactly that and half Custom, or First Class. The Custom section was screened off with a curtain, and a peep through this revealed more generous seats, a slightly de luxe atmosphere, free newspapers and the service of tea, coffee and juice included in the ticket price. There was one smoking car, at the end of the train.

The Café remained open throughout the journey and, owing to the American habit of grazing steadily rather than eating at set times, it was heavily patronized. The menu offered a range of all-American fare, but my experience was limited to the smoked cheese and ham sandwich, which proved to be typically generous, large slabs of rye bread containing eight layers of sliced ham and a similar amount of cheese.

The tunnels that allow trains to move in and out of Manhattan, all built at enormous expense at the start of this century, are soon left behind as the train swings northwards along the Hudson. For the next 140 miles (225km), all the way to Albany, the route hugs its eastern shore. A vital trade link since the 17th century, the Hudson is an artery through American history. One of the first rivers to be explored by the early settlers, it rapidly became one of America's prime carriers of freight and passengers. Later, a network of canals linked it westwards to Buffalo and Lake Erie and northwards to the St Lawrence. Even when the railways came, the river traffic continued to thrive and it is only the last few decades that have seen the Hudson's decline as a commercial waterway.

The western shore, seen from the train, is a continuous line of steep and sombre cliffs, crowned occasionally by palatial mansions and grand summer houses. One such mansion is the West Point Military Academy. Another notable one is that built by the Vanderbilt family – Cornelius Vanderbilt made his fortune from railways, owning a variety of companies from the 1850s. However, his biggest holding was in the New York Central, then spreading its lines westwards from the Hudson. His son William took over the Central, and under his leadership it

grew to be one of the major systems of the eastern United States.

The history of American railways is dotted with famous companies and many of their names are still to be seen on the side of freight cars – Canadian Pacific, Delaware & Hudson, Erie Lackawanna, Burlington Northern, Norfolk Southern, Union Pacific and, above all, Santa Fe – that is the Atcheson, Topeka and Santa Fe of the Johnny Mercer song, immortalized by the Dorsey orchestra.

Alongside the line a series of tall bridges span the river high above the water. Built of a spider's web of iron girders set generally on concrete piers, these have a spiky elegance made exciting by their height. Most carry roads, but at least one has that particular quality of American railway viaducts, a mass of thin trestles floating high in the air and looking far too insubstantial to carry the weight of a train.

Mansions apart, it is the weatherboarded house, in all its forms, that is a feature of this route: decrepit shacks buried in the woods with missing boards and peeling paint, old farms functional and careworn or lovingly restored, suburban villas brand spanking new, complete with balconies and verandahs, and grand colonial palaces with pillared porticoes. Americans still seem to model their lives on their colonial past and a shack in the woods is part of the American dream, the ideal primitivism of Thoreau albeit tempered by barbecues, swimming pools and air conditioning. And even

the most basic shack proudly flies its stars and stripes from the flagpole.

The scene is initially suburban, but quickly smartens up. At Yonkers, where according to Ella Fitzgerald 'true love conquers', tennis courts and yacht parks are well in evidence, and by Croton-Harmon the commuter belt has been left behind. The train was now well behind schedule, but the conductor was very relaxed. 'Some days we eat the bear, some days the bear eats us', was all he had to say to one querulous passenger. In fact, the timetable is constructed along generous lines, with the built-in flexibility that is essential for long journeys along single tracks with passing loops far apart. On my return the next day the train was 1½ hours late at one point but by the time it reached New York it was, by some miracle of timetable juggling, precisely on schedule.

WOODLAND AND WATERFALLS

The train now follows the river's curving shore, sometimes running through rocky cuttings with tumbling waterfalls, sometimes through woodland and sometimes along causeways with water on both sides. After Poughkeepsie and Rhinecliff the scenery becomes more dramatic, with a distant view of the Catskill Mountains to the west, and there are plenty of echoes of the landscape that had so powerful an appeal to the early 19th-century romantic painters now known as the Hudson River School, who glorified the river and the wonders of nature that it encompasses.

After pausing at Hudson, where the decorative 1875 station is remarkable, like so many now, for its complete lack of platforms, the trains run steadily on beside the river to Albany-Rensselaer. Here our crew changed and the John Wayne conductor was last seen walking

BELOW, *pausing at Hudson to take on more passengers*

BELOW, *the Adirondack mountains are a popular holiday resort area, notably around Lake Placid*

FAR RIGHT, *Montréal city, a fine mixture of old-style and modern buildings*

off into the sunset, head held high. Albany is an industrial town that has seen better days. Formerly an important railway centre at the meeting point of several lines, its development was linked closely to the growth of trading on the Hudson.

The train crosses the river, and then follows the old Mohawk & Hudson route to Schenectady through a landscape of woodland and industry. Most people who had started the journey in New York had left the train at Albany or Schenectady, and so only the serious travellers remained for the dramatic stages ahead, 220 miles (354km) and seven hours of arduous single track. At Schenectady the line crosses the Mohawk and then industry is left behind.

IN THE WAKE OF COMMERCE

Passing the old resort towns of Saratoga Springs and Glens Falls-Fort Edward, the train runs through long stretches of marshy woodland, with occasional views through to distant hills. There are remote farms, and little wooden settlements hidden among trees and at the stations families gather to show their children the train, which then ambles off into the woods, wailing. South of Whitehall the landscape becomes more open, and the train follows the route of the Champlain Canal. This grand waterway, with its high bridges and brightly painted locks, was built to connect the Hudson with the St Lawrence, via Lake Champlain, and

thus to create a direct freight route between New York and Canada. Today, it is used mostly by fishing and pleasure boats, but its commercial side is underlined by the series of navigational beacons that mark the route. The railway curves through the hills, following the canal, and all around is a rocky, dramatic landscape. North of Whitehall it crosses the southern tip of Lake Champlain and then swings north to run virtually along the lake shore for the next 100 miles (160km).

This is the best part of the journey. The lake is huge and magnificent, a vast expanse of water stretching to the distant horizon formed by the Green Mountains. To the immediate west are the Adirondacks, often out of sight, but an omnipresent and powerful force as the train winds its way through their rocky foothills. The journey, pausing at little lakeside towns, Ticonderoga, Port Henry and Westport, is one for all seasons. Spring and autumn are probably best, but the winter can be just as splendid with the lake frozen solid and the mountain rivers either stopped in their tracks or piled high with ice flows. Solitary fishermen stand above holes in the ice and winter birds flap slowly over the frozen lake, isolated in a landscape whose colours are infinitely varied in their subtlety and delicacy. Along the lakeside the train climbs steadily, and so by Plattsburgh it is often high on a rocky ledge, with views out across the lake towards Burlington on the distant eastern shore.

The lakeside stations are small and decorative. Port Henry is boldly dated 1888, while Westport is all green and white painted timber, with a bell tower, and old baggage trolleys. At each one there is an excited group, often with video cameras at the ready, waiting to greet someone from the train.

From Plattsburgh the line leaves the lake to wander through woods and farmland, to make a more low-key approach to Rouses Point, and the border. Crossing frontiers by train is always interesting, and this was no exception. The train waited for as long as it took for the Canadian Customs officers to examine everyone's documents, and ask a few searching questions. While this was going on, all the crew, driver included, assembled in the Café car, each with his dinner ready in a plastic pot to be put into the microwave. When they had eaten they sat about gossiping, waiting for the Customs men to finish. On the return journey the Customs were even tougher, with the Americans now in the leading role. 'Where were you born'? the gun-toting officers asked everyone in turn, while Sacha the sniffer dog, having done her duty, sat on a seat looking out of the window.

When the Canadians were finally satisfied, the conductor picked up his intercom to tell the driver 'Train 69, OK to highball', and we were on our way again, for the last 50 miles (80km). The landscape is now radically different, a flat, agricultural plain stretching to the horizon, marked only by farms and grain silos. Soon, however, we were into the suburbs, rows of little houses, all with pools in the garden, and countless level crossings, over which the train crawls at walking pace, hooter wailing.

Suddenly, there is the St Lawrence ahead. The train crosses it on a long iron bridge, slowly, giving time to view the locks, the quays, the shipping, and then, elevated on a long viaduct, it makes its way into Montréal PQ, the city's central station, a new, raw concrete structure buried, as ever, beneath a tower block. With a final wail from the locomotive, it was journey's end. We were in another country, and the notices were all in French.

PRACTICAL INFORMATION

■ The Adirondack runs once a day in each direction between New York and Montréal, throughout the year, and the 382-mile (615km) journey takes ten hours.

■ There are two classes, Coach and Custom, and reservations are required in advance for all seats. Sit on the left for the best views of the Hudson.

■ There are strict border controls between Canada and the United States, but no facilities for changing money at the frontier.

■ The best time to travel is the spring or autumn, and the train may be heavily booked at these times. Winter journeys may offer exciting views of snow-capped mountains and the frozen Lake Champlain, with possibilities for skiing along the route.

■ The Adirondack is operated by Amtrak, the National Railroad passenger Corporation of the United States. For reservations and information call toll free 1 800 USA RAIL within the United States, or contact a travel agent. In Britain Amtrak is represented by Leisurail, Unit 1–3 Coningsby Road, Merlin Business Park, North Bretton, Peterborough PE3 8HY. Tel: (01733) 335599. Fax: (01733) 505451. Also by Destination Marketing, 2 Cinammon Row, London SW11 3TW. Tel: (0171) 978 5212.

inspecting them there was a slight jerk and we began to roll.

The suburbs of Toronto are no more exciting than those of any other big city so this seemed the right time to look at my fellow passengers and strike up a few acquaintances. There were a number of Canadians on my train taking a fresh look at their country, as well as a few Europeans and some Japanese. All appeared adequately prosperous and all were clearly looking forward to the trip.

Back in the Coach section the crowd was even more cosmopolitan and younger, though less raffish than I remember them being 30 years ago. I recall sharing three days with a lumberjack who whiled away each mealtime by bringing his new-fangled chain-saw to the table and slicing up the bread; one thing lead to another, and when he started on the furnishings they threw him off the train.

This train ride across Canada has always instilled a certain camaraderie into the passengers, and this time was to be no different. Within hours our compartment had developed into a rolling party which continued on and off for the next three days.

The train was now running through the very beautiful lake-and-woods country north of Toronto. Every bend in the track revealed another view, another lake or river, with little villages or whitewashed weekend cottages dotted about on the lake shores. This was the start of a

FAR LEFT, *a grain silo pierces the flat prairie landscape*

BELOW LEFT, *it's a comfortable life in the 'Bullet Lounge', just below the observation dome*

LEFT, *freight trains also use this route – this is one of the wheat carriers, apparently as endless as the prairie itself*

OVER, *The Canadian snakes through the passes amid spectacular Rocky Mountain scenery*

long, long stretch across the Canadian Shield country, that mass of pre-Cambrian rock that covers such a large part of central Canada. It is glorious, rugged country where the lakes and rivers are dotted with beaver dams and the train stops at little stations here and there to let off fishermen and trappers. Towards the west, along Georgian Bay and the northern shores of Lake Huron and Lake Superior, lie large areas of swamp or muskeg, which proved a sore trial to the builders of the railway. Whole sections of newly laid line would be swallowed overnight into the almost bottomless bogs until finally they drove piles 150 feet (45m) into the morass and then floated the track on great rafts of logs.

MINING COUNTRY

About nine hours north of Toronto is Sudbury, a mining town where they mine nickel for the coinage, and the whole town and surrounding countryside are dominated by the 1250 feet (380m) Superstack, which can be seen from the railway. The object of the Superstack is to remove, or rather deploy, the sulphurous smoke emissions which used to fall like rain. These produced such devastating effects that the American astronauts came here to train for the moon landings, finding the country around Sudbury ideally barren. Conservationists will be glad to learn that, thanks, to the Superstack, the sulphurous emissions no longer fall around Sudbury; they fall in Scandinavia.

A few miles north of Sudbury lies Caproel which is a rail junction, and we were rattling

over the points as I headed in for the Moonlight Dinner, the last of the three sittings. The food is good: Canadian salmon, good steaks or a vegetarian choice, and some of that excellent Inniskillin wine.

Canadians tend to go to bed early and since we had been crossing the Canadian Shield for most of the day, I did the same, anticipating that by daylight we would be out of it and on to the prairies. The pre-Cambrian Shield is certainly varied and beautiful country but there is a great deal of it.

Sioux Lookout is not as exciting as its name suggests, but the change from the rock-and-forest country of the Canadian Shield is nothing if not dramatic. At one moment you are in woods and then suddenly on the first of the prairies, which you spend most of the day crossing. At first small white-painted farms dot the view but gradually these pull apart and away, and once you are in Manitoba, the next province to the west, you are fairly launched across the Great Plains.

I like the Great Plains of North America. Some people say they are boring and produce a sort of cafard, a desert ailment caused by looking out for ever at miles and miles of nothing, but in truth the Great Plains of Manitoba and Saskatchewan are not like that at all. They *are* flat, but there is something in the quality of the light that makes the view marvellously clear and constantly changing. The countryside ripples under the wind as the great cornfields wave gently to and fro, spreading out for miles around the little farms. There is colour, too, in the red

and ochre painted grain elevators and barns which stand out sharply in that crystal air.

WHERE THE WEST BEGINS

There were of course diversions. There was some singing going on in the bar, and there were two cities to look at: Winnipeg, capital of Manitoba and, later that night, Saskatoon. Winnipeg is said to be 'the place where the West begins'. It stands at the junction of two great rivers, the Red and the Assiniboine, and has another old railway hotel, the Fort Gary, named after the fort built by the Hudson Bay Company to trade with the Plains Indians, feed the immigrants and barter for furs. The train stopped here for 20 minutes, a stop referred to in Canadian trainspeak as 'dwell time'. I used my dwell time to stretch my legs along the platform, buy a couple of books and take a swift peek at some people dressed in 19th-century clothes who were waiting outside the station in buggies. These were Hutterites, a religious sect rather like the Amish of Pennsylvania, who plough their land with the aid of horses, use carts and buggies rather than cars, and still wear long skirts and poke bonnets, dark suits and wide-brimmed hats, a curious sight in a young and modern country like Canada.

That second day was spent trundling across the province of Manitoba and into Saskatchewan. Parts of this journey are across country so flat it must have been ironed. After dark we arrived at the city of Saskatoon. Saskatoon was founded as a temperance town back in the 1880s, but the good intentions came to nothing when the railway arrived. Railway pioneer Cornelius Van Horne declared that the railway was built with 'dynamite and whisky' and he was not wrong. Saskatoon is a pretty place, set astride the South Saskatchewan River, and has among other attractions a very good Western Development Museum, set in a vast hangar which contains a full-sized Western Railway Station, *circa* 1910.

Off again, while the three-day party roared on in the bar. That train-travel camaraderie was clearly taking effect and people were telling total strangers things they would have carefully kept from the folks back home. The Japanese had relaxed and were roaming the corridors in their underwear, shooting hours of video film.

Onward then, shedding passengers at smaller halts in this wide expanse of grass and grain fields, and across another provincial border and into my favourite part of Canada, the cowboy province of Alberta, green and rolling and dotted with ranches and great herds of cattle.

For Canada too has ranches and cowboys,

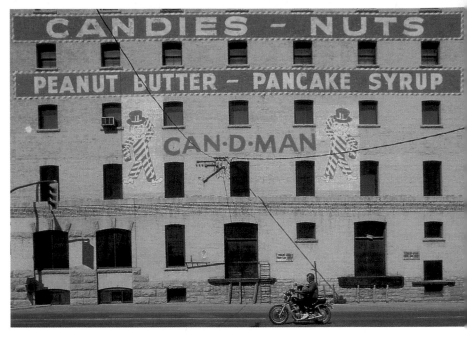

and Indians. The Sioux live to the south, along the US border. In Alberta, most of the Indians belong to the Blood tribe, one of the many tribes in the Blackfoot Confederation. To the north lies the country of the Cree, while to the west, in the foothills of the Rockies, the Stoney Indians still hunt and trap as they have done for centuries. Treated fairly by the encroaching whites, Canada's Indians never suffered the wars, deprivation and deceit which has decimated the tribes south of the border – which is not to say that Canada's original inhabitants welcome the curtailing of their lands and roving way of life.

We ran along the valley to the capital of Alberta province, Edmonton, where I was getting off the train for a welcome two-day

ABOVE TOP, *off the track in Winnipeg*

ABOVE, *preparing dinner on the train – almost a case of 'too many cooks'*

OVER, *looking high over the skyscrapers of Vancouver, on Canada's western seaboard, with the green headland of Stanley Park – and one of its famous carved and painted totem poles*

stop-over. Edmonton is an oil town and Alberta as a whole supplies much of Canada's energy. My main reason for stopping here was to stretch my legs and visit the West Edmonton Mall, a real experience. There are some 4000 shops and stalls in the Mall, plus a swimming pool, and penguins and an ice rink, cinemas, restaurants and jazz bands, and a submarine journey through a tank equipped with sharks.

RETRACING HISTORY

I spent the night in Edmonton and, deserting The Canadian for a short stretch, took a stopping train next day up to the resort town of Jasper in the foothills of the Rockies. The train runs along the Athabasca River and at every stop we disgorged fishermen or canoeists. The train arrives in the very centre of Jasper running in beside Main Street, and the population comes out to meet it as they must have met the stagecoach in days gone by. Jasper is pretty and surrounded by the mountains of the Jasper National Park, a paradise for skiing or fishing or walking according to the season, but my reason for stopping here was to spend a night at the famous Jasper Park Lodge. This is another railway hotel, famous among travellers for friendly deer and cycling waiters. The accommodation is in cottages and the deer come on to the verandahs and peer in the windows, while if you want a drink or a sandwich you call room service and in a few minutes a waiter appears on a bicycle, pedalling along, tray held aloft. Rarely is a plate dropped or a drink spilt.

The Canadian gets into Jasper in the early afternoon and waits there for an hour of dwell time to give the passengers a chance to shop and inspect the old steam loco, complete with cow-catcher, that stands beside the station. Then we set off again for the last night on the train and the most spectacular part of the journey, over the Rockies to Vancouver.

The route runs directly into wild mountain country and everyone is at the windows or up in the dome cars. Excitement rippling down the train announces the sighting first of a brown bear and a cub crossing a meadow by the track, and then of a moose, pacing the train at a fair gallop below the embankment before swerving off into the woods. In between the sightings there are glorious views, silver lakes and great peaks, as we climb towards Yellowhead Pass. There is the bulk of the 9549 feet (2910m) Mount Fitzwilliam and then the 7797 feet (2376m) peak of Mount Rockingham towering above Yellowhead Lake – but there are peaks and glaciers and lakes everywhere, every view one to eat up camera film.

The track splits a few miles west of Jasper with one line heading off north towards Prince Rupert and Prince George on the Pacific Coast, but we turn south and west to the mining town of Kamloops, giving up our vantage points with reluctance to go for dinner. I took the early sitting in order to see the mountains as the sun went down and then went to bed early. By 5 o'clock I was up and back in the dome car for the truly terrifying part of the journey, through the Fraser Canyon.

In Fraser Canyon, Cornelius Van Horne's 'whisky and dynamite' were both constantly employed for there was then no way through except for the river. Van Horne had hired thousands of Chinese labourers to work on the line and here they had to be lowered from the canyon rim on ropes, to hack and blast a track into the sheer walls of the cliff. Scores, maybe hundreds, died before the track was complete. Even seen from the train the canyon is formidable, the cliff falling sheer to the rocks and rapids in the river, one last defiant stand of Nature against Man before we are out of the canyon and running along the Fraser River, beside the great log rafts floating down to the mills and into the silver city of Vancouver, one of the most agreeable and beautiful of all the Pacific Coast cities.

This journey displays the sheer immensity and diversity of Canada as a flight never can. More than that, the trip is tremendous fun, with more than a touch of the vanishing world of real travel. 'Never go back' is a golden rule of travel, but to every rule there should be an exception; I might even do it again.

PRACTICAL INFORMATION

■ The Canadian runs between Toronto and Vancouver three times a week in each direction. The 2790 miles (4467km) are covered in 69 hours. The journey can be broken.

■ Classes include 'Silver and Blue' (available to sleeping accommodation passengers only) and Coach, both having access to the observatory or dome cars. Sleeping accommodation is in private cabins, shared couchettes or reclining seats. It is always advisable to book ahead, particularly for the spectacular Rockies section.

■ The journey can be enjoyed at any time, except perhaps the depths of winter. In July/August the Manitoba and Saskatchewan wheat fields are an endless yellow glory; in late September/early October the fall colours of the Canadian shield are ravishing.

■ The Canadian is operated by VIA Rail Canada. In Canada their offices can be found at any main line station or located through the Yellow Pages.

■ Abroad, VIA Rail general service agents can be contacted through travel agents or Canadian Tourist Offices, or at VIA Rail Canada, 2 Place Ville Marie, Montréal, PQ H3B 2C9, Canada. Tel: 514 871 6000. Fax: 514 871 6658. In Britain the agent is Leisurail, Units 1–3 Coningsby Road, Merlin Business Park, North Bretton, Peterborough PE3 8HY. Tel: 0733 51780. Fax: 0733 892601.

The Chihuahua Pacífico Train through Mexico's Copper Canyon

MONA KING

The Chihuahua Pacific Train (Nuevo Chihuahua-Pacífico) runs for some 406 miles (655km) through north-western Mexico, linking Los Mochis and Chihuahua. It travels from the tropical coastal valleys to the high plateau in the north, traversing the mighty Sierra Madre Occidental via the Copper Canyon (Barranca del Cobre). This is an area of exceptional beauty offering magnificent landscapes of great canyons and gorges, pine-clad slopes and deep rivers. It is also a region of great cultural interest, and stop-overs give the unique opportunity of exploring the homelands of the Tarahumara Indians, who still live in caves among the remote sierras of this wild and rugged region.

RIGHT, *boarding the Chihuahua Pacífico in the early-morning dark at Los Mochis*

FAR RIGHT, *flowering desert cacti are only one species of vegetation to be seen on this wonderful train journey to the heartlands of Mexico*

I T WAS HOT AND cloudless when we landed in Los Mochis. Cattle grazed peacefully in lush green pastures, tropical vegetation and flowers lined the route; this was mid-March and the scene looked decidedly cheerful.

Los Mochis, the starting point, or terminus, for the Chihuahua Pacific train, is also an important bus terminal for the region. A short stroll around the block revealed shops, colourful fruit stalls – and many buses.

Our hotel restaurant was lively with local Mexicans in cowboy hats, low-slung belts and tight-fitting trousers. There was even more action in the almost pitch dark bar where tourists were arriving in lively groups, the margaritas were flowing, the television was on full blast and there was an air of feverish expectancy. The band was about to come on. Reluctantly we decided to call it a day.

An unmentionably early hour next morning

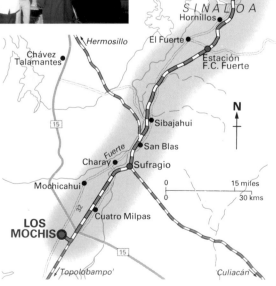

Map labels:

Nuevo Casas Grandes
Ciudad Guerrero
Miñaca
La Junta
Laguna Bustillos
Santa
CHIHUAHUA
Ciudad Juárez
Ojinaga
Pedernales
Anáhuac
El Encino
Isabel
Fresno
CUAUHTÉMOC
Lugo
El Charco
Terrero
San Miguel
General Trías
Torreón
Laguna de Los Mexicanos
Basaseachic
Sigoyna
C H I H U A H U A
Cajurichic
Treviño
San Juanito
Bocoyna
Los Ojitos
Creel
Laguna Arareco
El Lazo
Pitorreal
Tararécua
Posada Barrancas
El Divisadero
Barranca del Cobre
Batopilas, La Bufa
San Rafael
Sierra
Cuiteco
Bahuichivo
Tarahumara
Cerocahui
oris
Urique
Barranca de Urique

■ The Chihuahua al Pacífico line, linking Ojinaga, on the United States border, to the Pacific port of Topolobampo, opened in 1961. Plans for a railroad linking Texas with the Pacific had, however, been made as far back as the 19th century, and in 1898 the Kansas City, Mexico & Orient Railroad began construction of a line west of Chihuahua. It was not until 1952, when the Mexican government purchased the 'Orient', that engineers set about the daunting task of constructing the sector of the line through the Sierra Madre mountains.

Having the same gauge as the adjoining area in the US, the line serves as an important commercial link with the States and is in continuous use by freight trains. It has also played an important role in the development of the area in providing the only proper access to remote villages and communities in the Sierra Tarahumara. The passenger train, which travels only between Los Mochis and Chihuahua, is a big tourist attraction for visitors from all over the world.

The journey is one of contrasting landscapes and climatic changes. From the lush pasturelands around Los Mochis the train makes a gradual ascent to the mountains, entering a different time zone as it passes from the State of Sinaloa to that of Chihuahua. Then comes the Copper Canyon. Characterized by rugged peaks, plunging gorges, deep riverbeds and coniferous forests, this offers the most exciting scenery of the journey, which is often referred to as the Copper Canyon Railway. The last part traverses the plains of Chihuahua, passing through neat farmlands, fruit orchards and cattle.

Stops along the way include: the small colonial town of El Fuerte; Bahuichivo, for visits to Cerocahui and the Urique Canyon (Barranca de Urique); El Divisadero for magnificent views of the canyons; the lumber town of Creel, an excellent base for exploring the Sierra de Tarahumara; and Cuauhtémoc, to take a look at the Mennonite colony.

found us being driven through dark, deserted streets to the station. Undeterred, our fellow American travellers kept up a keen patter of conversation. The station was virtually empty, apart from a few people scurrying through to the platform where, awaiting us in all its splendour, was the train itself. Four blue coaches headed by a diesel engine were grandly labelled 'Ferrocarriles Nacionales de México' (Mexican National Railways), 'hecho en México' (made in Mexico), 'Primera Especial'.

We had scarcely settled into our seats when, with no fuss or bother, the train glided off on the dot of 06.00hrs. As we set off the sky became a gash of orange, revealing the ghostly outlines of palms and other foliage. Small huts and plots appeared to our left; trees and flowers abounded; washing was hanging out on the line. The odd woman peered out at us from the darkness of her doorway, while chickens, pigs and dogs poked about in the yards. A solitary horseman roamed the fields. The warm yellow glow of daybreak bathed the landscape, giving the whole scene an air of romance and making one reflect upon the merits of living freely in open nature – until, that is, the occasional glimpse of a huge satellite dish intruded upon the picture. Soon the sun peered over the hillside and the countryside took on a whole new lease of life. It was time to take stock of our immediate surroundings.

Our coach, the end one, was occupied mainly by local Mexicans, who were quiet and courteous, keeping to themselves. The men were dressed mostly Western-style, complete with Panama hats. Women tended to travel with children, generally very well behaved. Many locals slept; clearly they were not here for the scenery. Tourists, mainly Americans, were generally seated further up the train. Compartments are fitted out with very comfortable reclining aircraft-type seats and lunch trays; ours had 18 rows of seats. Windows allow for good viewing and have Venetian blinds. Heating, or air conditioning,

is provided and there are toilets at the back of each coach.

We soon made the acquaintance of conductor Sr Guillermo Cano, who came along frequently to point out anything of interest on the route. He advised us that the right-hand side of the train offers the best views most of the time and introduced us to three technicians sitting behind us, who were kind enough to let us out on to the rear end of the car whenever we asked. This is normally locked for safety reasons so we were privileged to be able to enjoy the feel of the warm breezes and the proximity of the countryside. Most of the coaches date from 1988. A few are slightly older and have been remodelled. There is also a freight/passenger train called the Mixto, which leaves an hour after the Primera Especial and stops all over the place, we were warned, with no reliable timetable. Added to that, of course, there are frequent freight trains sharing the same line, as we were to observe later.

At 06.50hrs we made our first stop at Sufragio, intersection point with the main north–south railway line from Nogales to Guadalajara, and then we were soon passing through fields of great organ-pipe cactus, where the horses and donkeys ran wild. Gradually hills and mountains came into view.

A temporary diversion was caused by the arrival of the complementary box breakfast, consisting of ham sandwiches, pasta, jelly and orange juice. Chilled beer, cola and other soft drinks were also available

Many locals left and joined the train at the next two stops, El Fuerte and Loreto, and we acquired an interesting new neighbour, a very tall Mexican dashingly attired in a large black hat, black trousers and waistcoat, high-heeled boots and silver-trimmed belt. The sky was blue, with not a cloud in sight. Strange rock formations could be seen, densely wooded peaks, with bursts of yellow blossoms and fluffy white kapok trees. Then, hooting loudly, we were crossing the El Fuerte bridge, with its 1637 feet (500m) span, and gazing down at the Río Fuerte far below.

A 15-minute stop, soon after, allowed us to stretch our legs. On the platform was a curious little shrine beside which smiling girls were selling bunches of purple bougainvillea. One of our technicians was down on the track, busily engaged in shunting manoeuvres that would free the line for a large freight train which duly passed by with a load of goats. We continued climbing gently until suddenly we plunged into the El Descanso tunnel, at 5966 feet (1829m) the longest on the track, to emerge about three minutes later into the mountainous terrain of Copper Canyon country. Soon after came the 345 feet (105m) Chinipas bridge, and a superb view of the river's pale blue waters beneath us.

A MOUNTAINOUS LANDSCAPE

The scenery became more dramatic as the train twisted and carved its way through numerous tunnels and over bridges across canyons with great jagged peaks and deep gorges reaching down to the riverbeds. Pink peach blossoms thrived high up on wooded slopes and tiny, isolated settlements could be seen down in the valleys. Just after Témoris the train made huge loops and curves as it continued its ascent, giving an impressive view over three levels of railroad, with a waterfall as an added bonus. Known as the 'Loops of Témoris', this stretch gives an insight into the ingenuity of the railroad's construction. Emerging from another set of short tunnels, we caught a glimpse of the striking rock profile of a 'cardinal', before passing through an area that boasts seven varieties of pine tree, apparently unique to the area. This was the start of a noticeable change in vegetation, with our journey continuing through beautiful coniferous forests, fields of pink and white blossom and small rivers. Following our next stop at Bahuichivo, the air became fresher and signs of habitation began to appear, small houses with corrugated roofs and large satellite dishes. Deciding a little sustenance was called for before the next stop, we ordered a box lunch (there being no dining car on the train) which turned out to be ham sandwiches again, with avocado and an apple instead of pasta and jelly.

Just after noon we reached San Rafael, a major stop where the crew change. While freight trains were shunted around, vendors crowded on to the train, noisily proclaiming their wares, which ranged from tacos, chocolates and drinks, to handmade baskets and souvenirs. Many of the passengers had scattered about the station, enjoying a '20-minute' respite, when the train moved off without warning. 'Let's go!' called out the tall man in the black hat as we all raced along the platform, chasing the train. With his

ABOVE, *Tarahumara Indian children glimpsed in a doorway – note the simple, weathered wooden shingles on the roof above their heads*

FAR LEFT, *a train pulls steadily across the high Chinipas bridge*

FAR LEFT INSET, *the railway curves above the river at the Loops of Témoris*

ABOVE, *the great plume of the Basaseachic waterfall pours some 1020 feet (310m) into a gorge on the Basaseachic River below*

RIGHT TOP, *trains travelling in either direction meet daily at the station of El Divisadero, where the platform has become a busy trading point for local women*

RIGHT BELOW, *a detail of Chihuahua's fine cathedral, which took almost one hundred years to build*

long strides he made it easily, while we only just managed to clamber aboard, rather breathlessly, to find the train stopping again a few yards up the track and remaining there firmly for a good while yet.

When Sr Cano came along, soon after, to advise us of our pending arrival at Posada Barrancas, our first stop-over, we realised we didn't want to get off. The comfort of the ride through such magnificent scenery had induced a state of semi-euphoria that we rather wished would continue for ever. However, Raquel was waiting on the platform at Posada Barrancas to escort us down the path to our hotel. Several Tarahumara women in colourful headscarves, blouses and wide skirts sat in the garden, quietly weaving tiny baskets from pine needles. A baby peeped out from its mother's shawl.

After lunch we were taken on a short ride to the canyon's rim at El Divisadero, where the spectacular view is a highlight of the journey. The panorama actually takes in the three great canyons of Urique, Tararécua and Cobre (Copper). While it is reminiscent of Arizona's Grand Canyon, wooded slopes give it a different character. Its grandeur is overwhelming and this first sight of it leaves a lasting impression. Our guide pointed out huts and caves inhabited by the Tarahumara Indians. Up the road, by the El Divisadero railway stop, is a lively little market where the Indians cook Mexican specialities and display pots and dolls, baskets and violins. From a log cabin back near our hotel, a scramble down the hill led to a large cave where three Tarahumara children lived with their parents. They were shy but conversed a little in Spanish, while long-haired pigs snuffled around. The following morning we took a horseback ride through Tarahumara settlements to another beauty spot overlooking the canyons.

Then it was time to move on. The arrival of the pilot engine caused a flurry of excitement and was followed shortly by the train itself, impressively punctual. Six minutes later we were at El Divisadero. The 20-minute stop gives passengers time to race down the slope for a quick look at the canyon and a brief browse around the market which we had visited the previous day. The southbound train from Chihuahua arrived and all was in order.

We set off again through vast pine forests, rocky hills and fresh green valleys. Far vistas opened up at every turn as the train continued its slow ascent. El Lazo (Lasso) is a dramatic spot where the track circles under itself, forming a complete loop. Soon after we came to Los Ojitos, which stands at 8071 feet (2400m) amid bizarre rock formations, the highest point of the journey. After that it was downhill all the way to Creel, which we reached at 3.15 in the afternoon. This tiny lumber town looks like something straight out of the Wild West and has a character of its own. We had decided to break the journey here again.

The town is surrounded by great open plains. In the vicinity are a number of curious rock formations, bearing such names as the Elephant, Lion and Mushroom Rocks. Near by is the deep blue Arareco Lake and several Tarahumara caves, where we saw the women sitting inside, cooking on an open fire. Creel is an excellent centre for exploring the Sierra de Tarahumara, homeland of the Tarahumara Indians. Known as great long distance runners, they are traditionally a nomadic race, cultivating their crops in the summer and moving down into the

canyons in the winter to their cave dwellings. They also produce wood carvings, musical instruments, baskets and other wares which are sold all over the place. They tend to be shy and modest, but are generally friendly to strangers.

A memorable excursion took us through awesome landscapes to the depth of the Batopilas Canyon and the old mining area of La Bufa. A few encounters with solitary Tarahumaras included a musical trio, who

entertained us by the roadside. A visit to the Basaseachic Waterfall, the highest in Mexico, was most worthwhile for the stunning setting of wild, rugged mountains that surround the cascade as it plunges steeply down to an emerald pool, with no human dwellings visible anywhere around.

The following afternoon we set off on the train once more, passing by stacks of lumber, curious rock shapes and pinewoods. Our next stop was the busy junction of La Junta, with more vendors and much activity. Our journey then took us through neat farmlands, grazing cattle and fruit orchards to Cuauhtémoc, where we again left the train for an overnight stop.

Locals in Western-style gear continuously sauntered in and out of the restaurant, conducting business on a mobile phone that was handed around by the manager, while tall, pale Mennonite men in blue dungarees provided an interesting contrast. Mennonite women wear wide-brimmed hats or headscarves, long skirts and white stockings. They are a religious sect who settled in the area in 1922 and farm the land, producing apples, cheese, oats and cured meats. Out in the countryside we visited a Mennonite library, a cheese factory, and a school where the children are taught High German and Plattdeutsch, but no Spanish.

On arrival at the station for the last lap of our journey we were told the train would be an hour late. The waiting room was locked: 'No one ever boards at Cuauhtemoc – they get off, but they don't get on!' The station master kindly unlocked it for us, however, and we waited in comfort as outside darkness fell and the temperature dropped. Delays are caused mainly by the single rail track, which means freight trains are for ever being shunted into sidings, which are far and few between.

Finally, after a few mournful hoots, the train appeared, an hour and a half late. It was fairly full, with the usual combination of local and American passengers. Sr Cano should have been on the train, but alas, there had been 'trouble in La Junta' and he had had to stay to sort it out.

The train crawled along at a snail's pace. It was dark outside, with few lights, but the full golden moon which lit our path brought a fitting end to a journey which had begun with the rising sun.

END OF THE LINE

There was a short stop at Anáhuac and then we spied the twinkling lights of Chihuahua in the distance. The train made a sweeping curve and pulled in with a flourish to its final destination. It was 10.30 in the evening and we had reached Chihuahua, a little late perhaps, but safe and sound.

Our arrival was tinged with sadness since this was well and truly the end of the line. So often, modern rail travel means hurtling through the countryside at high speed, creating a sense of total detachment from your surroundings, but what made the Chihuahua Pacific rail journey so special was the very opposite feeling; the leisurely pace of travel and single rail track give the sensation not only of travelling into the very depth of the countryside, but of being a part of it. It had been a unique experience, allowing us a brief glimpse of another world. Would we do it again? The answer is yes, without hesitation.

PRACTICAL INFORMATION

■ The Primera Especial runs once daily between Los Mochis and Chihuahua in each direction. If the train is on schedule, the 406-mile (655km) journey takes about 14 hours. To be sure of passing through the most scenic areas in daylight, start at Los Mochis. Travellers should make at least a couple of stop-overs en route, with El Divisadero and Creel specially recommended. (The railway company imposes a 15 per cent surcharge for two stop-overs.)

■ Good times to travel are February to March and September to November. The summer is hot and rainy and in winter it can be very cold at the higher altitudes.

■ There is one class. Reserved seats can be purchased at the station in Los Mochis or Chihuahua. For further information write to: Chief Regional Passenger Dept, Ferrocarriles Nacionales de México, PO Box 46, Chihuahua, (Chih), Mexico. Tel: (14) 12 22 84 or 15 77 56. Alternatively, the Mexican Tourist office in your own country can supply a list of tour operators. In Britain the Mexican Tourist Office is at 60–1 Trafalgar Square, London WC2N 5DS. Tel: (0171) 734 1058. Fax: (0171) 930 9202. In the US the Mexican Tourist Office is 405 Park Avenue, Suite 1002, New York. Tel: 212 755 7261. Fax: 212 753 2874.

The Central of Peru, the highest railway in the world

ANTHONY LAMBERT

Many travellers have been emphatic about the place of the Central Railway of Peru in the pantheon of great railway journeys. Whether or not the line deserves the title of 'the most wonderful railway in the world' as some have described it, the claim of the railway to provide a passenger service over the highest summit in the world, at 15,695 feet (4784m) above sea level, is incontestable. The highest point on a Himalayan railway barely reaches half this altitude, and Europe's Jungfrau Railway falls short by over 4000 feet (1220m).

H EIGHT ALONE would not win such an accolade, but the trains that leave Lima to scale the Andes and drop down the eastern slopes of the *cordillera* to Huancayo pass through thrilling landscapes of bleak majesty. The line, as it twists and turns through narrow defiles in its struggle to climb and reach higher

BELOW RIGHT, *brilliant colours light up the market at Huancayo*

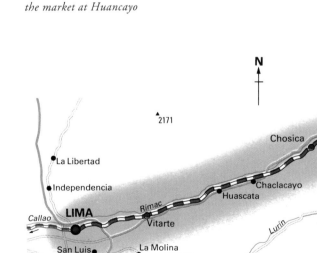

■ The Central owes its origins to one Henry Meiggs, 'Don Enrique', as he was known. Born in New York State in 1811, he made and lost several fortunes on the east coast before moving to San Francisco to take advantage of Californian gold discoveries. A financial crisis drove him to forgery and he had to flee the country in 1854. In Chile he made another fortune building railways, and became an honoured figure in Santiago. His attention turned to Peru, where the Government sought advice on railways from this already legendary figure and in 1869 gave him the contract for what was to become the Central line.

His ability to pick good engineers and inspire loyalty among his workers were key factors in the remarkable success he achieved, completing the line almost as far as Chicla by the time of his death in 1877.

Of the 61 bridges on the

valleys, leaves passengers astonished at the daring of the Victorian engineers who undertook to build the standard gauge railway (4 feet 8½ inches/1435mm).

Lima is not a place to linger. Well-armed soldiers and regular power cuts are constant reminders of Peru's political uncertainties. The colonial buildings built by the Spanish during the three centuries that followed the founding of the capital by Pizarro in 1535 have nearly all been swept away by bland development. But the city's only station, Desamparados, was built in neo-colonial style: situated behind the Presidential Palace, its exterior has a fussy grandeur with an elaborate clock equipped with 'Oxford Chimes'; it is also earthquake-proof.

Ideally, tickets should be bought in advance and a fine drizzle should give a grey pallor to the early morning scene; the coastal fogs known as *garua* that cloak the city between April and December are exchanged for clear, sunny

weather as soon as the train reaches the lower slopes of the *cordillera*. Equally, if you leave Lima in sun, it is unlikely to be shining in the mountains. Another paradox: to face the direction of travel for most of the journey, you need to find a seat with your back to the engine.

In common with train departures in many countries, the majority of people thronging the platform are not passengers. The five orange and yellow coaches are besieged by vendors, tearful relatives and friends bidding farewell, and locals for whom the single departure of the day is an event worth watching.

ABOVE, *the crest on this well-worn, wooden carriage is a reminder of the line's importance as a link with the mines*

Central, the bridge across the Verrugas Gorge is the most remarkable. When built in 1870, it was the third largest in the world, at 575 feet long (175m) and 252 feet high (76.8m). The first bridge was swept away after a cloudburst and rock fall in 1889. The second bridge was opened in 1891. Today's bridge is the third, built in 1937 on a slightly different alignment by the Cleveland Bridge & Engineering Co of Darlington, England, which

also built the Victoria Falls bridge across the Zambezi Gorge on the Zimbabwe–Zambia border.
Another bridge with a tale to tell is the Chaupichaca bridge. During maintenance work on the original bridge in 1909, the equipment train's

locomotive, No 33, had just been up to Tamboraque Station to fill up with water and was returning downhill when the wheels locked on the greasy rails and began to slide. The engine crashed at speed into a crane at work on the girders, bringing down the whole bridge, the engineers and 200 Jamaican labourers. The upturned locomotive can be seen alongside the twisted girders in the chasm below.

ABOVE, *for many the railway is a useful lifeline – these children are selling sweets to passengers at La Oroya station*

RIGHT, *the railway loops around settlements in a barren landscape*

The guttural throb of the American diesel quickens as the signal for departure is given at 07.40hrs. The locomotive's horn is in constant use as the train leaves the edge of the central district and enters the nether world of the *barrios*; stretching beside the line for miles, the dismal shacks are sad witness to a population increase in Lima from 200,000 to over 6 million in just 70 years. The filthy ribbon of water in the riverbed that parallels the line to the north is the Rimac, which the railway follows for 96 miles (155km) as far as Ticlio; in Quechua its name means 'the water that speaks'. At this point the river gives no hint of sound, but further east it falls 12,000 feet (3658m) in 80 miles (128km), in places a furious white cauldron during the wet season.

As the train ambles up the Rimac Valley, the *garua* gives way to blue skies, sometimes with a suddenness that startles those unfamiliar with the Andean climate. Though it is easy running for the first 25 miles (40km) to the first stop at Chosica, there is not a single downhill inch for the first 107 miles (172km). The pleasant climate at Chosica made the place an escape for wealthier families from Lima, who created a residential quarter in the railway town away from the capital.

Leaving Chosica the note from the diesel's engine indicates a steeper gradient, though much more taxing climbs are to come. The valley floor becomes greener as small farms create splashes of colour to relieve the pale browns of the hillsides. Purhuay tunnel is the first of 65 on the line, with a total length of over 5½ miles (9km). After a section of line that had to be rebuilt following freak flooding of the Rimac in 1925, the train pulls into Tornamesa, the first of 11 reversing points on the railway. It is from here that passengers with their backs to the engine will face forwards for most of the journey to Huancayo.

Tornamesa is unique on the Central in having a single reversal; the other ten are double

reversing points, most equipped with turntables though they have seen little use since the end of steam in the 1960s. While the diesel runs round the train, vendors ply the fruit which abounds in the area – guavas, paw paws, avocados and maracuya. The roar of the diesel's engine, pushed to give maximum power, signals the start of serious climbing. From here the gradient is seldom much below 1:25/30 until the continental divide is reached inside the tunnel through Mount Meiggs.

BEGINNING TO CLIMB

Tight curves increase the drag of the train, and steam locomotives sometimes stalled on this section to San Bartolomé, where the line crosses the Rimac. As the valley floor recedes, the view below looks ever more like an elaborate model railway. Sun-bleached pastel shades of green and red decorate the corrugated-iron roofs of the single-storey houses that make up the villages.

Fruit gives way to cactus and bunch grass, and the valley sides become progressively steeper until the line is built on a ledge of rock cut into perpendicular faces. Tornamesa appears directly below, a home for Lilliputians set amongst the massive brown hills. It is best not to let your imagination speculate on the consequences of rock falls at such points on the line.

Ten miles beyond San Bartolomé is the railway's tallest and longest viaduct, spanning the Verrugas Gorge. The present bridge is the third on the site and is named the Carrion bridge in honour of Dr Daniel Carrion, who

died after injecting himself with the blood of a railway worker infected with mysterious fever during his studies of the illness. Verrugas fever took a terrible toll of the Chilean labourers building the railway. Physically unsuited to work in high altitudes, they accounted for a large proportion of the estimated 7000 men who died from disease or accidents during construction of the railway.

Carrion bridge is one of the few on the railway to have guard rails; most have nothing, giving passengers the peculiar feeling of being suspended in air as they peer down a sheer drop of several hundred feet.

Beyond the small station at Surco are two 180-degree bends and a succession of short tunnels, cuttings and rock ledges, the sinuous course of the line making it ever more difficult to tell the direction of travel. Challape bridge, designed and built by French engineers, is crossed before arrival at Matucana, 56 miles (90km) from Lima and 7840 feet (2390m) above sea level. The Matucana Valley provides good grazing for cattle, and it was from the station here that flatcars loaded with milk churns made nightly descents to Lima – by gravity. Fatal accidents to the crews were so frequent that the service was curtailed.

Once out of the valley the terrain becomes much more inhospitable, although remains of terraces reminiscent of Inca cultivation survive, cut into the hillsides in a brave attempt to wrest a living from the soil. A narrow gorge takes the train to the first double reversal at Viso. Beyond is one of the most troublesome sections of line,

where in the early 1930s an entire mountain top came crashing down over the line, shutting it for weeks. Efforts to prevent slips on the precipitous slopes by planting trees have proved ineffective.

Passengers who are prepared may see the grim remnants of the first Chaupichaca bridge in the bottom of the chasm as the train emerges directly from a tunnel on to the present, more durable structure.

Another zig-zag commences at Tamboraque Station, followed by a further succession of tunnels, sharp curves and dizzy drops. It is noisy enough with a diesel at the head, but the cacophony of sound in steam days must have been defeaning. It certainly was for those on the engine; poor hearing among engine crews was common, and it was in tunnels that the ears were subjected to the greatest volume.

Blink and you could almost miss the Infiernillo bridge on the approach to the double reversal at Cacray; the train emerges from a tunnel directly on to the bridge and dives into another hole at the opposite end. By Cacray there are few trees, the rock and screes providing a purchase for little but hardy grasses. Adjacent to the upper reversal at Cacray is the old *Camino Real*, the 'Royal Road'. It was along this track, little wider than a mule, that the gold and silver from the mines at Cerro de Pasco, further north, were brought down to Lima. The erosion of profits by the difficulties and costs of carrying supplies to the mines, and the inability to transport economically other minerals such as lead and copper, were the principal reasons for construction of the Central. Ironically the money to pay for it was generated not by gold or silver but by bird droppings. Plans to build the line coincided with huge profits from the sale of guano, collected from Peru's offshore islands and shipped to Europe for use as fertilizer.

RIDING HIGH

Rio Blanco, 75 miles (120km) from Lima and 11,501 feet (3506m) up, was the destination for regular excursions laid on for sailors off foreign naval vessels which visited Callao, Lima's harbour. It is at about this altitude that some passengers may begin to feel the effects of mountain sickness, but most experience nothing more than a slight breathlessness, providing no strenuous exercise is attempted. The train is unique in having someone on board with an oxygen bag for anyone in need.

Another 4 miles and the train arrives at Chicla, foot of a 1½-mile-long zig-zag. This was the railhead for 14 years from 1878, while Peru fought unsuccessfully against Chile in the Pacific War, so bankrupting the country that no further

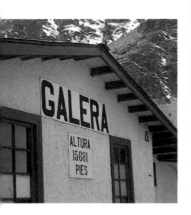

construction could be attempted. American and British creditors put together a complex deal whereby debts were liquidated in exchange for generous rights and concessions. One was control of all the railroads. Work on the line was resumed and the principal destination, La Oroya, was reached in 1893.

Though Cerro de Pasco is the main centre for mining, evidence of workings can be seen from the next station, Bellavista, up to La Oroya. A procession of downhill freight trains carrying the spoils of all this activity can be seen in loops and the headshunts of reversing points. Spoil tips mar the landscape in the immediate vicinity of mines, but the mountain views remain compelling. Snow decorates the peaks of mountains and lies in sheltered gullies, a startling contrast to the grey-brown rock.

After a crew change at the zinc-mining town of Casapalca, where the *Camino Real* forked, the train winds along a ledge to an isolated crossing loop named after the man whose name will always be associated with the Central, Henry Meiggs. With his confidence that 'Anywhere the llamas go, I can take a train', it was Meiggs who secured a contract to build what became the Central in 1869. The loop at Meiggs was an appropriate one to name after him, for it is ringed by the mountain peaks he struggled to conquer for the railway. A measure of the

challenge is provided by the view from the loop of Casapalca, already a collection of roofs the size of pinheads far below.

Eight more tunnels and the traverse of a ledge above a drop of vertigo-inducing height, and the train arrives at Ticlio, the highest junction in the world at 15,610 feet (4758m) above sea level. It is the sort of place to cure anyone disgruntled with their lot in life, for someone has to live and work in this dreary, featureless spot to control the junction and the entrance to Galera tunnel. There is little here, on the summit of the *cordillera*, to hold the eye. Mount Meiggs towers over the tiny group of buildings around the junction, but the last trees were left behind thousands of feet below.

A branch for mineral traffic goes off from Ticlio to the mining centre at Morococha, but the main line enters the longest tunnel on the Central which takes it through to the Atlantic side of the *cordillera*. Galera tunnel is 3861 feet long (1177m) and work started on it as soon as Meiggs began construction at the Lima end, in January 1870. The line climbs for 3000 feet (914m) from Ticlio to the summit inside the tunnel, providing a real trial for locomotives; it was made worse by water from an underground stream above the tunnel dripping on to the track and freezing. Steam locomotives on heavy freights sometimes slipped to a standstill and had to reverse for another try.

The descent down the eastern slopes to La Oroya is less dramatic. The train emerges into daylight at Galera, where some passengers photograph the nameboard on the gable of the station, which gives the altitude – 15,681 feet (4780m) at this point.

There is only one short zig-zag on the Atlantic side and the gradients are much easier. The valley broadens below the reversal at Rumichaca, but the scenery is unprepossessing until after the train has passed La Oroya.

The approach to La Oroya, the largest town on the journey and the railway junction for Cerro de Pasco, is disfigured by all the trappings of heavy industry. Yet without this there would probably be no railway, for the smelter here has processed much of the output of the nearby mines and those at Cerro de Pasco.

A DIFFERENT WORLD

The character of the 78 miles (125km) from La Oroya to Huancayo, completed in 1908, is very different. Following the Mantaro River all the way, the line passes through sheep and cattle raising country as far as Jauja. At the wayside stations, Indian women in broad-rimmed stovepipe hats stagger off the train with huge bundles. Tiles and mud bricks replace wood and corrugated iron as the building materials, and the size of farms is larger than those on the western slopes. Stands of eucalyptus provide a windbreak for farms and protect the soil.

Beyond Jauja, cereals are the main crop in the broad valley. The train bowls along between gently contoured hills towards the Indian market town of Huancayo, and the brilliance of colours in the clear air becomes more noticeable after the darker tones and the frequent shade of the mountains, already a world away.

After the encapsulated peace of a railway journey, the mayhem at Huancayo Station may come as a shock. Half the town, it appears, has come to meet the train, and willing porters outnumber customers by at least ten to one. Each, of course, knows of a very good hotel.

Essential to any visit is a trip to the market, where all kinds of useful and useless goods are on sale. The textiles are predictably splendid, while piles of attractive wooden spoons lie alongside tasteless plastic parodies of reviled world leaders.

Meanwhile, in the engine shed at Huancayo Station sits one of the Andes 2-8-0s that were built for the line by Beyer Peacock in Manchester, England. No 206 is still in working order. Perhaps when Peru's political tribulations are over, it will be possible to experience again the sound of a steam whistle echoing through the gorges of the Central.

PRACTICAL INFORMATION

■ Trains leave Lima for Huancayo daily from April to October; from November to March they run on Mondays, Wednesdays and Saturdays. The 208-mile (335km) journey takes 8–9 hours.
■ The train has First and Second Class coaches and food is available on the train. Seats should be booked in advance.
■ The best time to travel is from May to September. At the moment it is advisable to check with the Peru Tourist Office, Embassy or Consulate in your own country before travelling to Peru.
■ For travel arrangements contact a travel agent. In the US, contact the Peruvian Embassy at 1700 Massachusetts Avenue NW, Washington DC 20036.
Tel: 202 8339860.
Or contact the Peruvian Consulate at 10 Rockerfeller Plaza, 7th Floor, office 729, New York NY 10020.
Tel: 212 265 2480.

South from Santiago de Chile on the Rápido

CHRISTOPHER SAINSBURY

Squeezed between the Pacific Ocean to the west and the Andes to the east, Chile stretches 2610 miles (4200km) from Peru in the north to Cape Horn in the south, yet measures only 112 miles (180km) at its widest point. From the capital Santiago de Chile the Rápido follows the central valley between the Andes and the coastal *cordillera* on a 675-mile (1086km) journey south to Puerto Montt, passing through scenery which changes as rapidly as the climate. The only characteristics of the journey which remain constant are the views of the snow-capped Andes and the luxury of the train which harks back to the heyday of rail travel.

ABOVE, *the Chilean flag flies proudly above the signal post*

BELOW, *the attractive staggered windows and peeling paint of a bygone age – the Rápido is now a gleaming, modern and comfortable machine*

FAR RIGHT, *huasos – Chile's own colourful style of cowboys – are still a common sight along the route at local rodeos*

FLYING IN to Santiago's international airport is a breathtaking experience. The endless brown plains of Argentina abruptly give way to the snow-covered ridges of the Andes, dominated by the 2283 feet (6960m) peak of Aconcaguia, the highest mountain in the southern hemisphere and a magnet for mountaineers.

Santiago itself is a far cry from how most people imagine a city in South America to be. The summer heat may be fierce, but visitors are always surprised by its cleanliness. Only a few minutes' walk from the railway station is Quinta National Park, 100 acres of lakes and lawns with native and exotic trees offering secluded, shady places for a picnic and a siesta. It is also home to Santiago's railway museum, where enthusiasts can happily while away the hours until the Rápido makes its evening departure for the more congenial climate of Puerto Montt and the lake district. Be sure to allow enough time to explore the small area of shops and cafés next to the station, where you can stock up with mineral water and snacks for the journey and wander around looking at the stalls selling lapis-lazuli jewellery, stone or wood carvings, leather goods and felt cowboy hats. The station itself, opened in 1897, was designed by a Chilean, B Camus, but prefabricated in France by the Le Creusot company.

The locomotive which will pull the train as far as Temuco is a type 32 straight electric built by an Italian consortium in the early 1960s. The sleeping carriages, built in Germany between 1929 and 1935, are finished in handsome hardwood veneer with polished brass fittings. There is a main compartment in each with two tiers of bunks and four double comparments. Each carriage has an efficient hot water shower and – unusually for this continent – soap and toilet paper never seem to be in short supply. The Salon Class carriages, mostly built in Japan, have large, comfortable reclining seats with plenty of leg room. The double-glazed windows, heating and air-conditioning keep the carriage comfortable despite the extremes of temperature that can be experienced during the journey. An attendant is on duty throughout the

■ From the arid Atacama desert in the north to Antarctica in the south, Chile's landscape, climate and culture are never constant, but its shape makes it ideal for a rail system, a simple north–south main line with a few branches up into the high Andes and more leading down to the coast. With only 112 miles (180km) at the widest point separating the border peaks from the sea, the interior's vast natural resources are never far from a deep water port. The grain produced around

Talca is carried to the small port of Constitución along a branch line which follows the beautiful Maule River, while the timber that is grown on the rolling hills around the Bío-Bío River is taken to the busy port of Concepción along another attractive riverside branch line.
The first section of the main line from Santiago to Puerto Montt opened in 1857 and was extended to Rancagua in 1859. From San Fernando south the line is single track and the welded track terminates at Cabrero. The

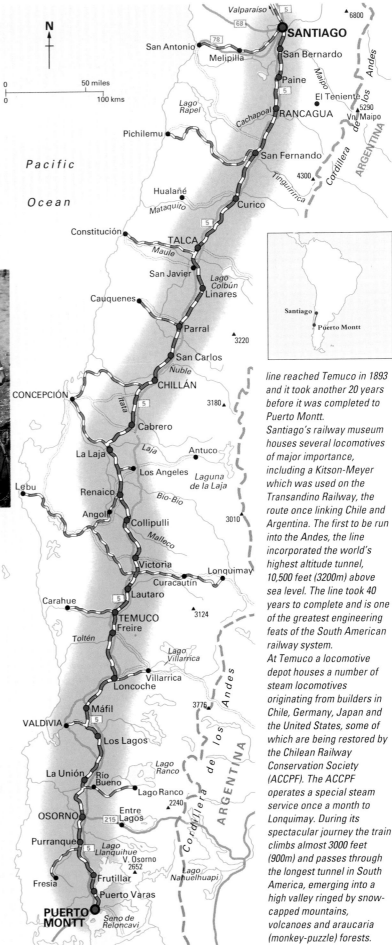

journey and will supply blankets if needed.

At every station during the trip chaos breaks out as hordes of local passengers fight to get into the Economica carriages, loaded down with babies, bundles and baskets (often filled with home-made sandwiches which they will readily sell to their fellow travellers). To appreciate fully the changing colours and cultures of the country this is definitely the best part of the train to be in. The Chileans are polite and considerate people and travelling in the cheapest carriages is a safe and thoroughly entertaining experience.

The Rápido rolls out of the station and passes through the dusty suburbs of Santiago. It is a good moment to wander along to the video bar and watch the 'maestro' mix a Pisco Sour, the national *aperitivo*. The preparation of this frothing cocktail is a Chilean ritual and barmen turn it into a theatrical event, often jealously guarding their personal recipe. Being able to relax at the bar and chat to a Chilean who may have been using the train since childhood or to other foreigners who will willingly exchange information abut their adventures in south America is one of the pleasures that gives the Rápido an almost legendary status. Chile has some of the most modern bus fleets in the

line reached Temuco in 1893 and it took another 20 years before it was completed to Puerto Montt.
Santiago's railway museum houses several locomotives of major importance, including a Kitson-Meyer which was used on the Transandino Railway, the route once linking Chile and Argentina. The first to be run into the Andes, the line incorporated the world's highest altitude tunnel, 10,500 feet (3200m) above sea level. The line took 40 years to complete and is one of the greatest engineering feats of the South American railway system.
At Temuco a locomotive depot houses a number of steam locomotives originating from builders in Chile, Germany, Japan and the United States, some of which are being restored by the Chilean Railway Conservation Society (ACCPF). The ACCPF operates a special steam service once a month to Lonquimay. During its spectacular journey the train climbs almost 3000 feet (900m) and passes through the longest tunnel in South America, emerging into a high valley ringed by snow-capped mountains, volcanoes and araucaria (monkey-puzzle) forests.

ABOVE, *Chile is the ideal shape for a single, criss-crossed railway line, carrying passengers, minerals and freight – including these bee hives – up and down*

RIGHT, *old steam engines patiently await restoration in the railway museum, their place now taken by modern, efficient electric and diesel locomotives*

fine neo-classical houses that contrast strikingly with the *haciendas* dotted along the edge of the railway line. Sadly, there are very few examples left of early Spanish architecture, violent earthquakes and frequent fires having spared only a few of the oldest buildings, but the plentiful supply of traditional local building materials and the range of climatic conditions have preserved styles of vernacular architecture which vary throughout the country. In this part of the central valley, windowless walls surround an open courtyard which often contains a fountain, shady palms and colourful shrubs.

Vineyards give way to fields of maize before the first major stop on the journey at Rancagua, a thriving commercial centre founded on land originally ruled by the Picuncha Indians. First

world, as well as very efficient internal airline services, but travelling in a state of solitary silence on them bears no comparison with the adventures a long rail journey can hold in store.

The train's very high standard of service is a reflection of the Chilean character. Many of the immaculately dressed staff have had jobs on the train all their working lives, and it is not uncommon to find someone with 40 years of service. Quite soon a waiter, in smart white jacket and black bow tie, will come around taking bookings for dinner. You will be offered the set meal of the day, the 'menu' or 'colaciones'. The local people, however, seem to subsist on the sandwiches that Chile is renowned for – steak, chicken, lamb, ham and hot-dog, with almost any kind of vegetable or melted cheese, served either in a large roll or between slices of toasted bread.

One thing to be sure of anywhere in Chile is a choice of the country's finest wines, and where better to be selecting a bottle than now as the train crosses the Maipo River which meanders through the heart of Chile's most famous wine producing area.

Silvestre Ochagavia first introduced French wines in the mid-19th century and they proved so suited to the soil and climate around Santiago that many other wealthy industrialists followed suit and their names still adorn the bottles of some of the finest vintages today. A number of these men are just as famous for their homes,

the Incas and then the Spanish came here to exact tribute in the gold that these Indians mined in the foothills of the Andes. However, the major source of the area's present day prosperity comes from El Teniente, the largest underground copper mine in the world. To Chileans the city's name evokes memories of a bloody slaughter during the war of independence against the Spanish, when almost the entire population died.

During dinner the *dormitorio* attendants will be making up the bunk beds and there is plenty of time to enjoy a sweet Vaina, Chile's second most popular cocktail, or perhaps a Manzanilla, prized as an aid to digestion. Insomniacs can while the night away watching a video. The sleeping carriages will have been transformed into a long tunnel of velvet curtains, but the ever-watchful attendant will have no trouble in remembering exactly which your berth is. It is worth paying the extra for a lower bunk, particularly in the summer when you can control the ventilation by opening a window.

With luck you will wake in time to watch the sun rise over an ever changing landscape. Between San Francisco and Talca enormous modern warehouses, bearing company names that can be found on supermarket shelves all over the world, stand in mile after mile of orchards that produce tonne upon tonne of fruit. In contrast, villages tucked away in the foothills of the Andes produce something that is unique to this area – tiny brilliantly coloured figures, animals, hats and flowers, all delicately woven out of 'crin' or horse-hair.

Talca was the home of Libertador Bernardo O'Higgins, the illegitimate son of an Irishman who once governed Peru and Chile. This colourful soldier and statesman has been immortalized on more street signs and in more portraits than anyone else in the entire history of the country.

The great plain narrows as the train travels south and the coastal *cordillera* rises to over 4000 feet (1200m) above the rolling foothills that grow most of the country's grain. Logs are piled high alongside the track and the barren hills of the north are soon exchanged for pine and eucalyptus plantations. Much of the timber will be exported as wood chips from Concepción, a bustling port that lies at the mouth of Chile's most famous river, the Bío-Bío. Internationally renowned for its white-water rafting expeditions, this enormous river has its source high in the Andes on the Argentinian border, and it is historically significant as the southern border of Spanish influence in mainland Chile.

The endless forests all the way from here to Puerto Montt were once the home of the Mapuche Indians. These peaceful nomads fiercely and relentlessly managed to resist Spanish domination, but once the country gained independence they found their lands encroached upon, and today their traditional settlements are restricted to a number of reserves or *reducciones*. The almost complete integration of the Mapuches with the European settlers in the south of the country has led to very marked physical characteristics which distinguish the majority of the population here from other Chileans.

The mountainous national parks and dormant volcanoes in this region make it one of the most beautiful in the country. Large areas of araucaria forest have survived the logging which transformed southern Chile into an area of almost endless farms. The monkey-puzzle tree, as the araucaria is commonly called outside Chile, is the oldest tree species in the world and their once extensive forests were the most heavily populated region of the Mapuche empire. The trees' nuts are still a traditional Indian food and

the species has now been declared a 'Natural Monument', with the strictest preservation order placed upon it.

One of the most spectacular engineering feats in the country is the 1337feet (408m) viaduct across the Malleco River near Collipulli. Opened in 1890, it was designed by a Chilean, Victor Lastarria, the steelwork being prefabricated in Le Creusot, France. As the train crosses the viaduct there are stomach-churning views of the river 300 feet (90m) below. An hour and a half later the Rápido will have quite a lengthy stop in Temuco, an excellent opportunity for a leisurely breakfast. What is in fact the longest electrified stretch of track in the Americas soon comes to an end, necessitating a change here to a type 18 diesel electric locomotive, built by ALCO, USA, in 1961.

South of the Bío-Bío River more of the towns, rivers and lakes have names with an

BELOW, *passengers wait to board the train at Frutillar*

BOTTOM, *wooden tiles like scales adorn the church at Frutillar*

Indian derivation, often recognizable by the two suffixes, -co and -hue, the former meaning 'water' and the latter 'place' in the Mapuche language. Temuco marks the northern end of the country's lake district, a region that attracts more summer visitors than any other. The distance between the Andes and the coastal mountains narrows as one travels south until both are easily visible from the train; condors gracefully soar above the ski slopes of the Andes within sight of the Pacific Ocean.

The railway line meanders between fields that become smaller and more lush with every mile. The regularity with which collisions occur on the endless twisting curves, plus many years of

RIGHT, *the spectacular volcano of Villarica, with tranquil Lake Pucon in the foreground*

BELOW, *the Rápido beginning its crossing of the Malleco viaduct, pulled by a type 16 diesel – before this section of the line was electrified*

BELOW RIGHT, *a mountain of wood chips at Puerto Montt*

experience, seem to have given the Rápido's staff an extra, sixth sense. Suddenly staff in the bar will leap to their feet and grab bottles on the shelves before the unwitting passengers have the slightest idea that a collision or derailment is imminent.

LAKE DISTRICT

Regular rainfall, rich soil and industrious settlers have turned an almost impenetrable temperate rainforest into Chile's richest dairy farming area. The first pioneers in this part of the country came from Germany and their influence is everywhere. Stone and tile houses have all but vanished by now and the dominant building material in the lake district is wood, with a Bavarian influence to be seen in the design of the churches and the older farm buildings.

The huge forests have been felled in all but the most inaccessible areas of the south, and the stumps of once great hardwood trees can be seen everywhere in the emerald green fields. Uncultivated areas of land beside the railway line have in places been invaded by one of the native species of bamboo, while in the mixed evergreen and deciduous oak forests trees are draped with epiphytes and lianas. Huge red fuschia trees flash past the window and the train sends flocks of

international investment in lake resorts, spas and ski centres has brought a new vitality to what was not so long ago an area of sleepy farming communities.

After passing through Osorno and the heartland of German colonization, the train briefly stops in Frutillar, named after a native plant, *fragaria chilensis*, which produced the first commercially cultivated strawberries. The south of Chile was also the source of *solanum tuberosum*, the potato, which the Mapuche Indians traded with the Incas and which eventually found its way on to dinner plates throughout the world.

The last few miles make a fitting climax to the journey. The train borders Lake (Lago) Llanquihue with breathtaking views of Osorno volcano's perfect conical peak, permanently covered with snow and ice, before the penultimate stop on the journey at the picturesque town of Puerto Varas, where Spanish remains a second language for many of the inhabitants.

Long grass sprouts between the sleepers almost completely hiding the line, and the Rápido creeps around the sharp curves as it descends towards the ocean, passing the trunk of an enormous alerce tree, nicknamed the 'President's Chair', where Pedro Montt sat and watched the construction of the railway at the beginning of the century. For the last ten hours the average speed of the journey has dropped to 20mph (32kph); in the days of President Montt engines were capable of five times this speed.

Suddenly the Rápido rounds a bend and there is a stunning view of Reloncavi Bay (Seno de Reloncavi), with mountains and volcanoes stretching away to the horizon and endless islands which merge to give the impression that this inland sea is just another lake.

The train slowly snakes its way down to the coast, the view of the busy port of Puerto Montt dominated by an orange mountain of wood chips, before crawling to a halt in the most southerly main line railway station in the world.

PRACTICAL INFORMATION

■ The Rápido operates daily in both directions between between Santiago and Puerto Montt. The 675-mile (1086km) journey takes approximately 23 hours.

■ There is a very high demand for berths in the sleeping carriages during the Chilean summer (December to February), which is the best time of year to make the journey. Classes include Salon, Primera, Segunda and 'Economica', all of which are heated and air conditioned.

■ The line is operated by the State-owned Ferrocarriles del Estado (EFE). It is best to buy tickets in Chile, the day before travel, at the station in Santiago or Puerto Montt; at the Hotel El Libertador, Alameda 853, Santiago; or Metro Estacion Escuela Militar, Santiago.

golden ibis and southern lapwings screeching up from the fields. Oxcarts, often accompanied by a *huaso*, or Chilean cowboy, may be seen trundling by.

One of the most colourful sights in the south of the country is a local rodeo where *huasos* will gather from miles around, wearing brightly coloured and beautifully woven ponchos, wide-brimmed hats, leather breeches, boots and enormous jingling spurs.

The midday meal, *almuerzo*, is the most important and largest for most Chileans. In the late afternoon they have *onces* which might include cold meats, cheese and *kuchen*, the delicious cakes and pastries which are famous in the south due to the German influence. All this is washed down with cups of tea or *mate*, a strong herbal drink made from an Argentinian shrub and drunk through a metal straw. The staff on the train will be enjoying their *onces* as the journey draws to an end, probably engrossed in that favourite of all Chilean pastimes, card playing.

Only a few miles away a chain of lakes stretches from Temuco to Puerto Montt, source of myriad rivers which the train crosses and one of the most famous trout and salmon fishing areas in the world. All along the border with Argentina large areas of the Andes have been designated national parks, and enormous

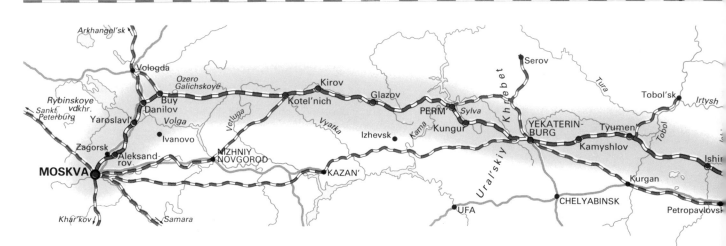

The Trans-Siberian from Moscow to Irkutsk

RICHARD SALE AND TONY OLIVER

There is little doubt that for the layman or the casual railway enthusiast the Trans-Siberian is the greatest railway in the world. It is also the world's largest continuous track, Vladivostok being 5866 miles (9440km) from Moscow. The journey takes seven nights and arrives in a time zone eight hours different from that of the start point. The journey crosses European Russia, then climbs over the Urals, the traditional 'border' between Europe and Asia. It crosses the steppes, goes close to the peaks that separate Russia from Mongolia, and traverses the wilderness of southern Siberia to reach the Pacific Ocean. With the recent changes in Russia offering more opportunities for exploration at towns along the way, the Trans-Siberian is now, more than ever the trip of a lifetime.

FAR RIGHT, *one of the sturdy locomotives on this, the longest continuous railway in the world*

WE SAT BACK and waited with anxious anticipation. With articulated, if not articulate, tongue we had just ordered a meal, but a second look at the phrase book suggested that we may have asked for a shampoo and set, with side salad.

We had flown into Moscow (Moskva) late afternoon the day before, and had been treated to a drive into the city that was remarkable for its ferocity. At the hotel the process of converting our travel vouchers into train tickets began. At each stage of the proceedings our details were laboriously handwritten into huge ledgers of a uniform blue-green. Wondering what would happen to the ledgers eventually, we had retired to bed on a hot and sticky Muscovite night. In the morning we finished breakfast and ambled down to collect our train tickets, which, despite – or perhaps because of – all the writing in all the ledgers, had not been ready last night. The tickets were ready now but, hardly to our surprise, we found that the train would leave an hour earlier that we had been told at home. And we had to be at Jaroslavski Station an hour before that. That gave us barely enough time to see Red Square and the Kremlin.

Negotiating the Moscow metro is not easy if you do not know how to pronounce Cyrillic place names, but with some pointing and some inspired guesswork we managed. The Metro

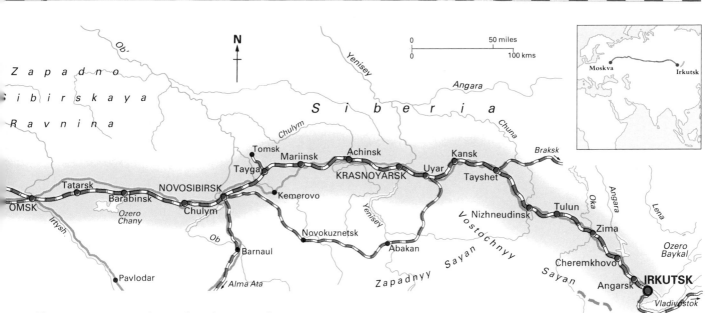

itself is impressive: escalators that drop 200 feet (60m) or more at speeds twice those you are used to take you to luxurious, marble-tiled platforms lit by cut-glass chandeliers. The platforms are usually overcrowded, but are swept clean every couple of minutes by clean, quick-moving trains.

A short walk from the metro exit brings you to St Basil's Cathedral at the edge of Red Square. No photograph of the cathedral can convey the elegance and beauty of St Basil's. The first impression is of smallness, but this is an illusion created by its being very compact, and the impression is rapidly replaced by wonder at the intricacies of the domes. The cathedral is actually a series of nine separate chapels, the outer eight topped by a turrets and domes. It is tempting to call them onion domes, but that is too simplistic for the coloured mass of twisted spirals, pineapples and zig-zags that form them. The cathedral was built by Ivan the Terrible in the mid-16th century, but is named for Basil the Blessed, a travelling monk who died a couple of years before building work started. Until recently the cathedral was closed to visitors, but the interior has now been restored and can be viewed: yet it cannot compare with the wonderful exterior.

To reach Lenin's tomb we walked past the Place of Skulls, so called because in days gone by it was used for public executions – Ivan the Terrible is said to have had a wooden grandstand built beyond the Kremlin's wall, the

■ *Railways had been built in European Russia in the second and third quarters of the 19th century, just as they had been built in the kingdoms of western Europe. At the time of this first surge of building the thought of a line to the east was not considered. Siberia was hostile, largely uninhabited, and furs – its great wealth – could readily be transported by conventional means, a combination of lake and river*

boats, and horses. By 1880, however, the situation was different. Railways now went as far east as the Yekaterinburg, Siberia had revealed its mineral wealth and, most specifically, there were problems in the east. Russia had annexed the provinces of Amur and East Siberia from China, and the Pacific port of Vladivostok – very important to Far Eastern trade – was attracting the attention of the Japanese.

The Tsar, Alexander III, decided to investigate the possibilities of a railway and in 1891 work began on the almost 6000 mile (9500km) railway across one of the world's most inhospitable wildernesses. In some areas the long harsh winters reduced building time to four months each year. Permafrost caused endless problems, tigers ate the workers in Amur, and the requirement for cheapness meant long detours to avoid tunnelling. Worker shortages caused convicts to be brought in, but conditions were so harsh that drafting soon replaced volunteering. Eventually, 25 years later, the line was completed, to open in 1916.
The Rossiya takes the traveller through European Russia with its arable land and stands of pine and birch, and through the Ural Mountains (Ural 'skiy Khrabet), low hills with beautiful woodlands and river valleys, to reach the steppes of Asia. In Siberia the track goes through the taiga, the magnificent forested area of the Siberian Plain. Beyond Lake Baikal (Ozero Baykal) the country is still taiga, but becomes more varied as the line goes through the Transbaikalian Mountains. Finally the track crosses Ussuriland, last stronghold of the Amur, or Siberian, tiger.

better to watch. The tomb is squat and massive. Implicit in its unimaginative architecture is the permanence its builders considered to be the destiny of their system; we wondered what the future held for both the tomb and Lenin's body now Soviet communism has been discredited.

We were among the first visitors to the Kremlin that day and several times had treasure to ourselves – the Emperor's Bell and Cannon, the Terem Palace's façade and the three cathedrals. Too often the expectations of a visit to a famous landmark lead to disappointment but, arriving here without preconceptions, we were overwhelmed by the beauty of the site and buildings. Only with difficulty could we tear ourselves away, but we had lunch to fit in before

catching the train. Our meal arrived. It was not a shampoo and set.

Jaroslavski Station, in contrast to the Kremlin, is not great architecture, though it is certainly interesting – a massive structure capped by roofs copied, it appears, from several film sets. Inside it is a madhouse. Half of Russia, or so it seems, is in transit through the station, and most of them want to walk in front of us. We have no idea where to go, and our grasp of Cyrillic is still not good enough to allow us to interpret the timetables. We try at a couple of ticket booths; mostly we get shrugs, but eventually a series of hand signs indicates we should be outside and to the right. We have read beforehand that the train usually leaves from

We worry a little. But there is no problem: the board flicks up a platform number, a train pulls into the corresponding platform. Our carriage is as labelled on the ticket, our compartment likewise. We have found home – for the next few days.

HOME FROM HOME

Home is 6 feet 6 inches (2m) by 5 feet 6 inches (1.5m) and mostly occupied by two seats/bunks. There is a small folding table and storage space above the corridor. Tatiana, our *provodnitsa* (carriage attendant), a dark-haired amiable girl – one of two, we are to discover – takes our tickets, scrutinizes the linen vouchers and fetches a pair of sheets, a wool blanket, a pillow case (but no pillow) and a tiny towel for each of us. The latter is for use in the toilet – enthusiastically referred to as a bathroom – where water emerges from a piece of rusty pipe set in the steel panel above a small sink. The toilet is stainless steel, the 'flush' operated by a foot pedal that merely opens a flap valve to the track below.

We barely have time to take it all in before our train, the Rossiya ('the Russia'), starts to move. It is hauled by a Czechoslovakian Skoda electric engine (in the far eastern section of the journey, Russian diesel engines will be used). There is a flurry of activity at the open windows, some waving, some tearful goodbyes. Then Tatiana bolts the windows tight to assist the air conditioning and starts to stoke up the coal-fired

FAR LEFT, *St Basil's Cathedral in Moscow is an architectural confection which defies description – and which should not be missed*

LEFT, *the Rossiya's nameplate and destination are stuck proudly on the side of the carriage – note the curtains at the windows*

Platform 2, but the grass and old concrete on the line there suggest that nothing has passed that way for years. A large airport-style timetable shows a train at 14.00hrs and much searching through our phrasebook produces a Cyrillic match for Vladivostok. No platform is mentioned, so we settle in to wait, feeling conspicuous with our Western clothes and rucksacks. Why have we been told to arrive an hour early? Just to form a queue perhaps.

We buy ice creams to combat the dehydrating affect of the sun and strike up a conversation, in poor French, with three Polish students. They confirm our reading of the timetable (good news) but can offer no information on what we should, perhaps, be doing (not such good news).

РОССИЯ
МОСКВА—ВЛАДИВОСТОК

samovar at the carriage's end. One of the journey's best features, we are to discover, is the constant hot water supplied by the samovar for making tea and coffee – although for a very small charge your *provodnitsa* will make tea for you.

The train pulls through the harsh, high-rise blocks and forlorn open spaces of Moscow's suburbs before emerging into pleasant wooded country dotted with Muscovite *dachas*, wooden chalets in various stages of disrepair. We miss the first milepost (actually a kilometre post), which is sad. When the last post is going to say 9000+, seeing the one that says 1 is nice for reference. The posts are on the southern side of the track (to the right if you are travelling from Moscow), occasionally so close to the track that they are difficult to see, let alone read.

Beyond the woods is Zagorsk, once the centre of the Russian Orthodox Church and where, to the north, the spectacular blue and gold onion domes of the cathedral dominate the skyline. It is a stunning sight, but there is no stop here, the train continuing to reach, soon after, the 60 miles (100km) post. Just beyond we stop briefly at Aleksandrov.

Outside the window now are endless fields, broken up by stands of weeping birch and dark pines. Ahead of us is the Volga, Europe's longest river at over 2235 miles (3600km) and a river that is burned into the Russian psyche in much the same way as the Nile must have impressed itself on the ancient Egyptians. We cross on a bridge of latticed steelwork, built, it seems, from the world's biggest Meccano set. The Volga is huge, packed with boats and the perfect backdrop for the gaunt city of Yaroslavl. It would be nice to stop for a while, but the Rossiya rolls relentlessly on, eating up the kilometres to Danilov. There it stops for 15 minutes, time to inspect the kiosks and to worry about the glances this brings; time to buy ice-cream (at 10 roubles, the very best value on the trip) from the woman on the platform with the cardboard box.

Later, in the restaurant car, where a hand-written sign tells us our waiter is Sacha, we meet Steve and Alistair, a pair of British students spending a year in Russia to improve their grasp of the language. This good fortune allows us to understand the menu. We order under the watchful smile of a man with teeth that represent a fortune in gold. Sacha brings soup. Its surface is a mix of curious white crumbs and yellow oil patches. A dredge around in the depths brings up a spoonful of small bones with skin attached, and some odd tubes. Too much thought about the origin of these and other bits that lurk at the bottom of the bowl takes away our appetites so we talk of other things. Alistair and Steve have spent 10 months in the country, travelling at ludicrously low Russian prices. Steve is in love with the Caucasus, Alistair with Central Asia, where he has visited Tashkent,

BELOW, *the only shower on this trip – improvising with a hose-pipe linked directly to the carriage water supply taps*

Samarkand and Bokhara. They both like the people and the pace of life, but find the material poverty and the tendency to regimented thought difficult to take.

Sacha brings chicken with potato slices that have been turned over briefly in a fat-filled frying pan, and a mash of vegetables, mostly pickled cabbage. There is strong brown bread that needs Russian beer (barely palatable) or Russian cola (excellent) to ease it down. When it is time to pay, Sacha calculates the price on an abacus, his nimble figures totting up our varied list with ease. The total is just a few dollars between four of us. Back at our carriage we drink milkless tea and organize our bedding. Outside, Lake Galich (Ozero Galichskoye) passes by, its beauty enhanced by the light of the setting sun. We are already far enough east of Moscow to have moved into another time zone and have lost an hour of sun time.

The lights, which work only at night, come on when we operate the switch. We make pillows from our jackets and begin the difficult job of adjusting to our rocking, lurching beds. And there is the endless clickety-click of the short rails. Then light filters under the bottom of the blind, bringing a new day of cloudless skies, bright sun and clear air. Outside the carriage window the birch forest is carpeted with purple lupins.

In the corridor the radio is playing. It played in the compartment last night too, but we found the switch to turn it off. Now, on the hour, it plays over and over again the opening bars of

ABOVE, *the fabulous blue and gold domes of the Trinity Monastery of St Sergius, at Zagorsk*

FAR LEFT, *passengers wait patiently, below a network of electric power cables*

'Midnight in Moscow' before returning to its diet of Russian folk music occasionally interspersed with Western pop tunes. Thankfully Tatiana often takes pity on us (or herself) and turns it off. The train's cook arrives with an aluminium yoke loaded with pots. Each holds an unappetizing breakfast, so we settle for two cartons of *smeetana*, sour cream that tastes like a tangy yogurt and really cleans the mouth out first thing in the morning. It also has the advantage of our not being able to tell if it has gone off or not, since it always tastes like that.

ROCKING ACROSS TIME ZONES

The Rossiya keeps Moscow time throughout its journey, and as a result all of the stations have clocks showing Moscow time, a bit disconcerting when it is clearly at odds with body or sun time. At present this effect is on our side, the train rolling over the Kama River into Perm in mid-morning – or so it feels, despite it being lunchtime locally. On the platform Russian women in their drab 'uniform' of thick headscarf, long coat and long wool socks, are selling vegetables and bread. One old woman approaches us with jars of pickled objects of dubious origin. We decline, settling for less adventurous fare of cucumber and tomatoes. Beyond Perm the train moves into the Urals, the country becoming more scenic with each kilometre, low hills covered with birch and pine forests separating lush valleys. Beyond Kungur the track runs along the Sylva River, in which families swim and splash, and beyond which rise low cliffs of crumbling white rock. For today at least, this small part of Russia seems at peace with itself.

Further on, the more usual aspects of Russian life return. An old lorry kicks up clouds of dust as it passes a pair of even older motor cycles with side-cars. In small vegetable fields old women with gnarled hands and faces crouch over long hoes. They wear clothes faded to a standard brown, and heavy woollen head-scarves. An old man leads a cow on a rope leash past an old woman herding four goats. Here, a man is drawing water from an old-fashioned well. There, in a yard beside a field of cows, sheep and goats – no more than 20 animals in all – another man is tinkering with the engine of a car whose body shows more rust than paint. In a small station two men are carrying a huge and misshapen load wrapped in a muslin bag. We pass a group of dilapidated wooden sheds, the ruins of a concrete building, a lumber yard full of logs stripped of their bark and polished by the weather, a small town with its own shanty village of lock-up garages.

At the 1104 miles (1777km) post a stone obelisk to the south tells us we have reached the point where Europe officially ends and Asia starts. The Urals seem very slight hills to separate continents and the obelisk undis-tinguished for such a grand job. We know the obelisk is there, and count the posts into it. But we miss one, and fail to catch it on film as it flashes past. Beyond, we have better luck at Yekaterinburg, formerly Sverdlovsk, where the train stops. It was here that the Russian royal family had been brought, early in 1918, to forestall rescue attempts just before the Revolution.

RIGHT, dining on the train is hardly an exciting gastronomic experience, for the food is basic and the menu simple – but it is also freshly cooked, wholesome and inexpensive

Sverdlov, a prominent local communist, decided that their presence was a threat to his town, and on 16 July 1918 he ordered their killing. The murder was brutal, the disposal of the bodies unpleasant, yet the town was later renamed for Sverdlov. But times change: Boris Yeltsin is a native of the town and has already ordered the demolition of the house where the killings were carried out and its replacement by a plain wooden cross. And the town has reverted to the original name.

Back on board we make our way down to the restaurant car. The carriages are non-smoking, so the tobacco addicts congregate at the carriage ends where a pair of doors gives access to an exciting step over the track. This makes our journey a perilous one. In the restaurant Sacha offers us yesterday's menu again. We pass on the soup, going for the pleasant crumbly cheese, a salad topped with sour cream and the chicken again. As he is bringing our chicken, Sacha pauses and stamps vigorously on something that has crawled out from beneath a stove.

Some of the folk from our carriage drift in. Next to us, in compartment 2, are a Russian

LEFT, *a typical wooden station building on the route, apparently in the middle of nowhere*

BELOW, *a platform vendor offers a variety of home-grown and home-pickled vegetables*

151

couple. He is huge, she a faded woman in a faded dress who rarely emerges, but can be seen staring out at us when we walk the platforms at stations in search of ice cream or tomatoes. Next are a pair of Germans *en route* to Japan. They had spent four days on trains – Berlin, Warsaw, Moscow – before joining the Rossiya. One of them tells me that by the time they reach Khabarovsk (from where they will fly) they will have spent 11 days on the train. He shakes his head wearily. Two more silent pairs of Russians occupy compartments 4 and 5, then come the English students. Beyond, a lone Australian, heading for Lake Baikal for some birdwatching, shares with a young Russian sports physiotherapist who has a nice line in black market watches and a good rate for roubles against the dollar. Later, at Omsk, the Russian departs and is replaced by another Sacha, this one a native of northern Siberia, a navigator who regales us with tales of life in the Russian merchant navy.

Outside, the steppes of the West Siberian Plain drift by, complete with occasional mounted men herding horses, though it is only at the 1299 miles post (2078km) that we actually reach Siberia, its arrival unheralded by signs and inauspicious as a light rain starts to fall. Tyumen, the oldest Siberian town and once a centre for exiles and prisoners, is dark and wet. Those they brought here died in their thousands from the cold and appalling conditions. They would have recognized it tonight.

Sleep is not easy, and there is a long and noisy stop at Omsk. We wake ragged, but spirits rise when the first milepost shows us to be beyond

1875 miles (3000km). The low light though the birch is beautiful, and as we pass some marshes we startle huge clouds of white butterflies into flight. We get down at Barabinsk and buy for our breakfast fresh, warm potato cakes and smoked fish (wrapped in pages from an old ledger! so is that their fate?). When we return to the compartment Tatiana is vacuuming our strip of carpet.

The weather is still damp and dark and time drags a little as we head for Novosibirsk. We cross the Ob River on yet another girder bridge. Below, huge barge convoys, looking like small floating towns, are being marshalled by tugs. Novosibirsk is big and modern, its station brighter. The platform sellers have hot boiled potatoes and beans, meat and vegetable pasties and drinks.

EDGE OF THE TAIGA

The country beyond the city shows signs of the taiga, the vast coniferous forest that lies south of Siberia's Arctic tundra, for which the next town was named. Taiga (Tayga) itself was once one of the prettiest stations on the route, but the old wooden chalets have now been replaced by utilitarian concrete and Taiga looks like all the other stations. Or even worse in the steady drizzle. We talk, play backgammon, drink tea, go visiting to exchange travel stories with the Germans and the Australian. Stations come and go in the gathering gloom. At Krasnoyarsk, with sun (or rather, moon) time at 02.30 in the morning, but the clock showing 22.30 the previous evening, the rain has stopped and the

FAR RIGHT, *Young Pioneers patrol outside the elegant old museum church in Irkutsk*

RIGHT, *a typical old wooden house in Irkutsk, with beautiful carving around the window frames*

lights of the city penetrate the darkness. The station is cold and smells of fresh sawdust, and an old man sells loaves of dark, heavy bread.

We sleep better than on the previous night, for although there is just as much banging and lurching, it is somehow easier to ignore. The first morning stop, at Tayshet, is disappointing but Nizhneudinsk is the best so far. A row of blue shacks offers nuts and big cedar seeds, biscuits and cakes — deep-fried, batter-covered 'cakes' that look like samosas and taste as good. An old woman sells home-made lemonade that tastes as fresh as the morning air. The train has stolen ten minutes in the night and we have a long stay in warm sunshine. The rain has rolled away and life is good. The countryside too has improved, not as open as the steppes, but with long views between the birch groves. Far away are the high ridges of the Sayan Mountains (Vostochnyy Sayan) that form the border between Siberia and Mongolia. Closer to the train there are bold, globe-headed orange flowers, lavender-like blues, and huge patches of yellow. Here and there farms and villages have been built, wooden houses surrounded by wooden stockades. Herds of goats with long, curved horns stand knee-deep in grass and flowers. Children play. A pair of steppe eagles circles overhead, and three falcons chase each other through the trees. This is glorious country.

The train is slower now, more in keeping with the pace of life. We rattle past lumber yards where the dark-trunked pines and weeping silver birches end their days. At Zima the platform sellers form a whole supermarket. Sacha treats us to *pelmen* (pronounced 'pe-el-me-en'), a typical Russian snack, a pasta pouch filled with mashed potato and herbs. A handful of roubles buys a whole bag and we munch away in the sunshine. Young boys hover near us asking for chewing gum. We close in on Irkutsk, wide expanses of steppe replacing the taiga as we move closer to Mongolia. A beautiful black and white northern harrier follows the train for a while, then wheels off towards the faraway ridge. We reach the Angora River. A building across the water looks like a lighthouse, but a closer look shows it to be a church. The train stops for two minutes at the village of Angarsk, beside the river, before covering the short distance to Irkutsk, where we leave the train.

Irkutsk was once the 'Paris of Siberia' though today's visitor will find this difficult to understand. Some of its older houses have survived, but their carved woodwork is now peeling into terminal decay. Yet it has a charm that the concrete jungles to the west do not possess. As if to underline it, as the Rossiya pulls out for Lake Baikal, the world's largest lake and home to the world's only freshwater seal, a flock of Pacific swifts chatters and darts overhead.

PRACTICAL INFORMATION

■ The Trans-Siberian leaves Moscow (Moskva) daily, all year round. All trains go to Khabarovsk and two trains a week continue to Vladivostok. The train takes seven nights, eight days to cover the 5866 miles (9440km) to Vladivostok.

■ The trains are sleeping berth only, i.e., the daytime seats convert to beds at night. For non-Russians there are two classes: First Class has two bunks to a compartment, Second Class has four. Bedding and towels are supplied, but not changed during the trip. Hot water is in constant supply: take a cup and a supply of tea, coffee etc. The restaurant offers simple, but reasonable meals and food is easily obtained at all stops.

■ Many choose to make the journey in winter, when the snow-covered landscape is of course, enchanting. In late spring/early summer, however, the scenery is equally beautiful, with the blossoming birchwoods carpeted in wild flowers.

■ Restrictions on travel to and within Russia are easing.
In Britain contact: Intourist Travel Limited, Independent Travel Department, Intourist House, 219 Marsh Wall, Meridian Gate II, Isle of Dogs, London E14 9FJ.
Tel: (0171) 538 8600.
Fax: (0171) 538 5967.
In the US contact Intourist Travel, 630 5th Avenue, Apt 868, New York, NY 10111.
Tel: 212 757 3884.
Fax: 212 459 0031.

Across the Mongolian Plains from Beijing to Siberia

KIM NAYLOR

❋

The first leg of the Trans Mongolian, from Beijing to Ulaanbaatar, the Mongolian capital, is stage one of a marathon rail journey which continues its route northwards into the *taiga* forest of Siberia to Ulan-Ude. Bearing westwards as the Trans Siberian, it then skirts the southern shores of Lake Baikal (Ozero Baykal) to Irkutsk, before traversing the vast expanse of Russia to Moscow – five time zones, roughly along latitude 55° N; 970 miles (1561km) and 1½ days from Beijing to Ulaanbaatar, 5593 miles (9001km) and 5½ days from Beijing all the way to Moscow.

RIGHT, *this Mongolian child has the distinctive features of her proud race – a nomadic people with a glorious past*

FAR RIGHT, *China, where the route starts, is one of the last outposts of the great steam locomotives*

BELOW, *insignia on the Chinese train to Erlian*

'TRAIN NO 3, 706 miles shorter than No 19 (the Beijing-to-Moscow Trans Manchurian route), but preferable.' Concise and to the point, Mr Lee could reduce the romance of rail travel to mere train numbers. As a station inspector, he had travelled throughout China by rail. Trains were his life and he saw his world through the train, or more precisely, its number: name a place and he would tell you the train which serves it. Far more interesting though: give him a train number and he would tell you all about the places along the route. It was like keying into a computer to gain access to a vast store of information. 'This is my index', said Mr Lee patting his train timetable, and then, tapping his temple with his forefinger, 'to the encyclopaedia of China'.

Wiry, fastidious Mr Lee, so immaculately dressed in an oversize brown suit with a white handkerchief pointing sharply from the breast pocket, was sharing my table in the dining-car. Our Soft Class appeared full, mainly with Chinese, from both home and abroad. A mixture of Westerners and a few Mongolians and Russians made up the complement of passengers. It was 09.30hrs and we were among the last to take breakfast; the waiters looked jaded, the table-cloths were stained with soya sauce. Mr Lee commanded respect: a pot of tea and two large bowls of noodles were promptly delivered and a paper tablecloth was brought to cover the clumsiness of earlier diners; a futile attempt to clean the window of the greasy marks left by foreheads, noses and fingers resulted in a

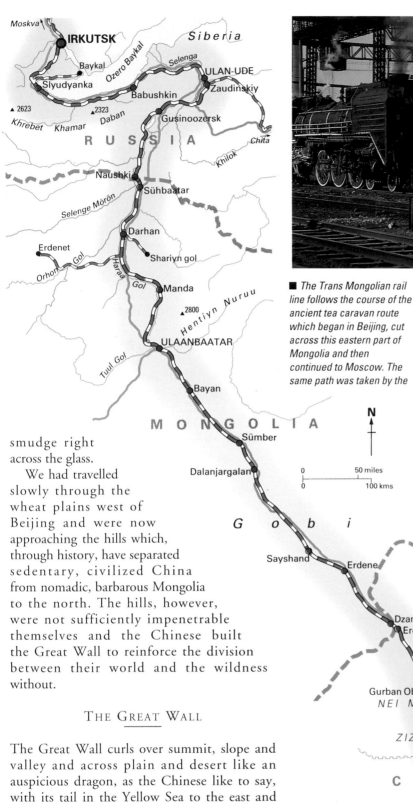

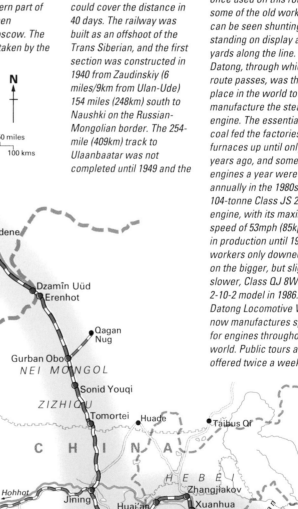

■ The Trans Mongolian rail line follows the course of the ancient tea caravan route which began in Beijing, cut across this eastern part of Mongolia and then continued to Moscow. The same path was taken by the royal messengers, who, changing horses at the post houses which dotted the way at frequent intervals, could cover the distance in 40 days. The railway was built as an offshoot of the Trans Siberian, and the first section was constructed in 1940 from Zaudinskiy (6 miles/9km from Ulan-Ude) 154 miles (248km) south to Naushki on the Russian-Mongolian border. The 254-mile (409km) track to Ulaanbaatar was not completed until 1949 and the

976-mile (1570km) stretch of rail across the Gobi to Beijing, which was laid by Soviet, Mongolian and Chinese workers, was finally inaugurated on 1 January 1956. Of the Trans Mongolian's 1390-mile (2236km) length, half is in the Peoples' Republic of Mongolia (Outer Mongolia). Diesel locomotives have replaced the steam engines once used on this route; some of the old work horses can be seen shunting or standing on display at station yards along the line. Datong, through which the route passes, was the last place in the world to manufacture the steam engine. The essential local coal fed the factories' furnaces up until only a few years ago, and some 240 engines a year were made annually in the 1980s. The 104-tonne Class JS 2-8-2 engine, with its maximum speed of 53mph (85kph), was in production until 1989 and workers only downed tools on the bigger, but slightly slower, Class QJ 8WT/12WT 2-10-2 model in 1986. The Datong Locomotive Works now manufactures spares for engines throughout the world. Public tours are offered twice a week.

smudge right across the glass.

We had travelled slowly through the wheat plains west of Beijing and were now approaching the hills which, through history, have separated sedentary, civilized China from nomadic, barbarous Mongolia to the north. The hills, however, were not sufficiently impenetrable themselves and the Chinese built the Great Wall to reinforce the division between their world and the wildness without.

THE GREAT WALL

The Great Wall curls over summit, slope and valley and across plain and desert like an auspicious dragon, as the Chinese like to say, with its tail in the Yellow Sea to the east and head in the Yellow (Gobi) Desert to the west. Its earliest section was built by the Qin dynasty in the 3rd century BC as protection against the Xiongnu (Huns) nomads of the steppelands, who, a minister of the day informed his emperor, 'live on meat and cheese, wear furs, and possess no house or field. They move like birds and animals in the wild. They stop only at places which abound in grass and water, want of which will start them moving again.'

Despised, but feared, these people were a constant menace to the Chinese.

Turkish tribes originating from the west – such as the Uighurs, Khitans, Tanguts – succeeded the Huns on the steppelands and the Chinese were compelled to build more wall to keep them out. But the success of the defence was limited. The Khitans (from which 'Cathay', as Marco Polo called his China, is derived) broke through and settled near Beijing in 938 and took the name Liao. More significantly, in the 1220s the Mongol Genghis Khan, the greatest ever steppeland nomad, conquered China; his grandson, Kublai Khan, moved the Mongol capital away from Karakorum, on the plains, to Beijing in 1279 and founded China's Yuan dynasty.

Within a century the Yuans had been usurped by the Mings, who drove them back north across the Wall, beyond the Gobi and home to Karakorum. The Ming then established their own rule over China in 1368, but they always feared the return of the Mongols and added to the Wall during their dynasty to give it its greatest strength and most spectacular proportions: 12,000 *li* (4000 miles/6400km), a length of wall requiring one million men to defend it.

Forty miles (64km) out of Beijing, after the town of Nankouzhen, the Juyongguan Pass cuts through the Jundu Mountains (Jundushan). The pass has always ben a main way from China into the interior and, as a consequence, it was of paramount strategic importance. For the Mings the pass with Mount Badaling, the eastern flank rising above the northern entrance, was the key defence point along their wall; for today's tourists, it is the most accessible section of the great sight from Beijing, drawing thousands daily. The train stops briefly at Qinglongqiao Station. The wall (really a southern or inner loop of the older wall) can be seen here, before the train doubles back a short distance and continues through a tunnel under the fortification to Badaling.

I had seen photographs of the Great Wall taken of and from Juyongguan and Badaling, a grey line twisting along the undulating contours of the green hills as far as the eye could trace it; I had read the wall was the only man-made structure on earth visible from the moon; 'nothing', I had been told, 'prepares you for the wall'.

My first view of this wonder of the world was from the dining-car. Through our grease-smeared window it looked hazy, rather like an Impressionist painting, as it crawled up a dun-coloured, scrub vegetated hillside a mile off. It was frustrating, I commented, that we had no time for closer scrutiny. 'I am a man of the train', replied Mr Lee, 'I have learnt to be seduced by the glimpse'.

As it pushes northwards the railway descends to flatter lands and to Zhangjiakou (75 miles/ 120km from Badaling), a 2000-year-old city on a stretch of the outer Great Wall. Ancient gateway on the Beijing-to-Russia trade route (the Mongols called it Kalgan, meaning 'Gateway' or 'Frontier'), Zhangjiakou is, today, an industrial city with a million inhabitants.

BELOW, *waiting at Quinlongqiao station, near one of the more accessible sections of the Great Wall*

The train follows the course of outer or northern wall for 111 miles (178km), crossing from Hebei into Shanxi province, and to Datong, a dusty, sand-coloured coal city. Also an ancient, strategic point on the inner side of the northern wall, Datong was scene of many conflicts. Among them was the famous siege at nearby Baiden in 200BC, when the Huns surrounded the Hans, inflicting much death over seven nights and days, only to lose the battle after the wife of their leader betrayed them to their enemy.

Mr Lee·left the train at Datong to attend to his duties. Besides giving me a history lesson, he had told me of the city's sights, including the extraordinary Yungang Caves which riddle the base of the Wuzhou hills 10 miles (16km) to the west. Here the Northern Wei dynasty, who ruled northern China between 386 and 534 from their capital at Pingcheng (modern Datong), crafted their characteristically smiling Buddhas: over 51,000 were carved into these caves, the largest being 56 feet (17m) high.

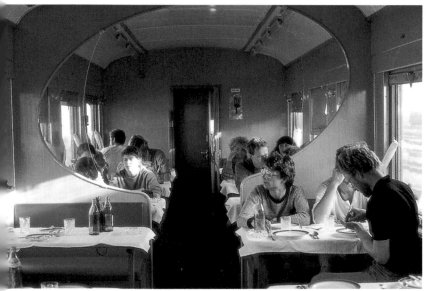

Beyond Datong and the outer wall lies the interior and the expanse of Mongolia. Mongolia is divided into Inner and Outer: the Inner Mongolia Autonomous Region (Nei Mongol Zizhiqu), which is part of China and is hardly 'autonomous', especially as now only 10 per cent of its 20 million population are Mongols, most of the rest being Han Chinese; and the independent Mongolian People's Republic, which was essentially part of the former Soviet empire for most of this century (Mongolia became the world's second Communist state in 1921). The train travels through the former to reach the latter.

Heading north from Datong, the train takes just under two hours to cover the 73 miles (127km) to Jiningnan – from where there is a branch line westwards to Hohhot, the capital of Inner Mongolia – and a further four hours ten minutes to reach Erlian (Erenhot) on the borders of Inner and Outer Mongolia.

We rolled gently into Erlian after dark. Mozart, local and universal favourite of the day, blared through the loudspeaker system; a neat row of smart, short soldiers stood 30 feet (9m) apart alongside the track to stop people 'running off'. Who would 'run off' in the blackness of the night into the emptiness of Mongolia? I pictured a nightmarish scenario of running on and on, breathlessly, without ever actually reaching anywhere.

The Chinese railways are standard gauge and the bogies have to be changed to the wider Russian five foot gauge, as used in Mongolia, before the journey can be continued. The train is shunted into the bogie yard and carriages are lifted up as the standards are replaced by the five footers beneath them.

Bogie changing is a lengthy procedure taking several hours and passengers are requested to adjourn to the station to sit out the wait. Sound advice is given on a hoarding above the currency exchange kiosk: 'Do not worry the time. After exchange to the bar'.

The inspecting of visas is conducted on board: one 'checks out' of China, takes the train for the 6 miles (10km) to Dzamïn Uüd across the border, where one 'checks into' Mongolia. It was around midnight before all the necessary formalities had been completed and we were on our way again.

We travelled through the night across the Gobi, more a desert of arid scrubland than sand dune, and by dawn we had reached the fringes of steppelands. The sun rose quickly and by 9 o'clock, as the train drew into the pink and white Choir Station, the sky was already a rich translucent blue.

Our first contact with Mongolian culture was the Mongolian dining-car which replaced the Chinese one at the border. The waitresses wore the attractive *del*, the traditional gown tied at the waist by a wide cummerbund-like sash which is worn by both men and women; the bottled drinks bore Mongolian labels, and chunks of meat replaced noodles as the cuisine. It was

LEFT, passengers in the dining car of the Trans Mongolian Express

rather like changing airlines: the basic features remained the same, only the cosmetic details of national identity differed.

A horseman appeared at the window, galloping in pace with the train. After some minutes he slowed, waved, laughed cheerfully and turned his horse towards a *gher* (the Mongolian term for a *yurt* tent) which was no more than a solitary white speck on a vast, rolling landscape. Suddenly, train travel seemed quite absurd. What did he think of us, crammed in a long metal tube, trundling along a well-worn route through a land of such immense, breathtaking space?

We reached Ulaanbaatar ('Red Hero'), the present Mongolian capital which had the pre-Communist name of Urga, about an hour after the scheduled 13.20hrs arrival time. I disembarked: I wanted to see beyond the rail line, to feel the soil, breathe the air, experience the land.

One needs a horse, a 4-wheel drive car or a plane to travel beyond the Trans Mongolian. From land or air one feels the illimitlessness of the country. Mongolia (Outer Mongolia alone) covers more than 600,000 square miles (1.5 million sq km). That is a country over six times the size of the United Kingdom and almost three times that of France; and there it lies, like a forgotten void in the heart of Asia, landlocked between the even larger China and Russia.

Once, though, Mongolia was the centre of the world. The rise of Genghis Khan as leader of the Mongol tribes from 1211 to his death in 1227 was like a bolt from hell to the rest of mankind. He and his hordes of horsemen seized the world by fear as they stampeded out of their steppelands. In February 1220 they razed Bokhara – 'they came, mined, burnt, killed, plundered and left', observed a witness. The impenetrable Samarkand fell a few days later; the entire population of Herat, numbering hundreds of thousands, was slaughtered; at the fall of Baghdad the massacre was so great that the blood of the slain flowed in a river like the Nile. In a letter to the Pope, Queen Russudan of the Georgians described the Mongols as 'a savage people, hellish of aspect, as voracious as wolves and as brave as lions'. They were dubbed 'Tartars', derived from Tartarus, the hell of classical mythology. And even long after Genghis' death, a rumour of a Mongol attack in 1238 struck a note of terror in far-off lands: Scandinavian merchants did not dare leave their shores to buy herrings and as a result there was, that year, a glut of the fish in the English east-coast port of Yarmouth.

With such deft speed had the Mongol cavalry whipped across half the world to create for themselves an empire which would stretch from Siberia, the Yellow Sea and Borneo in the east, to Poland, the Adriatic and Egypt in the west. No one has ever controlled so much of the earth before or since.

HEIGHT OF AN EMPIRE

As nomads, the Mongols did not build where they conquered. Signs of their presence in their empire are scarce. However, their steppeland capital of Karakorum, which was completed in 1235, was a major caravan crossroad in Asia, reputedly a splendid place which drew the world's greatest artists and philosophers. William of Rubrouck, a Franciscan monk and envoy of France's Louis IX, visited Karakorum

RIGHT, *the comfortable interior of a Mongolian gher, including a polished iron bedstead*

in 1251 and reported its great opulence. The *pièce de résistance* was the magnificent silver fountain, crafted by silversmith William of Paris: mare's milk, wine, honey beer and rice mead were channelled through separate pipes and then gushed through the spots of carved lions' and serpents' heads, splashing into basins below; a silver angel with a trumpet stood atop the fountain, and a man hidden down in the base would blow through a connecting pipe to sound the instrument.

Karakorum was destroyed by the Chinese Ming when they overthrew the Yuan dynasty in the late 14th century. By then the Mongol Empire was in irreversible decline; the hurricane which had ripped apart the world had subsided. Karakorum's ruins were plundered in the

16th century to build the nearby Buddhist monastery complex of Erdene Dzuu ('Hundreds of Treasures'), which still stands – though much was damaged by the Communists in 1937 – as a testimony to Mongolia's strong lamaist tradition. Nothing at all was left of Karakorum, which according to explorer Marco Polo had a circumference of 3 miles (5km). Indeed, only in 1889 was its site discovered by archaeologists.

I befriended an old nomad couple about half a day's horse-ride from Karakorum. They lived in a traditional white, felt *gher* which they would soon dismantle as they moved their animals on to fresh pastures. (The Mongolian herd numbers about 23 million head of livestock, predominantly sheep and goats, as well as horses and camels.) Namdag and her husband were both in their sixties. As a mother of ten (and grand or great grand mother of over 65 children), she had been awarded Honoured Mothers badges for doing her duty to increase the Mongolian population: Mongolia has barely 2 million people (90 per cent are ethnic Mongoloid-Mongols) and the fact that over 70 per cent are under 35 years old indicates the successful drive to raise the birth-rate in recent decades.

Several of Namdag's children lived in *ghers* scattered within a 20-mile (32km) radius, and on the day of my visit they arrived on horseback from across the horizons. I was welcomed and given the honoured seat to the right of the male host on the far side of the stove which forms the centre of the home. The party began, we drank *airaq*, fermented mare's milk, and ate chunks of cheese and the freshly slaughtered lamb.

Our sobriety remained reasonably intact. My hosts spoke in gentle, kind, hushed tones, only increasing the volume when they laughed. The hospitality was warm and generous. Were these really the descendants of those 'savage people' who had ravaged the world?

All that survives of Mongolia's extraordinary past are the stories. And the tales of wanton terror and kitsch silver fountains are so far

ABOVE, *a Russian steam locomotive stands preserved at Ulaanbaatar – note the narrow gauge*

ABOVE, *the nomads of Mongolia slowly cross and recross the plains in search of fresh pastures, living in their traditional white felt ghers*

RIGHT, *this great monument at Ulaanbaatar was built as a symbol of Soviet–Mongol co-operation*

removed from the realities of today as to give Mongolia a sort of unreal mythical quality. Indeed, the most celebrated account of the Mongols was a hallunicatory creation. When Samuel Taylor Coleridge composed his rich version of Kublai Khan's Xanadu with its 'stately pleasure dome' in his poem 'Vision in a Dream', he was so high on opium that afterwards he had not a clue what he had written.

I returned to the rail line, always a thread of reassurance in mysterious lands, and caught the evening northbound train out of Mongolia. The Trans Mongolian-Trans Siberian, a Russian service, departs from Ulaanbaatar six evenings a week bound for Moscow; it would be the early hours of the next morning before we reached the northern Mongolian towns of Darhan and Sühbaatar (approximately 5½ and 7 hours respectively from Ulaanbaatar), and Naushki across the border in Russia. Out of Ulaanbaatar, the train gathered speed in the empty countryside; the crisp sky was tinged with a rich magenta.

They say earth meets heaven in these high steppelands. Mongolia is like a breath of fresh air compared to China and Russia, its lumbering neighbours, which seem so weighed down in

culture, history, sights, industry, politics, populations, fame.

Sitting on one of the two beds in my compartment was an excessively bulky Russian. His clothes barely contained his body and patches of hairy pinky-grey flesh bulged between the gaps of his shirt buttons; his face was a series of flabby folds divided by deep furrows and it sagged, giving him the sad look of a bloodhound. I suddenly felt intensely claustrophobic at the prospect of a long journey in a small room with a large man.

We nodded our greetings. He mopped the glistening beads of sweat from his brow with a podgy hand and, wheezing heavily, reached down to his plastic hold-all and produced a brown paper bag containing a bottle of vodka. He poured two good measures, handed me one – a sort of symbolic compensation, I reasoned, for occupying more than his fair share of the compartment – and raised his glass. With a cheerful smile, which lifted his whole face and revealed a set of crooked teeth, he said in strongly accented English, 'Bottoms up to God, King and Country' and swallowed his drink in a single gulp.

By day, a country reveals to those on a train its landscape, its people, its flora and fauna, its history and its culture like a documentary film. But as dusk gives way to darkness, the traveller must look within for his entertainment. Boris, the Russian, had also enticed a quiet Mongolian from along the carriage into companionship with an offer of a drink. We were an unlikely trio, brought together by boarding the same train and consolidated in friendship through a bottle of vodka.

Our conversation, mainly conducted in English with the help of sign language, somehow progressed on to 'nationality'. Suddenly we realized our common ground: our respective countries had each ruled over, at one time in their histories, vast empires. Sensible debate dissolved as the vodka took effect. We gave each other nicknames. I, the Briton, became 'Victor' (from Victoria); the Mongolian, whose real name was unpronounceable anyway, became 'Genghis'; and Boris, refusing connection with any of the Soviet leaders, was called the 'Bear', the symbol of Imperial Russia.

By midnight we had created a game based on 'Monopoly', drawing a board on a paper tablecloth with squares denoting the different countries of our empires during the height of their powers. Of course, Genghis' Mongol and Bear's Soviet empires, carved out some seven centuries apart, did overlap considerably. But territories were eventually decided upon and the Bear, the most astute politician among us, argued successfully to gain the likes of Cuba and other more dubious Soviet satellites.

And so, as the locomotive pulled us through the blackness across the steppelands towards Siberia, we three empire builders sat in the empty dining-car with the world spread before us. Using sugar cubes as dice and toothpicks as currency we each embarked upon winning global supremacy.

Between sessions of 'Universal Empire', as we called our game, Boris had taught me the Cyrillic alphabet. At one stop I idly put my newly learnt skill into practice and after spelling out the name of the station I translated ВОЗАЛ into a word sounding like VAUXHALL. I was told later that in the 19th century a tsar despatched a delegation of engineers to England to learn about railway construction.

They met their British counterparts at Vauxhall, at the time a main London station. Their visit over, they returned to Russia and set about building their country's rail network. And, believing 'Vauxhall' to mean 'station', the Russian word for 'station' became 'Vauxhall'.

Back in England I telephoned Vauxhall Station, now little more than a underground stop on the Victoria Line, to see if they could confirm this story:

'I am trying to find out about a Russian delegation…'

'Had any Russians here?', shouted the man at the end of the line to a colleague. 'Sorry, guv'nor, no Russians have been here as far as we know', came the reply down the phone.

'No, this was during the tsars' time in the…'

'I'm new here, guv, he must have been before my time.'

The train and most of its passengers were travelling all the way to Moscow. By Omsk, Genghis had become Universal Emperor, having had the luck of the sugar cube and acquired Moscow and London from the Bear and me for a total of 79 toothpicks.

In defeat we promised Genghis a slap-up dinner when we reached Moscow. But as we finally neared our destination the fantasies of the train slipped into the background. After so long in our artificial world we were abruptly awakened to the realities of life. We all had other people to meet, other things to do, other places to go to. We said hasty farewells on the platform and disappeared in our different directions.

Our friendship, like the scenes through the train windows, had left strong impressions, but had been fleeting. People chanced upon on board are unlikely to be met again; the places seen in passing will probably not be visited. Brief encounters are, after all, the essence – indeed, the very charm, or 'seductive glimpse', as Mr Lee would have said – of train travel.

PRACTICAL INFORMATION

■ The Trans Mongolian Train No 3 runs once a week from Beijing through Mongolia all the way to Moscow (Moskva). From Ulaanbaatar Russian trains leave for Moscow six times a week. The 970 miles (1570km) from Beijing to Ulaanbaatar is covered in 1½ days, and the whole 5625 miles (9052km) from Beijing to Moscow takes 5½ days.

■ Border controls between China and Mongolia take place on the train.

■ Accommodation is either Soft or Hard Class. The former, with two- or four-berth compartments, is usually used by Western travellers. The dining-car is attached to the Soft Class carriages and at the end of each carriage is a samovar (batchok) providing hot water for tea.

■ The Trans Mongolian is operated by Chinese Railways. Tickets can be bought in Beijing, Ulaanbaatar and Moscow at the government tourist offices. However it is more reassuring to obtain a booking in advance through a reliable agent. In the UK, Regent Holidays of Bristol are specialists in travel through China Mongolia and Russia, and can arrange advance bookings. Regent Travel, 13 Small Street, Bristol BS1 1DE.
Tel: (0117) 921 1711.
Fax: (0117) 925 4866.
In the US contact China Passage (Fred Caplin), 168 State Street, Teaneck, New Jersey 0766-3516.
Tel: 201 837 1400.
Fax: 201 837 1378.

The Japanese Bullet Train to Tokyo

DAVID SCOTT

The Tokaido Sanyo Shinkansen long distance, high speed rail service links Tokyo, Japan's capital city, with Fukuoka in Kyushu, its southernmost main island. It is the fastest and most punctual train service in the world. Aboard the Hikari Express (nicknamed the 'Bullet Train'), which stops only at principal stations, the 664-mile (1069km) journey takes 5 hours 57 minutes precisely. The train carries passengers from the temperate climes of central Japan to the subtropical warmth of the south-east, passing through the densely populated plains of Honshu, the spectacular scenery of the Fuji-Hakone-Izu National Park, and along coastlines of both the Pacific Ocean and the Inland Sea.

RIGHT, the role of the controller of the Shinkansen is perhaps reflected in his uniform, which is more like that of an airline pilot than the traditional engine driver

FAR RIGHT, the distinctive rounded nose, as well as its speed, has given the Bullet Train its nickname

F ROM CENTRAL FUKUOKA I took the subway to Hakata Station. On the underground platform birdsong was being broadcast over the public address system. Raised metal studs, set in patterns, ran along the platform edge, foot braille for the blind. The train arrived: it was spacious, smoke-free and new – not unlike Fukuoka itself.

The Tokaido Sanyo Shinkansen trains are 16 carriages long, with three non-smoking cars. Apart from their bullet-shaped nose fronts, a distinctive feature is their double-decker cars. At the top is a dining-room with large viewing windows that extend to the roof, and at the lower level is First Class accommodation (called 'Green Car' in Japanese trains), where individuals or small groups may reserve private compartments with a hotel-style 'room service'.

Excellent refreshment facilities are one of the delights of travelling on this service. In addition to the dining-car, there is a trolley service. At frequent intervals a young man or woman pushing a trolley will appear at the entrance to the carriage, bow and then slowly move down the passageway selling *eki ben* (lunch boxes), bean jam

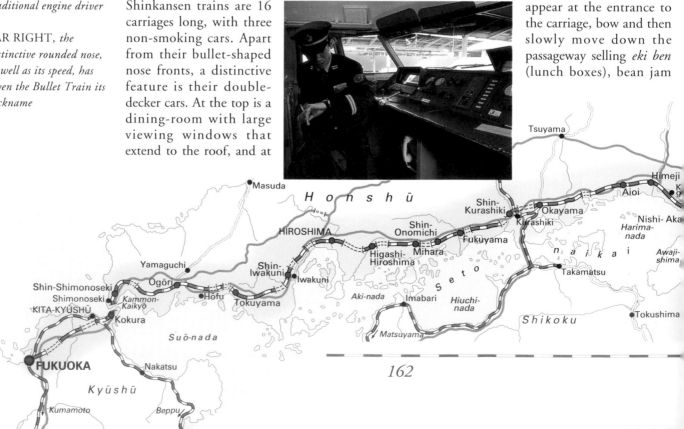

desserts, ice cream, beer and green tea. *Eki ben* are also sold at each of the Shinkansen stops, where they are at their freshest, and often contain a local delicacy. I bought one at Hakata Station before boarding the 08.49hrs Tokaido Sanyo Shinkansen for Tokyo, arrival time 14.36hrs.

Shinkansen train platforms are divided into carriage-length spaces, and above the exact place that each carriage door will be, once the train has stopped, hangs a numbered plate that relates to the passengers' tickets. Having found the correct one, and holding my suitcase in one hand (Japanese trains make allowance for only one medium-sized suitcase per passenger) and *eki ben* in the other, I stood in line to await the train's arrival. This is essential since the Shinkansen pulls into and out of the station within the space of five minutes.

The trains carry 1½ million passengers per annum between Tokyo and Hakata, and over 22 million between Tokyo and Osaka. On working days the passengers are mainly professional or business people, but during weekends and holidays the trains can be just as busy with tourists and city workers returning to their country homes.

It comes as no surprise that wheelchair-bound passengers are exceptionally well catered for on the Shinkansen. A private room is provided

separates the island of Kyushu from Honshu, Japan's main island, and then follows the northern coast of the Inland Sea (Seto naikai), avoiding the wooded, mountainous interior of western Honshu.
The line passes through Hiroshima, the target of the world's first atomic bomb; Osaka, major port and commercial centre; Kyoto, the spiritual capital of Japan; and then goes south across densely populated plains to the coast of the Pacific Ocean.
On its final stage the train runs along the coastal fringe of the Hakone-Fuji-Izu National Park, when Mount Fuji (or Fuji-san) may be glimpsed through the train windows. Past the tea plantations of Shizuoka, it finally enters the environs of Tokyo, to end at Tokyo Station, the biggest and busiest in the world.

■ The Tokaido Sanyo Shinkansen rail service opened in 1964 just before the Tokyo Olympics. It linked Tokyo with Osaka, a distance of 320 miles (515km), and followed for most of its length the route of the old Tokaido highway.
The Tokaido was just a narrow cobbled road but in its time was the most

important highway in Japan. It joined Edo (old Tokyo), the seat of the Shogun warlords, with Kyoto, home of the emperor and the spiritual heart of the country.
Wheeled vehicles, except for the emperor's carriage, were banned and on foot the journey took several weeks. The new Shinkansen 'Bullet Train' Nozomi, introduced in

March 1992, takes less than 2½ hours.
Since 1964 the Tokaido line has, in stages, been extended and linked with the Sanyo line, to terminate in Fukuoka, a bright, architecturally modern city

with a busy 'soapland' district of bars, nightclubs and restaurants.
The west–east route starts at Hakata Station in Fukuoka. From here it quickly tunnels under the Kammon Strait (Kammon-kaikyo) which

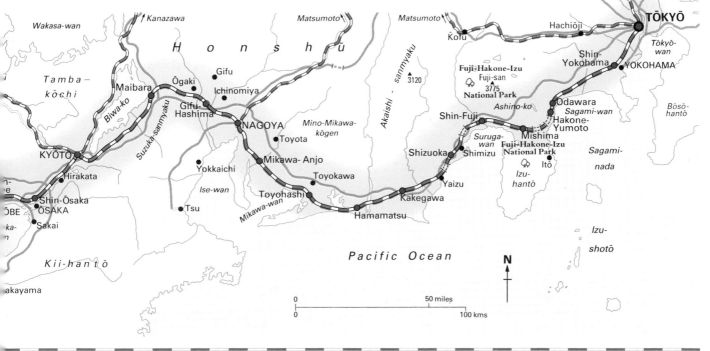

between the exit and the toilets in the buffet car, and seats in this room may be folded down into a bed. Those who want a regular seat will find that their wheelchair can be folded and stored next to a row from which seat C has been removed. Automatic doors on the train are wide enough for wheelchair access. I sat down between a soberly dressed businessman and a young woman wearing jeans and a T-shirt bearing the slogan, in English, 'Apple Closet Mode Selection' – English words that make no linguistic sense are a common fashion motif in Japan. Further down the carriage I saw a tall *gaijin* (foreigner), immediately distinguished by his height and thick moustache.

(240kph). The ride remained smooth. I learned later that the Shinkansen track consists of welded steel rail on a rubber pad, with the whole set in pre-stressed concrete. This, together with the use of individually powered axles on the trains, gives extremely smooth traction.

Despite their very high speeds and high passenger volume, trains on this service have a record of no deaths and no injury to a passenger in 27 years of operation.

Shinkansen are the fastest trains on this route but for the budget traveller in no particular hurry there are cheaper and slower trains which stop at many more stations. A good compromise train is the 'limited express', which travels on conventional lines and completes the journey in 14 hours 50 minutes. The service is frequent and there are stops at all the medium-to-large stations en route. From these stations there are efficient local services for exploring the immediate area.

Over the loud-speaker system a courteous female voice informed us in Japanese and then in English that the train would be arriving in Hiroshima in four minutes precisely. We were advised to 'have a nice day'. Soft,

ABOVE, *the Shinkansen carries more than 22 million passengers – including these school-children – each year between Tokyo and Osaka*

The train moved off and we quickly passed Kokura Station on the northern tip of Kyushu before tunnelling under the Kammon Strait. The train hurtled into the light at Shimonoseki, on the western point of Honshu. The sea briefly came into view and I saw several moored squid boats. They were easily recognisable by the large light bulbs, strung out above their decks, which are used to attract the squid at night. The Japanese love squid: in Tokyo there are restaurants and shops that specialise exclusively in squid dishes and foods.

The train was now passing through a steep, hilly area where habitation is restricted to villages squeezed on to flat patches of land between hills that rise too sharply to build on or even to terrace for cultivation.

According to the speedometer display in the carriage, the train was travelling at over 150mph

soothing music followed the announcement. Even in the land of Zen, silence is a rare commodity.

WAR AND PEACE

The feudal lord Terumoto Mori built Hiroshima Castle on the present site of the city in the 16th century. From that time forward the area had a military significance. During World War II Hiroshima was a centre of weapons manufacture. On 6 August 1945, at 08.15hrs, it was the target of the world's first atom bomb attack. The city was completely and instantly destroyed and 200,000 people died. Six thousand people a year still die from after-effects. The Peace Memorial Park in Hiroshima contains a museum, monument and other memorials of the bomb.

The train now sped along a route parallel with the northern coast of the Inland Sea (Seto naikai) which separates Honshu from Shikoku, the smallest and least developed of Japan's four main islands. Out of the window I saw a large, neon-lit hoarding which read 'Love is Needing to be Loved. John.' John Lennon or John the Baptist, I wondered.

The seat next to the *gaijin* was now empty and I went to speak to him. He was an Englishman called Terry who had lived and run a business in Fukuoka for the last ten years. He spoke fluent colloquial Japanese. He told me he had learned much of it watching Japanese television, and his language was sprinkled with low-life Japanese. He was on his way to Osaka where he would buy lengths of discontinued kimono material. He had this cut and sewn into specially designed scarves in Tokyo. The scarves were then sold by demonstration in department stores in Kyushu by six housewives whom he employed. During the humid summer months Terry returned to England to bet on horses, watch cricket and attend Wimbledon. He must be an enigma to the hard-working Japanese who take only three weeks holiday a year and never more than one week at a time.

The train approached Okayama, a major city on the Inland Sea noted for the large landscape garden, Koraku-en. I was reminded of a clip I had read in the Japan Times the day before:

The tradition-bound world of Japanese banking has been shaken by the changes in Japanese society. For instance, bank president Kenji Yoshida of Sanyo Sogo Bank, Okayama decided one morning, over a breakfast of fried tomatoes, to call his bank Tomato! In the first month under its new name the Tomato Bank attracted more new depositors than in the whole of the previous year.

A party of well-disciplined schoolchildren joined the train on their way to visit the Zen temples of Kyoto. They sat down and immediately unpacked their *eki ben*. I followed suit. My box, wrapped in decorative paper and tied with string, was made from thin, unpainted wood. It was divided into neat compartments containing *sushi* rice, grilled chicken, *shiitaki* (wood mushrooms), smoked fish, pickled plums and a pair of chopsticks. Once I had finished, I re-wrapped the empty lunch box, following the children's example, tied it up again and put it in the refuse bin.

To complete the meal I bought a plastic bottle of very hot green tea. The screw-top doubled as a cup and the lip of the bottle was perforated to catch the tea leaves. Japanese packaging is often ingenious.

ABOVE, *a Shinto shrine in Osaka – note the shimenawa, the great rope of rice-straw, hung up after the harvest season*

We passed through Kobe, famous throughout Japan for the quality of the beef produced from the local cattle who are fed on beer (Japanese brown ale). Cows are a rare sight in Japan and sheep are kept only in zoos, but in this district they may be seen, complete with *Kanji* (ideograms) brandmarks.

The Japanese describe Osaka, our next stop, as *shominteki*, a place of the people where appearance is less important than substance. (Osakans consider Tokyoites effete). Seen from the train window, the city looked grimy, chaotic and cramped. It is not a town popular with tourists, but for a keyhole view of real Japanese city life, and the closest there is to a working-class Japan, it is worth a visit.

From Osaka it was a short hop to Kyoto, the religious capital of Japan and, until the end of the Edo period in 1868, the home for many centuries of the imperial family. It is a lovely city of temples, Zen gardens, Shinto shrines and, in the quiet back streets of the old quarter, craft shops, traditional houses and Japanese inns. Unfortunately the area around the station is faceless and modern, and I was glad when the train left for the next leg to Nagoya.

It started to rain and raindrops on the train window distorted the view of wooded hills and flat, rice-growing paddies around the shores of Lake Biwa (Biwa-ko), along which we now travelled. The hills gradually flattened out and the landscape became a dull jigsaw of rice fields, unused urban land, low-roofed villages and small towns. Roads, railway tracks and pylon lines criss-crossed the plain. I turned to my female seat companion for conversation.

On the street of any Japanese city the man walking past you in a white shirt and a blue suit – indistinguishable from the men around him dressed in the same way – is probably a company or salary-man. They are the backbone of the Japanese economy. There are salarywomen but

PREVIOUS PAGE, *the Shinkansen leaves a green, local train standing in Tokyo's busy heartland*

RIGHT, *west of Tokyo the Shinkansen passes through the scenic Hakone region, an area popular with Japanese holidaymakers*

FAR RIGHT, *the train becomes a blur as it speeds past beautiful Mount Fuji, a dormant volcano revered for centuries as a sacred peak*

BELOW, *commuters wait in orderly lines at Tokyo Station*

they are fewer in number than men. A salaryman joins a company between the ages of 18 and 22. The understanding on both sides is that he will remain with the same company until he retires. A person who leaves a company position is considered potentially unreliable, and an unemployed ex-companyman over the age of 30 will find it very difficult to get a new position.

Etsuko, the young lady next to me, had trained as an osteopath. She told me that her first interview for a salaried job was at a Tokyo hospital. At the interview she was told her salary expectations up to the age of 60, her pension details and even how much she might expect for her funeral expenses. She was 18 years old at the time! The thought of her life being mapped out was so depressing that she had turned the job down. She was now a self-employed businesswoman, selling computer software.

Nagoya is Japan's fifth largest city. Flattened during World War II, it was rebuilt according to city planning theories of the time and, I am told, is an agreeable, if uninspiring, place to live.

A DIVERSE LANDSCAPE

From Nagoya the train travelled south, fringing the mountainous terrain of the Hakone National Park, and then east along the Pacific coastal plain. Here the land is heavily cultivated with crops such as tomatoes, aubergines and courgettes, grown under acres of ugly blue plastic sheeting. The Japanese appreciate perfect form as much as taste in their fruit and vegetables, and for commercial growers it is important to prevent the vagaries of the weather from causing distortions in the shape of their produce. The plastic covering has the desired effect, but certainly mars the beauty of the countryside.

We now travelled into the Shizuoka area, where most of Japan's tea is grown. Every available patch of land is planted with tea bushes. The best tea is made from the first spring shoots that appear at the top of the bush. They are hand-clipped and the tea made from them is extremely expensive, the province of the connoisseur. The second-quality tea is made from hand-cut secondary shoots, and the ordinary grade from machine-trimmed cuttings. Green tea ice cream is popular in Japan.

We passed through Mishima Station, entrance way to the Izu peninsula which juts out into the Pacific Ocean. It is not far south from Tokyo and the area is a popular summer resort for the city's residents. Ito, an old spa town on the north-east coast of the peninsula, was the home of Will Adams, the English ship's pilot who inspired the novel by James Clavell, *Shogun*.

The train sped through Fuji, Hakone and Odawara Stations. All are stops on slower trains for the Hakone National Park. This is an area of high mountains with Lake Ashino-ko nestling in the centre and Fuji-san (12,388ft/3775m) nearly always in view to the north-west. The Japanese believe that the symmetrical reflection of Fuji-san in the calm surface of Ashino-ko is the most beautiful sight in the world. From the train window I could see the summit wreathed in wispy cloud. A moving sight, even for a *gaijin*.

The official Mount Fuji climbing season is July and August, when the weather conditions are not too severe. Most people climb Mount Fuji in the hope of witnessing a sunrise from the top. This means that they either have to climb up overnight or have to climb during the day and stay on the summit overnight. It is an arduous climb and the mountain at close quarters is not beautiful. The rock is black and volcanic and there is no vegetation. Only the view outwards can lift the spirits. The Japanese say that to climb Fuji-san once is wise, but to climb it twice is foolish.

As we moved east, the open spaces between urban developments grew smaller until the landscape became one continuous urban sprawl. We were now in the outer environs of Tokyo, one of the world's largest cities and certainly one of the most dynamic. First impressions are that it is a city without any particular distinguishing features. Closer investigation, however, will reveal it to be a complex metropolis formed of a series of connected towns, now districts, each with its own individual neighbourhoods, character and energy.

The train pulled into Tokyo Station, it stopped and the electric carriage doors opened. It was 14.36hrs exactly.

PRACTICAL INFORMATION

■ The Tokaido Sanyo Shinkansen operates daily between Tokyo Station and Hakata Station in the city of Fukuoka, three or four times an hour. Reserved tickets are recommended for all trains, especially for a non-smoking seat.

■ Good times for general travel in Japan are April and May, which are warm, dry months, and autumn (September/October) which is also a time of clear skies and comfortable temperatures. It is worth bearing in mind that from late March to mid-April the cherry blossom ripens northwards from Kyushu to Hokkaido, and celebration cherry blossom festivals are held all over Japan to mark the event.

■ For foreign visitors, a rail pass, which allows unlimited travel on rail, bus or ferry services for between one and three weeks, is a good investment; this can only be purchased outside Japan. Anyone using Japanese Airlines can buy a voucher for one through them. Otherwise, apply to any branch of the Japan Travel Bureau. Individual tickets for the Tokaido Sanyo Shinkansen can only be purchased within Japan, from any major travel agent or at a railway station from the 'green window' counters (*midori-no-madoguchi* in Japanese).
The London branch of the Japan Travel Bureau is at 10 Maltravers Street, London WC2 R3EE.
Tel: (0171) 395 6600.
Fax: (0171) 836 6215.
In the US contact any branch of the Japan Tourist Board. The New York office is at JTB Americas Ltd, 1 Rockafeller Plaza, Suite 1250, New York, NY 10020-1579.
Tel: 212 887 9300.

Crossing New Zealand's Southern Alps

ROY SINCLAIR

In a little less than five hours the TranzAlpine Express crosses New Zealand's South Island from east to west joining two coasts and two vastly different destinations, the very English 'Garden City' of Christchurch and Greymouth, a quaint West Coast coal town at the mouth of the Grey River. In between, 145 miles (233km) of narrow gauge 3ft 6in (1067mm) single track twists and turns through the Southern Alps, across high steel viaducts spanning deep river gorges and through 19 tunnels. Flat cultivated plains on one side of the mountains contrast with lush rain forests on the other. To ride the TranzAlpine Express is to experience a diversity of spectacular landscapes compacted into a relatively short, coast-to-coast journey.

RIGHT, *heading west, the TranzAlpine Express approaches Arthur's Pass via Cass Bank*

FAR RIGHT, *driver Garry Martin at the controls of the 'Tranz'*

I FIND MYSELF the sole New Zealander in my carriage. As the foothills of the Southern Alps slowly loom larger, I am enjoying breakfast and Devonshire teas in conversation with new found friends across the table. An American tourist tells me how delighted he is to hear the expression 'as good as gold' in New Zealand: 'Why' he says, 'I haven't heard that back home since I was a kid!' Some English people tell me it is still the ambition for many of their young to visit Australia and New Zealand, the far-flung members of the British Commonwealth. The TranzAlpine Express, known locally as the 'Tranz', is clearly going to live up to its enviable reputation of being a very friendly train.

It is also a railway success story. The brain-child of one John Bennett, a Westcoaster and one-time InterCity rail manager who for many years believed the trans-alpine railway would attract tourists, the 'Tranz' was introduced in November 1987 and has led to a revival of rail travel in New Zealand.

Yet, compared to many of the world's great trains, the TranzAlpine Express is almost unpretentious. Its usual consist is three or four carriages hauled, at present, by a Dc class diesel electric locomotive. The pre-World War II, steel-clad carriages have been refurbished and fitted with large panorama windows, and a former guard's van has been rebuilt to provide an open-sided observation platform. At certain times during the year a club car with a buffet, or connoisseur car with a large rear window, is added.

On board the facilities and service are designed for tourists rather than regular travellers. Seats, in bays of four around a table, have sheepskin covers. A licensed buffet provides a choice of boxed lunches at reasonable cost – Canterbury Lamburgers, a Gold-miner's Lunch and, of course, the once in-famous Railway Pie. Sought after chiefly for reasons of nostalgia, it none the less makes a quality and filling meal. Devonshire teas of scones with jam and cream are served at passengers' seats.

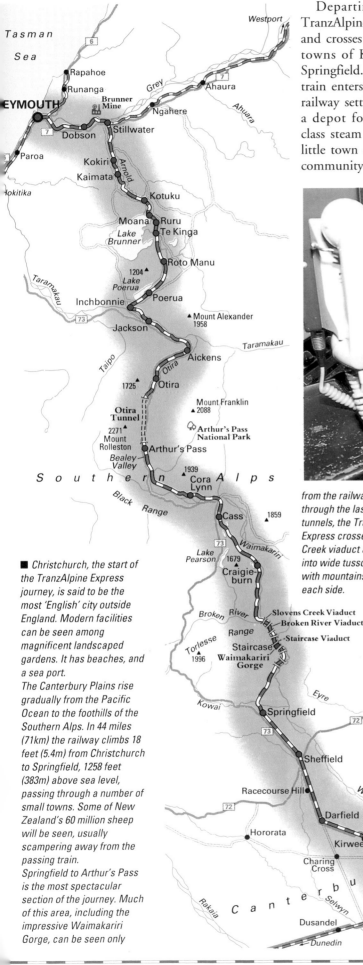

Departing Christchurch at 07.40hrs, the TranzAlpine Express soon leaves the city behind and crosses the Canterbury Plains, through the towns of Kirwee, Darfield and Sheffield to Springfield. Springfield is the last stop before the train enters the mountains. Once an important railway settlement with refreshment rooms and a depot for servicing magnificent 4-8-4 Kb class steam locomotives, Springfield is a sleepy little town surviving to serve the sheep farming community.

Christchurch, the start of the TranzAlpine Express journey, is said to be the most 'English' city outside England. Modern facilities can be seen among magnificent landscaped gardens. It has beaches, and a sea port.

The Canterbury Plains rise gradually from the Pacific Ocean to the foothills of the Southern Alps. In 44 miles (71km) the railway climbs 18 feet (5.4m) from Christchurch to Springfield, 1258 feet (383m) above sea level, passing through a number of small towns. Some of New Zealand's 60 million sheep will be seen, usually scampering away from the passing train.

Springfield to Arthur's Pass is the most spectacular section of the journey. Much of this area, including the impressive Waimakariri Gorge, can be seen only

from the railway. After going through the last of 16 tunnels, the TranzAlpine Express crosses Slovens Creek viaduct and emerges into wide tussock valleys with mountains rising on each side.

Arthur's Pass in the heart of the Southern Alps, rising at this point to almost 8000 feet (2428m), is the highest station on the journey. The township, 2417 feet (736m) above sea level, is head-quarters for the Arthur's Pass National Park. The Tranz-Alpine Express enters the Arthur's Pass portal of the 5⅓ mile (8.9km) Otira tunnel soon after leaving the station.
Otira, 1178 feet (359m) lower than Arthur's Pass, is a fascinating railway settlement that may have seen better days. People who live here either love it or hate it. Annual rainfall is about 200

inches. Otira is a Maori word meaning appropriately 'out of the sun'. In January, the steep, bushed mountain-sides are splashed with scarlet rata.
From Otira the railway gradually descends to Greymouth. Special features are the Taramakau River, famed for its greenstone, and lakes Poerua and Brunner.
Greymouth is a principal commercial centre for the West Coast. The town is sited on a narrow strip of land bounded on three sides by limestone hills, the Grey River, and the Tasman Sea.

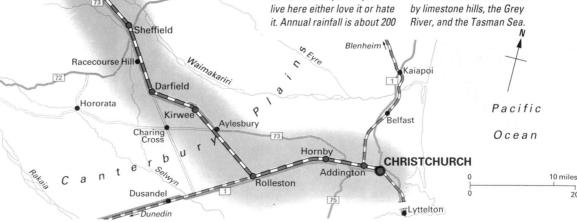

ABOVE, *the spectacular view from the train of the Waimakariri Gorge*

CENTRE, *looking down the length of the 'Tranz' towards the mountains*

Springfield is also home for Rosie. Just before 9 o'clock in the morning and again late in the afternoon, Rosie, a 17-year-old border collie, pricks up her ears, beats her tail furiously, and waits in eager anticipation. She meets the TranzAlpine Express every day, and was introduced to the railway many years ago by her master, the railway's Springfield traffic officer. But Rosie's master has retired, and Rosie now goes alone to meet the train. She is rewarded with a yesterday's beef pie.

Even if the TranzAlpine Express does not need to stop for passengers, it will always stop for Rosie. Our train manager, Bob Ewing, has stopped trains for Rosie for as long as he can remember: 'She used to come to the station when we ran the old trains to the West Coast', he says. 'We all took Rosie for granted. We saw her every day and we gave her a pie. Then a journalist working for the *International Herald Tribune* was on the 'Tranz' one day and asked about the dog. I said she was just an old mongrel that meets the train. He went home to Singapore and wrote a story about Rosie. We daren't call her a mongrel now; she's a celebrity!'

Sit on the right-hand side of the carriage for the best views on the next stage of the journey. During the 43 miles (69km) between Springfield and Arthur's Pass the TranzAlpine Express clings precariously to the top of the

Waimakariri Gorge, passes through 16 tunnels, and crosses five high viaducts before emerging into a wide valley bordered by brown mountains of tussock, scree and, sometimes, snow. The final ascent to Arthur's Pass is in the narrow Bealey Valley, beneath sharp rock peaks that rise above steep mountainsides of beech forest.

For railway builders the Southern Alps, leading up to the main divide overlooking Westland, were a formidable barrier. A government-built railway reached Springfield from Christchurch in 1880. At first, the railway west of Springfield was built by the Midland Railway Company, founded in London in 1886. But only 5½ miles (8.8km) of railway was completed before the company abandoned the project, leaving the larger part of the construction to the Government. The company apparently had more luck on the western side of the mountains, where it constructed some 65 miles (104km) of railway in Westland between 1886 and 1894. Today the company's name is immortalised in the 'Midland Line', the official name given to the trans-alpine railway.

Our driver takes the TranzAlpine Express slowly through tunnels and over viaducts. This is, he tells me, what people travel half-way round the world to see.

Sitting in the club car, a visitor from Bellingham in the United States says he could almost imagine he is travelling through the Rockies. His wife cannot believe that stock can graze so high up in the hills. Bob Ewing, the train manager, reels off the names and heights of viaducts; the most impressive is the 235ft (72m) structure spanning Staircase Creek, at the point

where the creek flows into the Waimakariri Gorge. The view from the viaduct, through high windbreaks, is of the aqua-blue Waimakariri River. All 16 tunnels are short, the longest being just over 30 chains (600m). One-time steam drivers, who were repeatedly almost asphyxiated while working on the footplate, say the tunnels always seemed much longer.

Bob, a jovial man, was previously a guard. Like most of the world's railways, those in New Zealand no longer have traditional guards, and guard's vans (cabooses) have been eliminated from freight trains. In his new role, Bob enjoys meeting people from overseas; he has met people from as far afield as Bermuda, Israel and Iceland. As train manger, he is ticket collector and raconteur. He is well versed in local folklore and especially that which relates to the few people who work and live

along this isolated section of railway. Not so long ago the railway provided the only link with the outside world. Shortly after crossing Broken River Viaduct, Bob points out a farm dwelling down on the far side of the river. 'Whenever we came up here in the railcar we always looked over to that house. A tea towel hanging in the window meant that someone wanted to go to town (Christchurch) and we were to stop on the way home.' Now that lonely property is accessible by a narrow road, and there is no signal for the TranzAlpine Express to stop.

On time, at 10.15hrs, the 'Tranz' stops at Arthur's Pass, the highest point on the journey. We are 2417 feet (737m) above sea level. The chalet-style station is a short walk from the township at the centre of the Arthur's Pass National Park, which covers 245,300 acres (99,270ha) of alpine wilderness. A number of passengers with heavy backpacks or bicycles leave the train. Some will stay, and rejoin the rails another day. Others will return to Christchurch later in the afternoon.

Arthur's Pass, a favourite haunt of railway enthusiasts, was once a place where thundering New Zealand-made Kb and Ja class steam locomotives stopped. Their trains were taken over by electric locomotives for the next section to Otira. The sound of those steam whistles echoing off the high mountains was really something! On certain winter days it can still be heard, when steam excursions run to Arthur's Pass from Christchurch.

In just 8 miles (13km) the railway descends 1178 feet (359m) from Arthur's Pass to Otira. Much of the distance is in the 5⅓-mile (8.5km) Otira tunnel. Up to four electric locomotives assist freight and unit coal trains up the 1:33 gradient between Otira and Arthur's Pass. The lighter TranzAlpine Express is the only train hauled through the tunnel by a diesel-electric locomotive.

The railway reached Otira from Greymouth in 1900 and Arthur's Pass from Christchurch in 1914. Horse-drawn coaches plied between the railheads, over the summit of Arthur's Pass and down through the treacherous Otira Gorge. Work on the Otira Tunnel started in 1908, at first under a private company contract, but in 1912 the Public Works Department took over the tunnelling.

On 20 July 1918 an iron rod was pushed through a drill hole from the Otira side of the workings. The meeting of work faces revealed headings were only 1½ inches (3.75cm) out in level, and less than one inch (2.5cm) in alignment.

According to a popular story, on 20 August 1918, the day before the official tunnel-piercing ceremony, the tunnellers blasted a hole and had their own private ceremony – they did not want some bigwig walking through the hole before them. The hole was then filled in ready for the big event the following day.

When the Otira tunnel was officially opened on 4 August 1923, it was the longest tunnel in the British Empire and the seventh longest in the world. Two slightly longer railway tunnels, the Rimutaka and Kaimai, have since been built in New Zealand.

The tunnel divides entirely different landscapes. Westland, known locally as the 'West Coast', is a land of lush bush, rainforests, and lakes teaming with sizeable trout. But it is not just the landscape that changes – the inhabitants are also different. Westcoasters, generally no-nonsense people, are well-known for their hospitality. But over the years they have been deprived of their resources in timber, gold and coal. Even today, each year more than half a million tons of West Coast coal is railed in large unit trains to Port Lyttelton near Christchurch, and exported to Japan. The TranzAlpine Express, carrying tourists, is endeavouring to put something back into Westland.

Otira, an often dismal railway town confined in a narrow valley, is the first stop beyond the long tunnel. Rusting sheds built to maintain steam locomotives and dilapidated dwellings with back gates leading to the railway recall a time when Otira was a much more lively town. In days long gone, a bottle of beer left on a gate post was the cue for an engine driver to throw off a few shovels of coal for the home fires. But there are still signs of life here. Electric locomotives are often seen waiting to assist the next coal train up to Arthur's Pass and, just occasionally, someone carrying a travel bag will come through one of those back gates and take the 'Tranz' to town.

In recent times, in an effort to make railways pay, numerous stations along the Midland Line have been closed. However, railway officials met more than they had bargained for when they attempted to close Inchbonnie Station, reached a short distance after crossing the Taramakau River. Inchbonnie people were furious and were prepared to fight. A little research established that Thomas Whillians Bruce, a Scot and one of the original settlers, had given the land to the government to build a railway station with a proviso that the train stopped at Inchbonnie when required, for all time. Railway officials could not argue with that. Inchbonnie is the stop for trout fishermen heading for the famous Lake Brunner Lodge, formally known as Mitchells.

Westland is sparsely populated. Miles of countryside pass by but no people are to be seen. Only occasionally is there a fence, a track, or some other sign to suggest that someone has been here before us.

As the 'Tranz' pulls out of Moana, on the shore of Lake Brunner, a Westcoaster has a very tall story to tell us. It is about an unlikely

FAR RIGHT, *the tiny station of Ruru, on the west coast side of the mountains, was built around 1894*

BELOW, *the preserved and privately owned steam locomotive Ka 942, built in New Zealand, on a special winter excursion to Arthur's Pass*

Australian (or was it an American?) who went fishing in the lake: 'He had caught half a dozen very good trout, and was packing up when he saw a huge eel swimming towards him. Alarmed, he picked up a large willow stake and thrust it into the back of the eel. He then watched the willow stake swimming out on the lake until it was out of sight. Some years later, returning to Lake Brunner for another spot of fishing, he got quite a shock when he saw a willow tree swimming towards him!'

Next stop is Stillwater, where the railway tracks divide. One goes north through the Buller Gorge to Westport and the coal bins at Ngakawau. The other follows the Grey River down to Greymouth. We see trains of large aluminium CB wagons coupled behind pairs of Dc class locomotives waiting to carry export coal to Lyttelton. Coal keeps the Midland Line in business.

The remaining few miles beside the Grey River pass quickly. A short distance from Stillwater the TranzAlpine Express passes remnants of the Brunner coal mine, the scene of New Zealand's worst mining tragedy. Sixty-seven miners died in 1896 when an explosion ripped through the underground shafts. A footbridge leads across the river to the old coke bins and interpretative displays.

Arriving at Greymouth, exactly on time at 12.25hrs, seems almost like an anti-climax. More than one glib journalist has attracted considerable ire from Greymouth people by referring to their town as a dead end for rail travellers.

A short walk from the station, however, and you are on the coast where the wild Tasman Sea crashes on to the beach. Ahead lies more than 1000 miles (1500km) of ocean. Next stop, the east coast of Australia.

We take an hour's bus tour with a local guide. A diehard Westcoaster, Sarah unashamedly tells us all we would wish to know about her small town that has many times been flooded by the Grey River. From a breakwater we watch a fishing boat cross the Grey River bar, the scene of numerous shipping tragedies; and we visit an impressive new jade factory.

Later we start to feel a little nervous as the TranzAlpine Express departure time approaches – and passes. But Sarah puts us at our ease. The 'Tranz', she assures us, has never once departed for Christchurch before her bus returned.

Really, it is a pity to be boarding the train again so soon, before seeing more of the West Coast with its old gold trails, two national parks (the Westland National Park has World Heritage status), and quaint towns with public bars reputed to be open all hours.

But for an amicable sort of traveller like me, with only the day to spare in Christchurch, a day excursion to Greymouth on the 'Tranz' is not to be missed. After all, didn't I once hear someone say of a rail journey, 'It's got to be the going, not the getting there that's good'?

PRACTICAL INFORMATION

■ The TranzAlpine Express runs daily (except Christmas Day) from Christchurch to Greymouth and return. The 145-mile (233km) journey takes nearly five hours each way. The train can be taken for a day excursion to Arthur's Pass, or to Greymouth.

■ Advance bookings are recommended.

■ A one-hour Greymouth sightseeing tour is available for day-trippers. Connections can be made for onward travel from Greymouth to the South Westland glaciers, Paparoa National Park, Westport and Nelson.

■ The journey is enjoyable any time, but is especially spectacular on a clear winter's day. Take warm clothing in winter.

■ The TranzAlpine Express is operated by New Zealand Rail. Tickets can be purchased at major stations and travel agents in New Zealand and through travel agents abroad. An InterCity travelpass, covering rail and many connecting coach services, is worth considering. Brochures are available from stations and travel agents in New Zealand and from Tourist Offices abroad. In Britain, contact: Leisurail, Units 1–3 Conongsby Road, Merlin Industrial Estate, North Bretton, Peterborough PE3 8HY. Tel: (01733) 335599. Fax: (01733) 505451. In the US contact New Zealand Central Reservations Office, 6033 West Century Boulevard, Suite 1270, Los Angeles, CA 90045. Tel: 1800 351 2323. Fax: 213 215 9705.

Across Australia on the Indian–Pacific

PAUL ATTERBURY

❋

The journey across Australia from Perth to Sydney by train was introduced only in 1970, yet it has already become a classic. For three days and three nights the train travels through 2461 miles (3960km) of extraordinary country, inhospitable, largely uninhabited and spectacular in its scale and changing colours. The Indian–Pacific is a very special train, a self-sufficient cruiser designed specifically for the journey, and it is the perfect platform from which to experience the Nullarbor Plain, the Flinders Ranges and the Blue Mountains. Its progress across the continent, in linking the Indian and the Pacific Oceans, is leisurely, and it is well-equipped for a journey whose sense of time and space will ensure relaxation.

―――――

RIGHT, *the great diesel engine of the Indian–Pacific*

FAR RIGHT, *Perth, capital of Western Australia and starting point of this extraordinary journey*

■ *The Indian–Pacific is a relatively new train and the route it follows was not finally completed until 1969, even though the first few miles had been laid as early as 1850. The history of railway development in Australia is complex, with many lines being built to different gauges primarily for the carriage of minerals from the mining regions to the coast.*
The route of the Indian–Pacific across Australia connects many mining towns. Most famous is Kalgoorlie, centre of one

THE TRAIN SLOWED to a crawl and then stopped. The doors opened and one by one the passengers emerged, climbing gingerly down the steps and on to the ground. Some stood by the doors, wary of leaving the security of the train, but others walked away, stepping over the tracks and kicking up dust from the ballast. The diesels throbbed and all around was a wall of heat, vibrating with the train. Away from the train there was just a huge arc of space defined by the straight line of the horizon, a rigid and unyielding circle unbroken for 360 degrees that separated the blue sky from the yellow brown earth. Cutting it in two were the tracks, parallel lines running away towards infinity in front of and behind the train. Beside the tracks the swooping telegraph wires curved away over the horizon. And that was that. There was absolutely nothing else to see. Passengers photographed the train, the straight line of the tracks and each other standing by the carriages or in the doorways, and then one by one they climbed back inside. The doors closed and with a whistle and a roar the train moved off.

We had stopped at Cook, not really a place, more a name on the map towards the eastern end of the Nullarbor Plain. We were on the longest stretch of straight railway track in the world, 287 miles (462km) without a curve, just one of the many superlatives and extraordinary facts associated with this strange journey.

The train journey across Australia represents a kind of Holy Grail for anyone who enjoys train travel. It is, quite simply, one of the best, if not the best journey in the world. It may not be the most luxurious and the route can hardly be called scenic, but its individuality has an irresistible appeal.

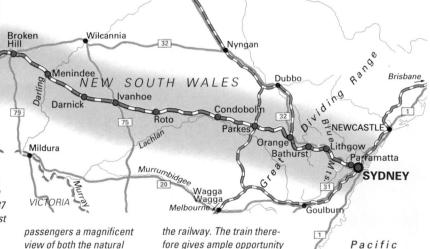

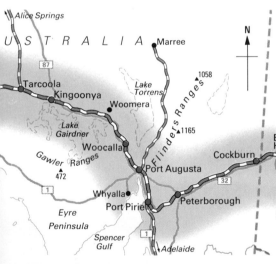

of the world's greatest gold rushes and still the centre of gold production. Also important are Port Augusta, Port Pirie, Broken Hill and Lithgow, towns that grew rich on the mining of silver, lead, zinc and other metals. A large part of the journey is taken up with the crossing of the Nullarbor Plain, hundreds of miles of limestone covered by low scrub, a huge colourful plateau as flat as an ocean. Crossing the Plain, the train goes in a straight line for 287 miles (462km), on the longest stretch of straight railway track in the world.

A total contrast in landscape is provided by the mountains through which the train travels in the east. Notable are the Flinders and Gawler Ranges, but most spectacular are the Blue Mountains, offering passengers a magnificent view of both the natural landscape and the engineering features that the route demanded. For much of its journey the Indian–Pacific is isolated from all but the smallest settlements, and these exist only to serve the needs of the railway. The train therefore gives ample opportunity for appreciating the harshness of outback life, a reality for anyone living or working away from the coastal regions. Because of their isolation, the train is literally a lifeline for those who live along its route.

ABOVE, *the tracks stretch away forever into the distant mirage*

I had booked my passage on the Indian–Pacific to travel from west to east, from Perth to Sydney (and this proved to be the best way to enjoy the route). Like much of Perth, the station is a modern building, and therefore notably lacking in the kind of romantic atmosphere that should accompany the start of so epic a journey. However, romance and long train journeys seem inseparable and even in the concrete surroundings of Perth Station it was impossible not to feel something on that warm spring evening. It seemed wrong to be setting out on this journey alone. I should have been stepping on to the train with an alluring and slightly mysterious companion, with whom I was deeply in love; but the script had gone wrong somewhere. The friend who had brought me to the station gave me a kiss and as the doors closed waved and walked off to find her car.

It was time to take stock of the train. The Indian–Pacific has to be largely self-sufficient for its journey and it has to have everything on board to keep its passengers happy. As a result, the staff-to-passenger ratio is much higher than usual. Coming from Europe, I was conditioned by the railway traditions of the 19th and early 20th centuries, when long distance train travel was a necessity made bearable by considerable luxury. The Australians have no such tradition, for no train had crossed the continent until 1969. The Indian–Pacific, which started its first run on 26 February 1970, was therefore purpose-built as a cruise train. By any standards, it is a very large train, with a series of First and Second Class cars which serve as sleepers and, for day use, restaurant cars, lounge and club cars, along with kitchen and stores cars, staff cars and much else beside. Tacked on the end there might be a baggage car or two and some flat trucks carrying vehicles belonging to passengers.

Broadly speaking, there are two types of accommodation, single or double, rather coyly called roomettes and twinettes. My roomette contained a deluxe armchair which in due course would convert into a bed, a cunning folding wash basin and lavatory, a little chair, a radio and a variety of hooks, shelves and bits and pieces designed to turn the space into something vaguely home-like. Most of one wall was a large picture window offering a private view of thousands of miles of Australia. Those lucky enough to have a cabin facing the right way can lie in bed and watch the world roll past. The twinette has all of this for two.

All the roomettes are set at alternating angles off a central corridor, so walking through a car, which one does many times a day, involves a curious zig-zag movement, unfamiliar at the best of times, and extremely difficult for those who have spent some time in the bar. At the end of each car there are shower rooms, large and well-equipped, with plentiful supplies of hot water. Further exploration led me to the restaurant car, a bar car complete with electric organ for those evening sing-songs, and a lounge or club car where one could take morning coffee or afternoon tea, eat ice creams, chat to fellow passengers and, from time to time, watch videos.

Not long after the departure from Perth a steward came round to issue meal tickets. There are three sittings for each meal and, once you have been allocated to one, it is very hard to change. Even changing your table causes considerable upset and so you get to know your table companions rather well. Selecting a sitting is a personal matter, for each seems to have its problems. The first is too early, the second too rushed and the third too late. However, by the time you have crossed two times zones and reached Sydney, you are two hours ahead of yourself and so the actual time you sit down to eat a meal has long since lost any sense of reality.

Days merge imperceptibly together and the train becomes the centre of the universe. The result is extremely relaxing.

Inevitably, eating was an important part of the day. First, the steward brought round an early morning cup of tea. Next was breakfast, a lavish spread that included rolled oats (Australian for porridge), steak and tomatoes and all the trimmings. Lunch and dinner were both four-course epics, good basic dishes efficiently presented at speed by waiters who carry nine bowls of soup the length of a swaying carriage without spilling a drop.

FOCAL POINT

The bar was the social centre of the train and it was impossible to enter it without being drawn into some kind of conversation. In fact, conversations, infinite in variety, sometimes casual, sometimes surprisingly intimate, passed the time very efficiently. The train always offers such a wide range of entertainments – conversation, the opportunity to read, ever changing scenery, food and drink, plus plenty of time and space for walking about. It is comfortable, it is entirely relaxed because the outside world has ceased to exist, but above all it offers privacy. Your cabin is always there, a secure escape, when you want to get away.

Among the souvenirs on sale on the train were some excellent large-scale maps, and tracking our snail-like progress across the continent was another restful occupation. Looking out of the window was also eternally fascinating, offering a unique insight into Australia's landscape, history and cultural development. There is no better way to grasp the scale of the country and its richness of landscape than to watch it rolling past the window for three days.

Each cabin was equipped with a brief guide to the route and its rather complex history. The Indian–Pacific may be new but railways in Australia certainly are not. The first part of the route to be built, a short stretch from Sydney to Parramatta, now virtually a suburb, was completed in 1850. It took

the next 120 years for trains to reach Perth. In the 1860s the line was pushed on to Lithgow, having crossed the formidable barrier of the Blue Mountains by a series of zig-zags whereby the trains climbed by alternately pulling and pushing up sections of track and then descending the same way on the other side. It was not until 1910 that trains could cross the Blue Mountains in a conventional manner. Elsewhere other parts of the route were under construction, mainly to link the gold, silver, lead and zinc mines to the coastal ports, passengers being a secondary consideration. With their largely local perspective, the engineers built their railways with different gauges. The final link in the trans-continental railway, the long stretch between Port Augusta and Kalgoorlie, was completed in 1917 and although crossing Australia by train then became a reality, it was a laborious and impractical journey because gauge changes made through running impossible. This chaotic situation remained in force until 1969 when the task of converting the whole route to standard gauge was finally completed.

The popularity of the Indian–Pacific is now legendary. For many it is almost a pilgrimage, often something to be done when work is over and the children have gone. However, passengers were not the primary reason for the

BELOW, *a quiet corner of Port Augusta*

BOTTOM, *much of the Blue Mountains area of New South Wales is designated a national park*

PREVIOUS PAGE, *rolling through lush, green cattle country*

ABOVE, *part of the mighty Flinders Ranges, where some of the earliest fossil sea-creatures have been discovered*

FAR RIGHT, *journey's end – Sydney, with its famous opera house and the Harbour Bridge*

line's rebuilding. There are three Indian–Pacifics each way each week, but the freight traffic is much heavier. Much of the route is single-tracked, and so we had many long waits in passing loops to let the freight trains pass, several locomotives hauling trucks loaded with oil drums, pipes, timber, containers from all over the world and, most remarkable of all, complete lorries and trailers with their grinning drivers still in their cabs.

We left Perth at 9 o'clock in the evening, and by the time we had passed through the suburbs it was getting dark. There was no dinner and so most of the passengers disappeared into their cabins, with only a few seeking out some conversation over a nightcap in the bar. The first dawn broke as we approached Kalgoorlie, and here there was a treat in store. At some very early hour, and before breakfast, those who were willing were taken on a rapid coach tour of the deserted streets of this gold town. Highlights included the red light district, where the girls conducted their business in rows of cabins that looked rather like small beach huts. The coach driver, far more awake than most of his passengers, gave a lively talk on the gold rush, Kalgoorlie's growth and decline, the surrounding ghost towns and the state of the industry today. Intellectually refreshed, we then returned to the train for our first experience of the substantial Indian–Pacific breakfast.

We travelled all day through an increasingly empty landscape with bushes and scrub

stretching to the horizon, enlivened by the occasional glimpse of a kangaroo or emu, and made exciting by the dramatic changes in colour as the sun began to set. By dinner we were well into the Nullarbor Plain, and this awesome limestone plateau was to dominate the view, and our minds, for some time to come. It is spectacular in its size and its unchanging quality, with the kind of timeless immensity familiar only to those used to travelling in the desert. The train became at this stage even more like a cruise liner, sailing across an interminable sea, with any conventional sense of time and space rendered meaningless. The meals came and went, conversation flourished, died and flourished again, we read our books, took showers and walked about, but outside the window nothing changed, except the light which was never quite the same from one hour to the next. Night came and went and there it was just the same.

A dusty track ran along beside the rails and this, freely scattered with empty beer cans and the occasional long-abandoned car, was the only sign of life. Every now and then the track led into a tiny lineside settlement, a siding perhaps and some rusty buffers, a few derelict sheds and a row of tin-roofed bungalows. Here there would be little groups waving and shouting, mums, children and excited dogs, sudden bursts of life, quickly forgotten as the train rolled on. These settlements, no more than a series of names on the map, Kitchener, Haig and Fisher (this section was built in 1917), Naretha, Nurina and Loongana, these were the homes of the maintenance crews, their lives wholly dependent upon the trains.

On the next day we finally left the Nullarbor behind and variety began to creep back into the landscape. At Tarcoola we passed the junction with the line leading north to Alice

Springs. This is served by the Ghan, another extraordinary Australian train, that travels north into the Great Outback from Adelaide several times a week. Hills and marshy lakes began to appear, and even trees. We passed Woomera, a famous name now lost in history, and then we turned south towards Port Augusta, with the Flinders Ranges filling the horizon to the east. We ran down beside Spencer Gulf, with the Gawler Ranges towering across the water, to Port Pirie. Here there was time to leave the train for a quick walk round the old seaport with its curious Wild West frontier atmosphere, a relic of the great days of the mining industry set against the dramatic background of the Flinders Ranges.

Now we turned east, to climb up through more mountainous country towards Broken Hill. The light slipped away and we reached this famous mining town in the middle of the third night. By the morning all was different. We had crossed the Darling River and entered a more fertile and greener landscape. We sat down for lunch, the last of the many train meals, and at each table the arbitrarily assembled group who at first had had little to say to each other ordered

bottles of wine. The train began to climb, winding its way up through rolling country that had more than a hint of England. All around were flowers and fruit trees in bloom, grass banks and clumps of wood, pretty villages with old bridges over tumbling streams, old clapboarded stations with rustic seats, and every now and then a glimpse of a bowling green, with groups of old ladies in white coats and hats, discussing the game like ancient schoolgirls. At the top we came to the Blue Mountains, and then it was a scenic ride down the other side, through ravines and rocky outcrops, through tunnels and round bends so tight we could see the front and the end of the train at the same time, and all through a landscape of wonderful colour, with sudden great vistas over wooded hills. It was a magnificent finale.

The end in sight, we ran quickly through the long miles of Sydney's suburbs, through the industrial belt and then into the city proper. Crawling and creaking, the Indian–Pacific jolted over the points and came to a final halt in the terminus, on time, after 68 hours of an unforgettable journey.

PRACTICAL INFORMATION

■ The Indian–Pacific runs three times each week in each direction between Perth and Sydney, throughout the year. The 2461 miles (3960km) journey takes 68 hours, and three nights are spent on the train.

■ There are First and Second Class cars, a restaurant car, lounge or club car and bar car, and every passenger has a combined sleeper and day cabin, available as singles or doubles and fully equipped with all necessities.

■ All places have to be reserved, and the popularity of the train means that bookings may have to be made up to a year in advance.

■ The journey is interesting at all times of year, but at the height of the Australian summer in February the temperature outside the train can be as high as 109°F (43°C). The best time to travel is probably October, the Australian spring.

■ The train is operated by Rail Australia. Bookings should be made through major stations in Australia or a travel agent. In Britain, contact: Leisurail, Units 1–3 Conongsby Road, Merlin Industrial Estate, North Bretton, Peterborough PE3 8HY. Tel: (01733) 335599. Fax: (01733) 505451. In the US contact ATS Tours California, 100 North First Street, Burbank, California 91502. Tel: 818 8411030. Fax: 818 8410345.

The Marrakech Express to Casablanca and Fès

PIERS LETCHER

Morocco's main railway line runs through all four imperial cities and the country's commercial capital Casablanca. From Marrakech in the south, via Casablanca, Rabat and Meknès to Fès, the journey takes you across scrub desert, along Morocco's Atlantic coast, and into the agricultural heart of the country, where cactus fields vie with olive groves, orchards and orange plantations. Marrakech and Fès both make great start or end points for the journey.

RIGHT, *a colourful market stall, a bright feature of Morocco*

FAR RIGHT ABOVE, *taxis hover outside the station at Marrakech – the train may be glimpsed through the station doors*

FAR RIGHT BELOW, *a water seller in Marrakech, bedecked with gleaming drinking vessels*

THE PLACE DJEMMA EL FNA is at its most deserted as we breakfast early on the roof of our hotel. It's a perfect platform from which to look down on the square where only a few hours before we were walking amongst fire eaters, scribes, magicians, snake charmers, story-tellers, acrobats and a cheerfully toothless dentist with a whole tray of filthy teeth to choose from, some of them perhaps his own. The food stalls are all closed up now, and the orange squeezers have not yet started selling the fresh juice. In the far-off haze, 40 miles (64km) away, the 13,665ft (4165m) summit of Mount Toubkal, Morocco's highest mountain, is just visible.

A clutch of Petit-Taxis (with 'Petit-Taxi' written across the roof-racks) fight for our custom as we leave the hotel, and one of us negotiates furiously with the drivers while the other watches the bags. A short but flagrantly dangerous ride later we are at

Marrakech Station. We recover with a mint tea, a few minutes to spare before the train leaves.

The Express train that is waiting for us, smart in freshly painted orange and yellow livery, is a great improvement on the so-called Rapide which brought us here from Casablanca. That train was late to leave and became progressively later with each stop. The seats seemed to have been padded with broken concrete, and the few windows which were not darkened by grime had volumes of water trapped between the double glazing, which petrified into unusual standing wave patterns with the motion of the train. Three raucously drunk Poles with giant Eastern Bloc rucksacks made up in volume for what the train lacked in speed.

This train, however, is marvellous; air conditioned, comfortable, quiet and fast, and there are great views out across the desert. Mustapha, a young Berber revolutionary, elects to share our compartment with us. He declaims

at great length about the country's problems, why the Berbers are so much better and more honest than the Arabs (on the next train we shall hear the opposite story, from the Arab side) and is insistent on trying to write down the titles of banned and dissident publications in my notebook. I resist this effort strenuously after what happened in Casablanca on my first afternoon in the country.

I was standing outside the Voyageurs Station, lining up a photograph, when out of the corner of my eye I spotted

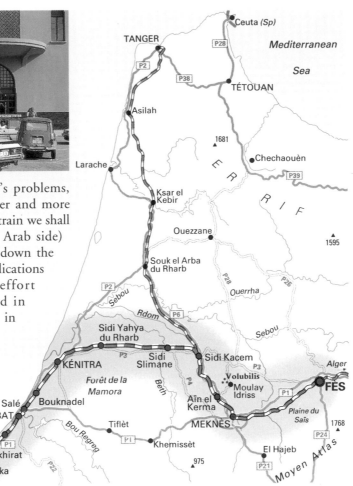

■ The history of the railways in Morocco dates back to the period dating from 1912, when the country was being brought under the control of the French army and an extensive system of narrow gauge military railways was built. In 1915 the 'main line' from Marrakech to Oujda on the Algerian border via Casablanca, Rabat and Fès was opened for public

service, but it was not until 1934 that a standard gauge line superseded the military narrow gauge route.
Marrakech, the southern terminus of the railway, is a marvellous city surrounded by desert and the spectacular mountains of the High Atlas. The city has a Berber rather than Arab flavour and is centred on the unique Place Djemma El Fna, where street dentists mix with storytellers, snake charmers, acrobats, fire-eaters and the smoke from the best outdoor food stalls in the country.
Casablanca – leave any thoughts of Rick's Café and Ingrid Bergman at home; with a population rapidly approaching four million Casablanca has practically nothing to offer the tourist. The nearest train station to the town centre is Casablanca Port, but most trains leave from Casablanca Voyageurs.
Rabat is the most recent and the most cosmopolitan of Morocco's four one-time capital cities, and perhaps the easiest place to visit; the king lives here and hustlers are banned by Royal decree. Rabat Ville is the train station you need.
Meknès is a provincial city, but the wonderful unrestored ruins of Moulay Ismail's Imperial City, partly destroyed in 1755 by the same earthquake that devastated Lisbon, make it worth a stop-over. The remarkable ruins of Volubilis, the last outpost of the Roman Empire, are a taxi-ride away.
Fès is a most exciting and unusual city. Inside the busy self-contained medina of Fes El Bali you will find every type of cottage industry and commerce, a throw-back to the Middle Ages with practically no concessions to the present.

ABOVE, *the engine of the express carries the five-pointed Moroccan star on the front*

RIGHT, *the line passes between leathery spears of cactus, near Meknès*

two officers of the Sûreté coming towards me. I made the mistake of showing them my Press Card and one of them rushed off with it to call his boss ('Hey, boss! I landed me a journalist!'). It was only a matter of moments before the wagon arrived and I experienced that unpleasant sinking sensation as I watched the railway station retreat behind the iron bars of the rear windows.

It was very difficult not to feel guilty after several hours of interrogations. I was passed from one uniformed or plain clothes officer to another, nobody quite sure what to do with me or why I was there. Perhaps they were expecting a small (or large) bribe. Finally, I was ushered into the big cheese's office – fancy carpets, ornate silver teapots on the table, hangers-on lounging in deep armchairs. After a close inspection of the camera ('Nice, very nice'), he implored me not to get arrested again and sent me on my way. It never was made exactly clear what I was arrested for ('That's alright sir, no charge'). From the police station it turned out to be a surprisingly long and expensive taxi ride back to the station.

So, I am not keen to carry around incriminating evidence such as Mustapha's list of banned and dissident publications, and since then I have been a good deal more circumspect with the camera and will avoid using my Press Card.

TRAVELLING ON

The train we are on is called the Tour Hassan, and runs between two of the three extant 12th-century Almohad Minarets: the Koutoubia in Marrakech and the Hassan Tower in Rabat. (The third is the Giralda in Seville, in service since the 15th century as the cathedral's bell-tower, and familiar as one of the recurring symbols in the Expo '92 advertising).

Just outside Berrechid ('Tell people you think they're from Berrechid,' laughs Mustapha. 'There's a huge mental hospital here.') we slow down and the compartment suddenly warms up. It takes a little while to work out that the air conditioning is no longer functioning. In compartments with windows locked shut in hot countries it rapidly becomes uncomfortable. After half an hour or so the train starts up again

and, rather than waste time fixing the air conditioning, an engineer comes along the train unlocking the windows with a special key.

Like most trains, ours has a soft drinks vendor wandering up and down (many also carry a buffet car). In Morocco alcoholic drinks can be bought only in the more expensive hotels and one or two licensed bars. Be careful to drink mineral water only, and check that the seal has not been broken; there is a small but vital trade in re-bottled water.

Morocco is a country, more than most, of contrasts. A huge generation gap is opening up between the young, half of whom seem to have visited France or Spain, and the old, who still wear the traditional costume of *djellaba* and *babouches*, skullcaps perched firmly on their heads. (And this is perhaps the most unsuitable

of all outfits imaginable for bicycle riding, yet cyclists dressed like this are ubiquitous.) In places like Fès you hardly see any women at all and those that you do see are secluded behind the *chador*, with sometimes just a dark pair of eyes visible amongst the cloth. In Rabat or Casablanca, by comparison, you can see women in Western dress, comfortable with themselves and the world.

As visitors, you should be careful to dress modestly; shorts are basically unacceptable off the tourist beaches, and you should keep arms covered too. Women travelling alone should prepare themselves for a moderately gruelling trip.

Mustapha, smart in a shirt and tie, jacket slung over one shoulder, leaves the train at Casablanca, and I sit well away from the window for fear of being recognized by the Sûreté again.

Ahmed, a railway worker, joins us, and explains that the electric engine died, and that we have been pulled along by diesel for the last 20 miles (32km). Fifteen minutes out of Casablanca we stop for an age in a small siding while the crew cast around for another electric engine. They find one, thus allowing us to

you have to be careful about where you get off the train. As soon as you have left Salé you cross a wide river (the Bou Regreg) and at this point you should head several carriages along the train towards the engine, especially if you are in First or Second Class. On all but the shortest trains you will soon come to a halt in a tunnel. This, unlikely though it seems, is where you must leave the train, to walk along the loose chippings in the dark beside the carriages until you reach the Rabat Ville platform. The tail end carriages are left stuck in the tunnel, and only start to move when the train is on its way to Rabat Agdal, the suburban station, or worse, Casablanca.

In the window seats are a couple who would have trouble looking more decadent if they tried. The man sports a rumpled business suit and has his white-socked feet out of his Louis Vuitton shoes and up on the seat next to his wife. She is wearing a voluminous white dress and dipping pudgy fingers into an enormous paper bag of sticky Turkish Delight. Every so often she wipes the back of her hand across her chins and cleans up with a range of perfumed

LEFT, *the great brass portals of the Royal Palace at Fès dwarf ordinary mortals*

BELOW, *taking a break for tea and a chat*

luxuriate in the comfort of the air conditioning again for the last half hour to Rabat. There are lovely views of the Atlantic about 500 yards away, and the abundance of smart villas and compounds here testifies to the strong commercial and diplomatic presence along this fertile stretch of coast.

Our train terminates in Rabat and it looks as though we have missed the first two of the possible three connecting trains today. Ahmed assures us that there will be an Express along shortly. He is right, of course, and the train we were parked alongside at Casablanca Port soon comes along to pick us up. Had we changed trains there, discounting further Sûreté encounters, we would have been able to get window seats. As it is, we are lucky to get the last two in a compartment; everyone else who climbs on board after us has to stand in the corridors.

Going the other way into Rabat, from Fès,

RIGHT, *Fès is the cultural and mercantile centre of Morocco, and the best preserved medieval Muslim city in the world*

pastel handkerchiefs. Beside them are two skinny students in jeans and clean white shirts, and a solo Spanish woman who silences the compartment by responding 'Cairo' when one of the students asks her where she is going. We all imagine the immense and difficult journey across the closed borders of Algeria, Tunisia and Libya, emerging, perhaps years later, somewhere like Tobruk. She settles back into *El País*.

And lastly there is Mohammed, a teacher from Fès on assignment in Rabat, who cannot stand the heat, even in this air conditioned compartment. He sweats prodigiously, and fans himself ineffectively with a newspaper while pursuing his cross-examination of us. He slyly indicates that he will, if we are lucky, guide us around the medina and the souks tomorrow morning, find us a hotel tonight, a good place to eat, and if, perhaps, we are lucky, maybe we would be interested in meeting his daughters…

This kind of thing happens all the time in Morocco (well OK, so I was exaggerating about the daughters), with a significant proportion of the population on the make to a larger or smaller extent. But we do Mohammed an injustice: he turns out to be as good as his word, and does find us a better, cheaper hotel in Fès than the one we had planned on using, and guides us around the souks the next day, not just showing us the handicrafts stalls owned by the immediate members of his family (which is what happened to us in Marrakech), and he even races back to the hotel on his moped to rescue my companion's glasses while we are waiting for the return train to Rabat. All of which is a salutary demonstration of the danger of being instinctively distrustful of everyone you meet in this country. (None the less, if you are arriving after dusk in any Moroccan city, you would be well advised to have a hotel reserved in advance, and to take a taxi there from the station.)

The route from Rabat to Sidi Kacem is as dry as anywhere we have seen, with sand-red, ochre and sunset-orange coloured villages, and scrub grass being grazed by scraggy sheep and goats; kids wave up at the train and one or two, in a show of extreme optimism, even hold out their hands for money. Small fields and backyards are fenced in by cactus, and shepherds stand in the middle of nowhere, transfixed by the spectacle of the passing train.

ABOVE, *dyed skins drying in the hot sun, just outside Fès*

FAR RIGHT, *the famous Bab Bou Jeloud arch, gateway to the old walled city of Fès el Bali*

From Sidi Kacem there is an as yet unelectrified branch line to Tanger (130 miles/ 208km), but there is no real reason to visit the city. The hustlers are the world's most accomplished, and there is little left now of the decadence that made the city so (in)famous in the 1930s and 1940s.

We take on board a weary-looking contingent of passengers fresh in from Tanger. Among these are three incredibly bewildered looking Czechs who spend the rest of the journey copying everything they can out of our guidebook, despite speaking no English. Throughout the country this time there has been a dearth of tourists; my previous visits have been fraught with problems finding accommodation, and marked by frequent encounters with other foreigners. I ask why and everyone has a different explanation – the long term fall-out of the Gulf War, says one; everybody's at Expo '92 in Seville, says another; Algeria's fault, says a third, enigmatically.

From here to Fès the route is as beautiful as any in Morocco. The railway winds its way up into the foothills of the Middle Atlas, crossing and re-crossing the River Rdom, with apple and peach orchards on either side, interspersed with olive groves and lush meadows.

We work our way up to Meknès, 1810ft (552m) above sea level, and watch two small boys leap on to the end of the train as we leave the station. They are stuck on the outside and grip tenaciously to the door handle, unable to open it against the wind and not being helped much by the crush of passengers inside. When I look again, 10 or 15 minutes later, they are gone; it is impossible to tell if they dropped off or if they fell.

The last hour of the journey to Fès is perfect. The heat has gone out of the day and at this latitude the shadows lengthen quickly, casting soft colours over the landscape as the sun goes down. The train comes into Fès, and although it carries on eastwards to the Algerian border it seems that everybody gets off here.

Fès is one of the most unusual cities in the world; an unforgettable assault of aromas and stenches, unidentifiable sounds, and a wealth of eye-catching detail. The animals alone are a shock to anyone of western sensibilities: turkeys and rabbits hobbled at the back of tiny shops, cloudy-eyed fish lying on glistening slabs, yard-high vats of squirming snails exuding slime, mules and donkeys and bony horses cluttering the streets, dirty glass tanks full of terrapins trying vainly to escape, skinny cats searching warily for food, and chickens breathing their last on the butcher's block. Take an official guide.

We are first off the train and are treated to the enchanting spectacle of hundreds of passengers flooding out through the station into the satin light of sunset over the ville nouvelle.

PRACTICAL INFORMATION

■ Between six and eight irregular trains run each day, with one through train. The journey time for the 362 miles (583km) between Marrakech and Fès varies from 8 to 10 hours.

■ Express trains are slightly faster than Rapide, have air conditioned coaches and are slightly more expensive. There are three classes of carriage: First (1); Second (2), which is fine; and Economy, which is very cheap, crowded and uncomfortable. First is rarely full, but Second Class air conditioned is worth reserving.

■ The best time of year to travel in Morocco is between May and November; the winter is colder than you might expect, spring comes late, and July and August can be phenomenally hot. Avoid travelling during Ramadan if possible.

■ Moroccan State Railways (ONCF) operate the route. As major upgrades are being made, the only real way of finding out detailed information is by asking at stations locally.

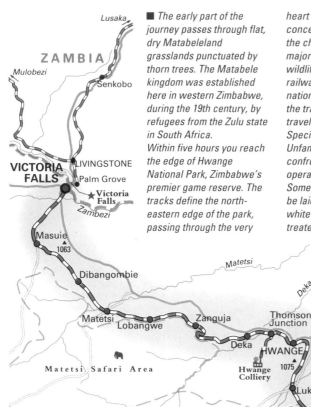

■ The early part of the journey passes through flat, dry Matabeleland grasslands punctuated by thorn trees. The Matabele kingdom was established here in western Zimbabwe, during the 19th century, by refugees from the Zulu state in South Africa.
Within five hours you reach the edge of Hwange National Park, Zimbabwe's premier game reserve. The tracks define the north-eastern edge of the park, passing through the very

heart of adjoining wildlife concessions. Visitors stand the chance of seeing all the major varieties of African wildlife here. Dete is the railway centre for the national park and provides the transfer point for travellers on the Zimbabwe Special railway safari. Unfamiliar conditions confronted the British operators of the railway. Some of the first sleepers to be laid were attacked by white ants and had to be treated with arsenic.

IT TOOK THE VICTORIANS to dream up a crazy idea like the Cape-to-Cairo railway. It was every bit as megalomaniac as an empire on which the sun never set or as eccentric as the notion of exporting British culture and customs to the tropics.

A chance of a trip on the Bulawayo-to-Victoria Falls section of this mad, unfinished rail-link was something we had jumped at. Nothing matches the adventure of buying a ticket in Bulawayo's echoing booking hall, waiting on the platform for the 19.00hrs scheduled service to the Falls and throwing in your lot with the erratic timetabling of National Railways of Zimbabwe.

Daily train services in Zimbabwe are immensely eventful and Bulawayo Station retains its century-old sense of occasion. Its status holds as a central junction connecting Zimbabwe's Matabeleland with the country's capital and the lowveld in the south-east but also, perhaps more importantly, it continues to carry human cargo from further north to South Africa's labour-hungry mines.

When the Bulawayo-to-Victoria Falls

A number of trains collided with elephants between Dete and Hwange (Wankie) colliery, where high embankments impeded the animals' escape.
Hwange (Wankie) town is an ugly coal mining centre but of immense importance to the railway in that, because of its promise of ready fuel, the line was diverted from the planned route. Matetsi is in one of Zimbabwe's major

hunting areas abutting on the north of the national park. Providing an appropriate climax, Victoria Falls offers both the most spectacular natural sight of the trip as well as an exceptional feat of engineering. With a braced arch spanning 500 feet (152m), the steel bridge was built in 1905 to carry the Cape-to-Cairo railway across the 400ft (122m) deep gorge of the Zambezi River.

Although passenger trains no longer cross the bridge, you can go on foot and get a taste of the experience of earlier travellers who could peer from the train into the dramatic gorge and even feel the spray from the massive waterfall.

section was completed at the close of the 19th century, it was one stretch of the Cape-to-Cairo link that, like a ribbon, was to gift wrap Africa for Queen and Empire. That, at least, was the fevered vision of Cecil John Rhodes, the sickly English vicar's son sent, because of his asthma, to Africa where he made a fine recovery and became a wealthy entrepreneur, Prime Minister of the Cape and an ardent expansionist.

Rhodes fulfilled the Victorian image of the businessman-hero. He had a dream, it was profitable and it conformed to the aims of Empire. A 19th-century Punch cartoon shows him as the 'Colossus of Rhodes', pith helmet in hand, with one boot resting on the Cape and

Through Central Africa from Bulawayo to Victoria Falls

TONY PINCHUCK

Aside from its romantic associations with turn of the century travel in central Africa, the rail route up Zimbabwe's western flank passes through some of the continent's best game country and terminates at one of the natural wonders of the world, the Victoria Falls. The railway was a central plank of a planned British colonization of the entire African continent and the route is rich in historical associations. Zimbabwe's pre-independence name, Rhodesia, was inspired by Cecil John Rhodes who, at the end of the 19th century, fantasized about a world dominated by Britain, Germany and the United States. The railway is one relic of that dream.

the other on Egypt. With hindsight, the Africans whose countries he annexed were less appreciative of his heavy footwear bearing down on their continent – although they do continue to make use of his railroad.

'The object', Rhodes declared, 'is to cut Africa through the centre and the railway will pick up trade along the route.' The tracks never reached Cairo, petering out instead somewhere just across the Congo River.

Like a graph, the railway registers the progress of Rhodes's business and political fortunes. The first leg of the iron road

from Cape Town to Kimberley corresponded to the discovery of diamonds in 1887. The precious gems filled Rhodes's pockets and set his sights north in search of more of Africa's buried riches.

Through his British South Africa Company, he bought, grabbed or conquered territory and soon the railway was passing across the dry Kalahari sands of eastern Botswana before veering right into Zimbabwe and the great central African junction of Bulawayo, where it lurched north again for the final leg to Victoria Falls. Here the line crossed the Zambezi and continued north-east to Lusaka and beyond to the Zambian copper belt, where it entered Zaire at Ndola before coming to an end.

Through trains no longer steam all the way from Africa's southern tip to Victoria Falls, but it is still possible to complete the journey along continuous track by changing trains and travelling on the railways of South Africa, Botswana and Zimbabwe.

Bulawayo is, nowadays, the usual starting point for the journey. And here you can still detect the dusty fingerprints of Empire. The buildings, from the sombre courthouse dominating the town centre down to the airy colonial residences in the once whites-only

ABOVE, *Main Falls – just one section of the breathtaking Victoria Falls*

FAR LEFT, *craft workers in down-town Bulawayo*

TOP, *dining in Rail Safaris-style – rather different from the service on scheduled trains*

ABOVE, *the population of Zimbabwe is predominantly of the Shona tribe, with some Matabele*

suburbs, all hark back to the heyday of British influence. The Colossus of Rhodes, however, has come down in the world, his statue in the town centre having been torn from its pedestal after independence in 1980 and reportedly kicked by irate bystanders.

Their annoyance was perhaps understandable. In 1893 Rhodes provoked a war and conquered King Lobengula's Matabele state, of which Bulawayo was the capital, driving local people off their land to make way for the railway. The current station stands on the site of one of Lobengula's crack regiments.

When we travelled, Zimbabwe's trains, drawn by ancient Garratt steam locomotives, were not always running on time. The authorities have since started phasing out steam on passenger routes, replacing it with diesel. If you are bent on steam then a packaged trip is your only guarantee.

Organized rail safaris, which have been running this route since the late 1980s, are well within the Victorian spirit as far as obsession goes. 'Read on to find out a little more about the Enthusiast Express', urges the Rail Safaris brochure. For a substantial fee you are invited to ride on the footplate of a Garratt locomotive, to spend the night in a steam depot and to dine in a shunting yard. It conjures visions of eating a meal as giant engines shunt goods wagons on either side of the table and a dusting of soot gently descends on to the blancmange.

Zambezi Special 'steam safaris', are less loco-centric and take passengers from Bulawayo to Victoria Falls re-creating, not entirely authentically, the elegant days of steam with 1920s rolling stock, luxury compartments, white tableclothed meals and champagne.

For a fraction of the price (about the cost of an average taxi ride across London) our scheduled train lacked the champagne, but not the adventure, I suspect. When it left the station about half an hour late, no one seemed too perturbed.

For Zimbabweans, the railway is more than a means of transport. It is a great point of family reunion and parting, an umbilical cord connecting city dwellers with their rural roots. Virtually everyone in the country has such ties with the countryside, making the railway a vital social and economic link.

It was about 7.30 in the evening and getting dark by the time the accommodation allocations were brought on to the platform by the station master, dressed in his well-pressed dark blue uniform and Omo-white shirt.

A SENSE OF CONTINUITY

On Zimbabwe National Railways, the lists are still posted up in the same heavily varnished, glazed display cabinets that for decades served the network when it was called Rhodesia Railways. Despite the new brown and cream livery and NRZ marque on carriages, the RR monogram is still etched into the glass of coach windows and often still appears on the mirrors inside compartments, mostly dating from the 1950s and 60s.

Classes are clearly distinguished. First and Second, with their sleeping car compartments, provide a roomy ride at one end of the train while Third Class crams passengers into a rolling ghetto at the other, cramped passengers being forced to sit out the overnight journey on wooden benches.

Third Class travellers struggle with goods packed in baskets, bulging boxes secured with string, tin trunks and poultry. Among them are usually a number of African women, the new entrepreneurs who have replaced the cigar-smoking British men who rode the rails with an eye to a business opportunity. In the same spirit of Victorian self-help and enterprise, these modern-day free marketeers ply a precarious trade by crossing the border to Francistown in neighbouring Botswana, where they exchange smuggled Zimbabwe dollars for consumer goods which they resell in their own country. Bulawayo Station bustles with these wives and mothers dressed in their fruit-salad tropical prints. Working to tight budgets and narrow profit margins, they frequently spend the night at Francistown Station, risking arrest for vagrancy.

We took the soft option in First Class, roughly the same as Second except there are fewer people in each compartment. Our coupé was intended for married couples; if you are not hitched, it is probably worth pretending in order to avoid bureaucratic confusion.

First Class compartments take four people, and second up to six. They are sexually segregated. Upholstered seats convert into bunks at night. A stainless steel handbasin, hot and cold running water and a mirror are

provided in each compartment. Blinds on the windows and locks on the doors ensure total privacy.

The whistle eventually blew and the engine heaved its long load out of the station, barely gathering speed as it left behind the illuminated cooling towers that stand like skyscrapers in a city where few buildings surpass three floors. The tracks snake through the townships of Mpopoma and Luveve with matchbox houses lining the route. Dim lights and smoky chimneys signal the way out of town and give the train its send-off into the darkness.

A bedding attendant comes round First and Second Class soon after departure. Working with remarkable speed, he pulls down the top bunk, making the bed with freshly ironed linen and pillows. He draws up the back-rest of the seat and attaches it out of the way to a leather strap to make way for the bottom bunk, on which he repeats his bed-making acrobatics. Once the beds are made, there is nowhere left to sit and you are forced to turn in for the night or take a stroll down the train.

Wool blankets may seem unnecessary given the hot daytime temperatures, which even in the 'cool' dry season (from May to September) remain warm. However, along some parts of

the journey, the temperatures can drop quite sharply after dark.

Out of curiosity more than hunger, I strolled down through Second Class to the dining car. *Sadza* and *nyama*, traditional maize porridge with meat stew, were being served by a languid waiter to a lone woman half-collapsed with a bottle of Lion Lager in one corner. None of the other more animated drinkers seemed to be eating at all. The retired British couple who arrived dressed for dinner seemed dismayed by the scene. They had fully expected a multi-course meal served by uniformed waiters, silver service and starched tablecloths, they explained. I quickly realized it was time for bed and made my way back through Second Class, where one or two drinkers were hanging out of compartments having good-natured conversations with neighbours and apparently telling jokes, to judge from the salvo of explosive belly laughs.

Through the night the train trundles across sparsely populated Matabeleland, where small-scale African farmers raise thin cattle and goats in the chewed back drylands of Zimbabwe's west. Inexplicably long delays and stops at the tiniest of junctions, some in the middle of nowhere, punctuate the journey. Small stations

ABOVE, *taking on water*

and sidings bear a veritable *mélange* of Ndebele and English names: Morgans, Igusi, Sawmills and Nyamandhlovu (with the curious meaning of elephant meat).

Around 11.00 at night the train is scheduled to pull in at Gwaai Station. Along the river valley white ranchers have battled for three generations against harsh conditions basically unsuited to farming, and the onslaught of predators. Many are now converting their land back to wildlife, but on a commercial basis.

You can tell you are near the national park itself when the sidings adopt Ndebele names for animals in a tantalizing hint of the denizens within: Ingwe (leopard), Isilwana (lion), Impofu (eland) and Intudhla (giraffe). You do not, of course, see these on the night train, but on the Zambezi Special you would be having mid-afternoon tea around here.

And for steam *aficionados* this region holds a greater delight: the 70-mile (112km) section of track from Gwaai to just before Dete was the world's most extensive 'long straight' at the time it was laid. If, like me, you are not quite so enthralled by this, you may be more interested in the fact that the long straight defines the north-eastern border of Hwange (Wankie) National Park, Zimbabwe's top game reserve. The entire section of north-western Zimbabwe around Hwange is an enormous patchwork of hunting concessions, private game ranches, safari areas and game parks, all thronging with animals.

From Dete to Hwange Town the line goes through dense bush and broken rocky country. Malaria-ridden, it is said to be David Livingstone's 'Valley of Death'. The survey work carried out at the turn of the century to determine the route often had to be carried out

on hands and knees, crawling through thick undergrowth – a hair-raising prospect given the abundance of dangerous animals.

Hwange Town lies in the middle of this stretch and in terms of fascination could not be less similar to the national park with which it shares a name. An ugly place, it is, nevertheless, the reason the railway comes this way at all. With its rich coal seams, it proved the magnet that drew the line away from its planned route further east and pulled it towards the Victoria Falls. Symbolizing the debt it owes to the railways, the town has a large locomotive standing on a plinth like a monument to a war hero. The chances are you will sleep through it.

Morning breaks between Deka and Matetsi, waking travellers to a very different world from the previous evening's. The Matabele drylands give way to savannah and mopane and teak forests, and game. Expect nothing but be prepared for anything. It was along a stretch of winding track bounded by some valleys that I watched through the window as a sable antelope

FAR RIGHT, the famous railway bridge spanning the Falls – spray from the tumbling cataract has created its own area of tropical rainforest

BELOW, palm trees and even a pond decorate the station at Victoria Falls

galloped across a wide expanse – floating almost, it seemed in my half-sleep state – as the sun burst out of the bleached morning. It was only a little later that I spotted a pride of lions, which nonchalantly watched the train go by from only 35 feet (12m) away. It is fair to mention that the guard only half-believed me, saying that in 17 years he had never once seen a big cat on the trip.

COLONIAL MEMORY

Only two hours after sunrise the train pulls into its ultimate destination, Victoria Falls. The station is a whitewashed Edwardian concoction shaded by flame-flowered flamboyants, sweet smelling frangipanis and syringas, with palm trees and ponds on the platform.

Designed with a carefully positioned ceremonial gateway, it leads out to Zimbabwe's most elegant hotel. Continuing through a procession of halls and gardens, the path pulls you relentlessly into the dripping rain forest and on to the very edge of Africa's greatest natural wonder.

The energy and power of over a mile's (1.6km) width of Zambezi River thundering over 325 feet (100m) down a sheer chasm, throwing up a spray an equal distance skyward, is awesome.

For a full mile (1.6km), one set of falls gives way to another until at last the path leads to the railway bridge connecting Zimbabwe to Zambia. Instead of allowing the bridge to cross the Zambezi at a convenient point, Cecil Rhodes decreed that train passengers on the bridge should not just see the great spectacle but also feel the spray. Despite the problems it created for the builders, the elegant steel structure spanning the swirling gorge was completed in 1905.

Rhodes never steamed across the bridge. He died in 1902 in Cape Town and his body was carried on its final journey along the railway only as far as Bulawayo, to his chosen resting place in the Matopo Hills.

PRACTICAL INFORMATION

■ On the scheduled service, operated by National Railways of Zimbabwe, trains leave from Bulawayo every day in the evening and take just under 13 hours to travel to Victoria Falls. All First and Second Class compartments have bunks for which comfortable bedding can be hired for the night.

■ It is not easy to make reservations from outside Zimbabwe, but places are generally available on trains. You can book up to 30 days in advance at any station in Zimbabwe.

■ The Zimbabwe Special, effectively a package tour on rails, runs between Bulawayo and Victoria Falls around 20 times a year. The return tour takes six days (five nights) and includes days off the tracks for game viewing and sightseeing. Overnight accommodation and full board are provided. The packages are very popular and booking is essential.

■ Contact the operators direct or book through a travel agent. The operators are: Rail Safaris, PO Box 4070 Harare. Tel: (Harare) 736056. Fax: 708554. In Britain, contact: Leisurail, Units 1–3 Conongsby Road, Merlin Industrial Estate, North Bretton, Peterborough PE3 8HY. Tel: (01733) 335599. Fax: (01733) 505451.

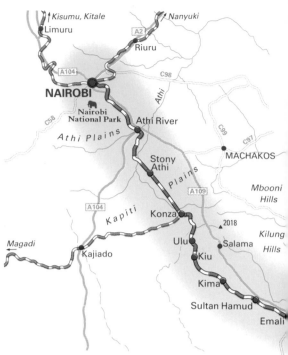

Taking Kenya's Lunatic Line

RICHARD TRILLO

The 'Uganda Railway' was built at the turn of the century from the seaport of Mombasa inland, a route through the high wilderness of Kenya before the country had that name, a route to the anticipated riches of Uganda and Central Africa. But soon it became less a means of access to the interior and more an avenue of escape to the outside world for the thousands of white settlers who had made their homes in the highlands after World War I. Today, it is still in the coastward direction that most visitors take the train, often after an exhausting stint on safari and as a prelude to a week under the palm trees, on a journey that still resonates with the echoes of a bygone era.

TOP, *the modern city skyline of Nairobi*

ABOVE, *the proud lion crest of the Kenya railways*

FAR RIGHT, *looming out of the darkness, Kenya's 'Lunatic Express'*

IT IS 6.45 IN THE EVENING. The worst of the Nairobi rush hour is over; the last rays of the sun are slanting through the jacaranda trees and the office blocks. A London-style cab deposits us in the station forecourt and an elderly porter has already beaten his colleagues to the door. There is time for a drink – cold Tusker beers on a white linen tablecloth – as the sound of the Maroon Commandos guitar band echoes around the station through the PA system.

On the platform, our card on the berthing board tells us which compartment is ours. Having squeezed ourselves in, we assess the circumstances: chrome and polish, sliding window (screened against insects), wardrobe, basin and well-upholstered, fold-down bunks. The drinking water spigot is dry and, down the

■ Nairobi, the capital of Kenya, was founded as a railhead site in 1899. Of particular interest to rail enthusiasts is the Railway Museum near the station. By day, in good conditions, there are clear views from the Simba district of the 19,340ft (5895m) Mount Kilimanjaro, Africa's highest mountain, some 60 miles (95km) to the south. The hotel-cum-service station on the road at Hunter's Lodge, Kiboko ('Hippopotamus') is the best rest stop along the

now among the most popular in Kenya. Access by train to Tsavo East is feasible (get off the train at Voi), but to tour the park you need transport. There is a variety of accommodation. Voi, set among rocky hills and the only town of any size along the route, is a centre for sisal production, with regimented rows of the cactus-like plants all around. It is also headquarters for Tsavo East National Park.
Mombasa may have been founded as early as 2000 years ago. There are good, cheap restaurants, some pleasant hotels and a likeable, low-key atmosphere. Visit the old city, the 16th-century Fort Jesus with its museum, and the cloth traders' Biashara Street.

corridor, there is no paper in the rather cramped squat-down toilet. There are shouts from the platform and a hand clasps the corridor window; it is the porter waiting for his tip. We give him ten shillings. He seems unsure whether we are going to give him more; then, after some hesitation, we discover he is asking if we want any change from the note. A steward comes hurrying down the corridor taking dinner reservations. We elect to go for the recommended first sitting. By 9 o'clock the third sitting diners will be wishing they had done the same as the food loses its shine and the staff come to the end of their shift.

At 18.59 the station loudspeakers start a monologue in Swahili. Precisely on the hour, with the announcement continuing, the train departs, jogging steadily through the city's industrial area and the poor, dry suburbs of east Nairobi – Kaloleni, Makadara, Doonholm. Outside it is already quite dark, though a full moon glares intermittently through speeding cumulus. The equatorial dusk is extraordinarily rapid, the sun diving vertically below the horizon to disappear in minutes without a trace. Out of the dark come voices and the occasional ragged child's figure trotting alongside the train through the tangle of sidings and

whole route, a shady oasis ringing with tropical birds, while Makindu ('Among the palms') is the site of a beautiful Sikh Temple. Kibwezi is a Kamba trading centre with honey and wood carvings much in evidence. The district is hilly farm and scrub land, cut through by seasonal streams.
Mtito Andei ('Forest of Vultures'), a sprawl of petrol stations, cafés and cheap hotels surrounded by stands of 'upside-down' baobab trees, is the headquarters for Tsavo West National Park. Tsavo West and Tsavo East National parks are the largest parks in Kenya, covering an area the size of Wales (8000 square miles/ 21,000sq km). The famous red elephants (red from the dust) were victims of poaching on a massive scale in the 1980s. This has been controlled by a new wildlife service and the parks are

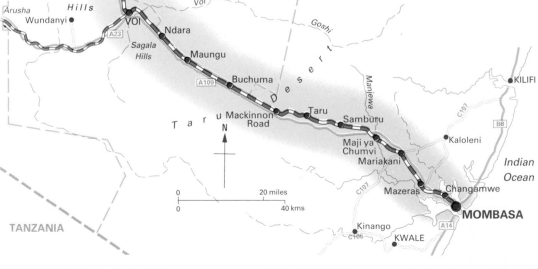

RIGHT, *catching some cooler air through an open window in the corridor*

wasteland. A steward in silver-buttoned white tunic strides through the carriages ringing a tiny bell. Time for dinner.

The dining-car is eight carriages down the train. Encumbered by camera and video bags (agile thieves have been known to board the moving train) we work our way forward, stunning our elbows and careening against the walls. Older, and wider, passengers experience some discomfort and it is well worth trying to get a convenient compartment when booking. In the dining-car you take pot luck. We find ourselves sharing with a lively group of French tourists. But the diners, who include anyone travelling First or Second Class (hard-seated Third Class travel separately), are a very mixed crowd. There is always a good selection of tourists of all nationalities, the occasional missionary couple (often American), various expatriate workers and members of the aid and voluntary community, and middle-class Kenyans (usually civil servants or businessmen).

Dinner arrives in fits and starts. The menu announces Cream of Tomato Soup (juggled, in large bowls), Lake Fish Italienne (a small, tasty course, dwarfed on huge dinner plates), and a choice of beef casserole or chicken curry with side dishes. The style is do-it-yourself silver service as the waiters lean across the tables with tottering trays. There is Kenyan wine, white or red, but it's expensive and there are few takers. We plump for more beer, reliable and cool and cheap. The curry side dishes have been forgotten. We prompt and they eventually arrive, but turn out to be tinned pineapple, chutney and desiccated coconut – more signs of a slight but noticeable decline in Kenya Railways in the ten years since I first used the service.

Outside, to the south, the big spaces have begun. The railway marks the northern boundary of Nairobi National Park, small by Kenyan standards but still covering 44 square miles (1145sq km), and large enough to provide sanctuary for most of Kenya's big game species except the elephant. Somewhere out there live rhino and giraffe, zebra, wildebeest, lion and leopard and there are muddy pools of hippo and crocodiles. Turning away from the cosmopolitan sputter of English, French and Swahili and putting our hands up to the window to hide the glare of the lights, we peer into the gloom – dark shapes everywhere under the moonlight but nothing convincingly animal-like. Then, just as we are about to give up, a whole herd of zebras comes into view – surprisingly grey and horselike in the dark, head to tail for insect-free sleep. It is a small triumph, but the rest of the meal (pineapple crumble and custard, followed by some of the most dishwater coffee imaginable) tastes better for it.

What makes this 13-hour overnighter so enjoyable is the dramatic contrast between Nairobi and Mombasa, between 'upcountry' and 'down-country'. Nairobi, the capital, is in the highlands, some 4700 feet (1700m) above sea level, hemmed in by high ranges to the north and west and giving on to wide plains of savannah and cereal fields to the south and east. With its gift shops, clubs and bars and its huge variety of safari operators, hotels and restaurants, it is a pacey, metropolitan city only as old as the railway line, and geared to the demands of the tourist and foreign investors. Downtown rents are high and development is vertical. Most of Nairobi's million-plus people survive in the teeming shanty towns that begin a mile or two from the skyscrapers and stretch with little planning and few amenities for thou-sands of acres across the dry plain. The people of Nairobi are a broad mix of the country's two dozen ethnic groups – Kikuyu and Luo, Kamba and

swaying motion at times. Long stretches of it are the original, laid between 1896 and 1903 by British engineers and over 30,000 Gujerati and Punjabi labourers hired in India. Many of the stations, sited every 10 to 12 miles (15 to 20 km) and now carefully maintained by lonely, under-employed station masters, are on the sites of the original railhead camps.

AFRICAN QUEEN

The idea of building a railroad from the island of Mombasa into the heart of Africa was conceived in the late 1880s, after Africa was partitioned by the European powers and Queen Victoria's government became bent on dominating as much of it as possible. The Uganda Railway proved to be a valedictory piece of Victorian engineering, executed at huge cost in money and lives – nearly 2500 lives, and another 6000 permanently invalided.

To begin with, it was the British fear of French and German efforts to beat them to the Upper Nile that drove the pace of construction forward. Radical MPs poured scorn on the Tory

Luyia, Kalenjin, Maasai, Samburu and Turkana, to name some of the largest – but in the city, family roots and mother tongue matter less than quali-fications and job.

The island port of Mombasa, by contrast. is old, relaxed and physically tropical in ways that could hardly be more different from Nairobi. The old part of the city, dating back over 1000 years, is a warren of narrow streets and hidden doorways. Most of the people are Swahili, a group whose origins stretch back to the earliest days of trading contact between East Africa, Arabia and the lands across the Indian Ocean. Women wear long, black *bui-bui* cloaks with veils over their modern clothes. Traditional dress for men consists of the *kikoi*, a woven cloth wrap, with a shirt on top and an embroidered cap. The Swahili language in its basic form is now the *lingua franca* for much of eastern and central Africa; but pure Swahili, the language of the coast, is the preserve of the few, the spoken sign of a unique, poetic and probably vanishing culture.

Back at the compartment our beds have been neatly made up with crisp linen and a single (but necessary) blanket. After the vaguely odoriferous meat-packing suburb of Athi River, Greater Nairobi has been left behind and as soon as the third sitting of dinner is over, the train starts to pick up speed, from a cautious 25mph (40kph) to a cantering 45mph (70kph). The metre-gauge track, just 3ft 3in wide, imparts a vigorous

government's plans and soon dubbed it the 'Lunatic Line'. And the project was beset by difficulties from the start: Mombasa Harbour was unsuitable for large ships and a new port had to be built; a bridge to the mainland was needed; then, having laid the first few miles of track up the slopes, the labourers faced a gruelling nine-month test of endurance pushing across the waterless Taru Desert; there was renewed urgency in the goading from London as a mutiny broke out in Uganda and the line was used to bring troops into the country; and no sooner had the mutiny been quelled and the Taru Desert crossed, than the builders came to the Tsavo River and a delay of nearly a year in

TOP, *a salutary warning in this country famed for its wildlife*

ABOVE, *zebras watch carefully from a distance – the track passes through the Tsavo East and Tsavo West national parks on its way to the coast*

constructing a permanent bridge, while lions terrorized the work gangs, killing 28 labourers and maybe 100 Africans, and eluding the guns of Colonel Patterson in almost supernatural fashion (he got them in the end, of course: they were stuffed and can be seen in Chicago's Field Museum of Natural History). Tsavo is Kamba for 'slaughter' and, although the banks are tree-lined and cool, local people have always feared its reputation.

The line proceeded during a terrible famine into Ukambani (the land of the Kamba people) and had more trouble with lions and innumerable rhinos: the railhead engineer Ronald Preston found them 'a regular nuisance in disturbing the work, by turning up at odd times and gazing at our workmen'. But with increasing altitude and a corresponding decrease in time lost through malaria, the railway made progress and, at the end of May 1899, the railhead reached a swampy bit of no man's land called Waso Nairobi ('Cold Water Stream'). By August of the same year, there was a regular passenger service between the nascent town of Nairobi and Mombasa. The Uganda Railway went on to its goal, Lake Victoria, which it reached in December 1901, though it was 1903 before all the permanent viaducts were

completed, all the temporary diversions removed and all the stations built. The total cost was not far short of £6 million.

The construction of the single line required one and a quarter million steel sleepers and some 200,000 30ft (9m) lengths of railing, each weighing 500 pounds (225 kilos). Under ideal conditions, with no steep grades or gullies to overcome, the railhead team could advance at the rate of about one-third of a mile (550m) per day, shifting camp every month to the new forward position. But only in the Taru Desert were conditions technically ideal, and here progress was slowed by the sheer heat, the need to clear away the dense thorn scrub, and the many injuries from thorns and brushwood under bare feet.

In the light of pre-dawn, I wake to a smell of

damp earth and switch ends in my top bunk. By craning my head over the side of the bunk, I can lie prostrate and look out of the window. We pass through Mackinnon Road in the middle of the Taru Desert, with its ornate Sayyid Baghali Shah Pir Padree Mosque, right by the track on

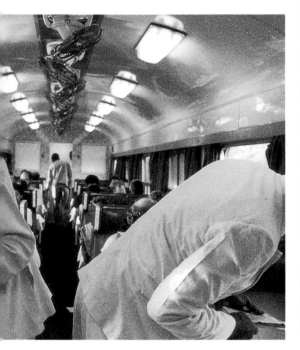

the compartment side. As we leave the Desert, the countryside is crinkled with small, still empty watercourses and speckled with the early green and yellow vegetation of the first rains. The track crosses the Nairobi-to-Mombasa highway and down the road there is a commotion of people around two lorries, tipped sideways on either side of the road. The narrow, pitted highway is a notorious killer, especially at night, and police and ambulance may be hours in coming to the scene. It is another reason why the train is always full. At Maji Ya Chumvi ('Salty Water'), the women are up and sitting by the fires; the children are still too sleepy to wave as we pass but stand in still clumps and hold themselves against the chill. Unlike the shacks you see around Nairobi and the small compounds of round huts in the rural highland areas, the houses here are rectangular, occasionally still the droopy, thatchwork cottages of traditional construction, but mostly built of mud brick or concrete blocks, whitewashed and roofed in corrugated-iron.

Through the station of Mariakani ('Place of the Poisoned Arrows'), everyone is up and starting the day, children brushing teeth, men gathering goats, toddlers

running down the embankment. By the time we reach Mazeras, with its delightful botanical gardens and coconut palms, the long vistas of scrub are ended and the coastal domain has really begun, with its mango and banana trees and dense coconut plantations. The sun comes up and starts to strike as the train loops down a steep escarpment, 560 feet (170m) in 15 miles (24km), to the sea. The humidity is soon high and all the fans are on in the dining-car as we breakfast in the full English manner under the glare of President Moi's framed photograph. The coffee is hot and stronger than at dinner (which suggests a gradual dilution through the day), and our brows are soon dripping – the neat, starched napkins prove very useful. Outside, factory workers walking by the tracks shout 'Jambo' and 'Happy Breakfast' and some raise the waving, two-finger salute of Kenya's largest opposition party, FORD, the Forum for the Restoration of Democracy.

The train crawls gingerly across the Makupa causeway, the railway running above the road of morning traffic, and on to Mombasa Island. Ancient hulks of loco-motives fill the shunting yards to the left as we draw into the station at 08.05hrs, just five minutes late.

Under the acute rays of the sun, the station forecourt is like a furnace. The cars here seem older than Nairobi's and jostle for road space with wiry barrow men hauling great loads and crowded, honking buses. Seawards, deep-set purple clouds herald the start of the monsoon season, when the streets are battered by torrential rain and rivers of refuse course down the alleys. There are black-veiled women walking home with bags of shopping from the over-spilling Mackinnon Market. Later in the morning, we hear the call to prayer from one of the city's 50-odd mosques. Mombasa feels like a different country and, but for the British and their imperial designs, it would be.

PRACTICAL INFORMATION

■ Two trains a day run overnight between Nairobi and Mombasa in each direction. The slower, stopping train takes 14½ hours to cover the 327 miles (526km), the quicker (the usual choice for tourists) takes 13 hours. A deluxe daytime service has operated recently, leaving Nairobi on Saturdays and Mombasa on Sundays (13 hours).

■ Trains run full, and advance booking is essential. First Class compartments are for two, with connecting doors for groups. Second Class are four berth, single sex compartments. Third Class travel is on hard seats only, but is a good way to meet less affluent Kenyans. The dining-car is for First and Second Class passengers only.

■ Travel is unaffected by the seasonal rains (the general pattern is 'long rains' from March to May and 'short rains' in November or early December), but the undulating savannahs are at their prettiest just after the rains have broken. Sunset is at approximately the same time all year round.

■ The line is operated by Kenya Railways and bookings can be made at stations in Kenya, through a travel agent or by contacting Kenya Railways, PO Box 30121, Nairobi.

On the Blue Train from Cape Town to Johannesburg

GUS SILBER

Three days a week, liveried in blue and cream, South Africa's Blue Train glides along the rails between Pretoria and Cape Town, its streamlined carriages whispering a seductive fantasy of escape. Behind the gold-tinted picture windows, in sound-proofed, fully carpeted compartments, the wealthy and the glamorous clink their fluted wine glasses and watch the hinterland go by. The mountains and winelands of the Western Cape, the brooding, primeval Karoo Desert, the diamond fields of Kimberley and the gold reefs of Johannesburg and the Witwatersrand; from the edge of the Atlantic Ocean north-east to the industrial and metropolitan heartland of the Transvaal, the route covers 1000 miles (1608km) of narrow gauge rail in one day, one hour, and 12 minutes.

ABOVE, *Table Mountain dominates the city of Cape Town, spread out along the shore*

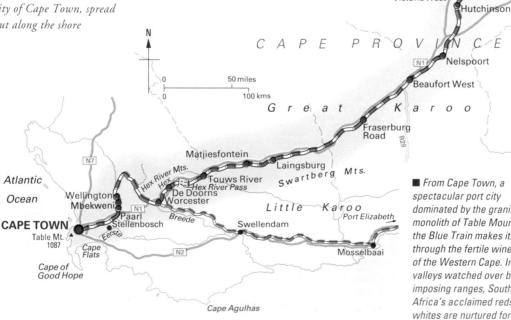

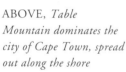

■ From Cape Town, a spectacular port city dominated by the granite monolith of Table Mountain, the Blue Train makes its way through the fertile winelands of the Western Cape. In valleys watched over by imposing ranges, South Africa's acclaimed reds and whites are nurtured for domestic and international consumption. Paarl is the centre of the wine industry, and is also renowned for the 'Taal Monument', a slender obelisk erected in honour of the Afrikaans language, which had its formal origins here in the 19th century. The route then winds around the breathtaking Hex River pass, a marvel of railway engineering that conquered gradients as steep as 1:31 when it was built by surveyor Wells Hood in 1876. Beyond the Hex River Mountains lies the semi-arid Great Karoo, a prehistoric landscape that covers one-third of the southern African subcontinent. With its strata of volcanic basalt, sandstone, fossilized shale

and glacial debris, the Karoo is of great interest to scientists and geologists, and South African literature frequently uses its eerie desolation as a metaphor for suffering and resilience.
On the northbound route, the Blue Train stops for an hour at Matjiesfontein, a Victorian village built as a refreshment station and health resort by railway official James Douglas Logan in the 1890s. At the massive railway junction of De Aar in the northern Cape, the Blue Train switches from electric to diesel locomotives for the flat stretch to Kimberley,

scene of South Africa's great diamond rush in 1869. At daybreak, the Blue Train enters the gold-rich terrain of the Western Transvaal, where fields of maize and sunflowers give way to the flat-topped minedumps and headgear of the world's deepest and wealthiest gold mines. Beyond lies the Witwatersrand region, the business and industrial heartland of South Africa. After passing through the railway junction of Germiston, the Blue Train heads straight for Pretoria, South Africa's jacaranda-lined administrative capital.

SPEED IS NOT THE ESSENCE of the Blue Train. In the early hours of the morning, when its cargo is asleep and dreaming, the train switches its motive power from electric to diesel, and girds itself for the flat stretch between De Aar and Kimberley in the northern Cape. Here, under cover of darkness, the Blue Train swallows up the landscape at its top speed of 62mph (100kph).

But the pace of the train is governed by its function: it is a luxury train, and the ultimate luxury of the supersonic age is time. So, one cold autumn morning, when it was spring in the northern hemisphere and the Blue Train had precious space to spare, I rose before dawn and hurried to catch the breakfast flight from my home town of Johannesburg to the port city of Cape Town.

It took two hours on the airbus, and all I saw was furrowed farmland, billowing clouds, and the white-capped waves of the angry Atlantic. In another 30 minutes, I was running through the

concourse of Cape Town railway station, glancing at my watch and heading for Platform 24. When I saw the red carpet, I began slowing down. When I saw the Blue Train, all that quickened was my pulsebeat.

Since 1923, the Blue Train has been synonymous with the opulence of First Class rail travel in South Africa, first as a steam express linking the Union Castle mailship service to Johannesburg, then as a British-built assembly of all-steel, air-conditioned saloon coaches, then as the electric and diesel driven vehicle built to 'a standard of luxury and workmanship equal to the best in the world' in South Africa in 1972. According to the legend of the Blue Train, when that draft specification was presented to the general manager for his perusal, he took out his pen and deleted two words: 'equal to'.

There were the 17 blue and cream carriages, including a lounge-car, a kitchen-car and a dining-car, and there were the three class SE1 electric locomotives, silhouetted against the grey skies at the mouth of the platform. There was a Rolls Royce engine humming to itself in the power car, generating enough electricity to keep

BELOW, *the splendid Blue Train awaits its passengers*

BOTTOM, *old buildings on the Cape Town waterfront, a reminder of the city's historic past*

107 passengers and 28 crew on the rails. I was in no hurry to go home, and I could think of no better way to get there.

It took just a few strides of the carpet to locate my fixed abode for the next 25 hours and 12 minutes, but I carried on searching, stealing glimpses of gold velvet and mahogany veneer and bottles of champagne nesting in silver ice-buckets.

There are four classes of accommodation on the Blue Train: the A-type suite, with bedroom, bathroom, sitting-room, and bar; the B-type, with bathroom and sitting-room; the C-type, with shower and sitting-room; and D-type, with communal shower and sitting-room. I was in a D-type. Of course, it was a Blue Train D-type.

I peered through the Venetian slats of the dining-car, where all classes would congregate for lunch, dinner, and breakfast. In the warm orange glow, white-jacketed stewards were putting the silverware on parade, and my view of the luncheon menu was obscured by a carnation in a slender crystal vase.

I was sitting inside my D-type compartment, sipping Cape sparkling wine and tracing the royal blue line on the route map, when I began to realize that the landscape outside the window was moving. It was just after 10.50hrs. As smoothly and quietly as a needle pulling thread, the Blue Train had set off on its great trek into the South African interior.

Behind us, seagulls swooped in the brisk autumn wind, and the surly hulk of Table Mountain wrapped a mantle of cloud around its shoulders. We picked up speed. At 37mph (60kph) on the Blue Train, all you can hear is a soft, insistent rapping on the door of your compartment. It was Johan

BELOW, the Blue Train snakes its way through the landscape

Stemmet, the steward. 'Is this your first time on the Blue Train, Sir?' I nodded.

THE MECHANICS OF LUXURY

The steward walked over to the window-panel and introduced me to the mechanics of luxury. Press this button for valet service. Turn this knob for climate control, and this one to raise or lower the electric blinds. Here are two stereo music stations at your fingertips. Here is hot water, cold water, iced drinking water. If you would like your shoes to be collected for cleaning, please place them in this box beneath your seat.

Outside, it was a grey, blustery Cape Town day. On the railway platforms, people looked up from their newspapers as we rushed by, steel wheels cushioned on friction dampers and 'a rubber sandwich integrally moulded into the

rubber air spring, thereby increasing the lateral flexibility of the spring and considerably improving the lateral ride'.

On the Blue Train, the most arcane technical specifications translate into passenger comfort. 'The inside of each coach structure is coated with graded thicknesses of Aquaplas resin-bonded anti-drumming compound, with floor pans of sheet steel fitted over the glass fibre layer on the bogies'. Translation: it's quiet in here.

Pneumatically sealed and insulated from the real world, I adjusted the climate, the light, and the sound to my own personal liking. Then, as the green outer suburbs of Cape Town gave way to the wind-whipped dunes and scraggy bushes of the Cape Flats, I took another sip of chilled sparkling wine.

Despite the anti-drumming compound, I could hear the rapping on the door, and I opened it to Reggie Wonner, manager of the dining-car. 'Your first trip on the Blue Train, Sir?' I nodded. Lunch at 12.30, dinner at 8.00, breakfast between 7.30 and 9.00. The dining-car was four coaches down, out of the door and to the right. Of course, I knew that.

Beyond the line, in prelude to the wine country of Paarl and the Hex River Valley, the first tangled vines were growing in the sweep of grimly chiselled mountains. These were modest farmsteads, their white porticoes guarded by cypresses at the end of rutted dirt roads. Here and there, roosting in the scrub, an ostrich preened its feathers among indifferent sheep and horses.

ABOVE, *the fertile wine-growing country of the Paarl, with the Drakensberg Mountains forming a dramatic backdrop*

ABOVE, *dining in luxury and style*

RIGHT, *the harsh Karoo landscape*

'Travelled with us before, Sir?' I shook my head. Renier Koekemoer, manager of the Blue Train, inspected my ticket and checked my name on his clipboard. Years of riding the rails had taught Mr Koekemoer the ideal ticket-inspecting stance: legs apart, shoes firmly anchored to the carpet, elbows coiled and shoulders slightly raised. The gun-slinger's position. The train could lurch, judder and sway, and Mr Koekemoer would stay on his feet. It was purely a matter of instinct.

This was the Blue Train, with its laterally flexible springs and compressed air disc-braking system, 'designed to give maximum braking on a dry rail just short of the point of wheel skidding'. Mr Koekemoer said we would be stopping for one hour at Matjiesfontein Station in the Karoo, for a late afternoon walkabout available only on the northbound route.

'This will leave us an hour behind schedule', announced Mr Koekemoer, scribbling away on his clipboard. He looked up. 'But don't worry. We'll make it up during the night.' The weather was improving. The curtain of cloud lifted over Paarl, and the midday sun shone like a spotlight on the floor of the Valley of Pearls. The name is a tribute to the glistening granite domes of the Klein Drakenstein range: the real pearls of the valley hang in bunches from the vine.

Wave after wave of Chenin Blanc, Riesling, Cabernet Sauvignon, Pinotage and Shiraz rolled by the window, the leaves of the vineyards tinted autumn gold in the shadow of the crags. Beyond the gabled headquarters of the KWV, the Cape Co-Operative Wine Farmers' Association, we raced the articulated trucks bearing crates of export wine and brandy, and then we sped our own way towards Wellington.

Just before Mbekweni Station, Renier Koekemoer spoke on the intercom: 'Good afternoon, ladies and gentlemen, if you look out of the corridor side now, you will see flamingoes.' He was right. On the fringes of a marshy pond, sinuous birds rustled their wings like exotic dancers, revealing fleeting glimpses of black and tangerine under-feathers.

A xylophone chimed. In three languages, a pleasant female voice confirmed the signal: Lunch.

It was low season on the Blue Train, and the dining-car was able to accommodate all 47 passengers in one sitting. Normally, 90 per cent of the passengers are foreign tourists, mostly from Germany, the United Kingdom, and the USA. But today the dominant accents were indigenous English and Afrikaans.

I eat at a table with a sprightly old lady from the garden suburbs of Johannesburg, and a 30-something Doctor of Mathematics from Birmingham, taking a short break from a university exchange programme in Zambia. 'I just like trains,' he beamed, the rush of sunlit mountains and rolling farmland reflected in his bi-focals.

The sprightly old lady shared my home-grown motivation. 'Sooner or later,' she said, digging a silver spoon into her fruit parfait, 'you've got to find out for yourself what the fuss is all about.' We were in the Hex River Valley now, awed by serrated peaks and swirls of mist, and it felt as if we were travelling straight into the jaws of a dragon.

These were the Hex River Mountains, the granite wall dividing the abundant orchards and vineyards of the valley from the barren plains of the Great Karoo, and the real marvel of the place was the way they had built a railway around it. Driven by the grand colonial dream of a Cape-to-Cairo route, the engineers of the British Empire began making tracks in 1859, and the line had reached the Eerste River Valley by 1862.

But the Eerste River was only 21 miles (34km) from Cape Town, and the granite ranges to the north seemed unbreachable. Until Wells Hood found a way. Hood was the surveyor who etched a path across the Hex River Mountains in 1876, and the parallel lines began their climb from De Doorns, 1565 feet (477m) above sea level.

By the time the narrow gauge track had reached 3150 feet (960m) above sea level, it had embraced enough curves for 16 complete circuits, with an average gradient of 1:31. And here we sat, admiring the view, taking the Hex River Pass as effortlessly as our hallmarked Sheffield knives cut into our Fillet of Salmon Trout Grenobloise.

'Sorry to bother you, lady,' said Renier Koekemoer. The sprightly old lady looked up. 'I just wanted to know if everything is going well with your painting.'

'Oh yes, fine,' she said. 'I have decided to leave it locked up in the shower.' Mr Koekemoer frowned slightly. 'Really, if you prefer, we can leave it in an unused compartment for you overnight. The train is not full. It will not be a problem.' But the sprightly old lady smiled and shook her head.

'Thank you, it's just that I prefer to have it travelling in the same compartment as myself.' Mr Koekemoer apologized once again, inquired about the fish, and made his way to the next table. The conversation could not go unexplained for long. It turned out that the sprightly old lady was not merely travelling on the Blue Train to see what all the fuss was about. She had loaned an oil-painting from her private collection to a waterfront gallery in Cape Town, and now she was escorting it home in the style to which it had become accustomed. This was not just any oil-painting. It was a Pierneef.

Jacob Hendrik Pierneef, 1886 to 1957, was South Africa's greatest landscape painter, a Dutch-schooled Impressionist who devoted his life to capturing the essence of the land on canvas. He painted the small towns and lonely farmsteads of the Karoo, he painted the thorn trees and fat baobabs of the Transvaal bushveld, he painted the mighty Drakensberg Mountains of the Natal escarpment. He painted the kind of landscapes you can see from the window of a train.

It is no coincidence that the largest single collection of Pierneef's works is in the hands of Spoornet, the semi-State concern that runs South Africa's railways. A different Pierneef reproduction takes pride of place on the wall of every compartment on the Blue Train. I had a view of Ladybrand, a small town in the Orange Free State. I had barely glanced at it; there was too much going on outside the window.

'Some people find Pierneef a little too sentimental,' said the sprightly old lady. She was carrying a canvas of Loskop Dam in the Eastern Transvaal. It was a big painting. But the Blue Train has big showers.

I had ample opportunity to ponder Pierneef's Ladybrand back in my compartment, because the Blue Train was burrowing like a mole through the fourth-longest system of railway tunnels in the world. There were four tunnels, and the longest was 21.8 miles (13.5km). Twenty minutes later, when we emerged from the claustrophobic blackness, I looked out of my window to see the dry, ravaged, bitter beginnings of the Great Karoo.

The name, in the aboriginal tongue of the Khoisan hunter-gatherers, means arid, sparse, parched. I turned the climate control slightly to the left, and I pressed the valet button for my cup of afternoon tea. For millions of years, drought has held the lease on the Great Karoo.

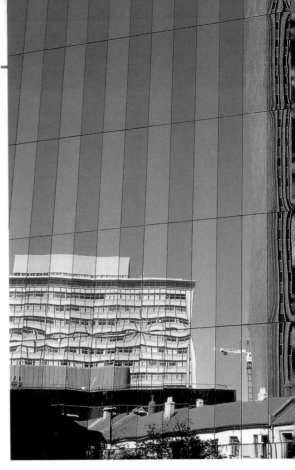

But there have been other tenants. Spiky leaved aloes and stapelias cling to the caustic, pebbly soil, and ephemeral wildflowers burst into bloom after the flash floods. There are ostriches, antelopes, birds of prey. Somewhere out there, beyond the railway tracks, there may even be people.

Beneath the searing blue sky, with its wisps of corrugated cloud drifting slowly towards the horizon, a whitewashed house with a red tin roof would be standing alone in the middle of nowhere. There would be a rusty-vaned windmill, waiting for the wind, and a concrete reservoir with dark green shrubs growing around the base. But as hard as I searched from the window of my compartment, I could never see the people who were living there.

We rolled past the scratchy carpet of yellow-green scrub, the jagged outcrops of scarred red rock, the flat-topped hillocks eroded by wind and rain. 'Ladies and gentlemen,' said the voice on the intercom, 'we have arrived at Matjiesfontein Station. Please move forward from your compartment, as the train is too long for the platform.'

I moved forward, stepped on to the platform, walked through a doorway, down a flight of stone stairs, and straight on to a bright red double-decker London omnibus. I couldn't miss it. It was the only bus in town, and the conductor was standing in front, splintering the bone-dry Karoo air with a blast of his dented bronze bugle.

FOREVER ENGLAND

'Could you tell me how long the tour lasts?' I asked the bus driver, but he just laughed. 'Don't worry. You won't miss your train.' We chugged into the main street of Matjiesfontein, which was also the only street of Matjiesfontein, and then we turned on to a dirt road, swung around, chugged down the street in the opposite direction, and spluttered to a stop outside the Lord Milner Hotel. That was the village of Matjiesfontein, a corner of a foreign desert that is for ever England. Well, parts of it.

The London bus and the Victorian street lamps; the Union Jack fluttering atop the turrets of the Lord Milner. From here, during the Anglo-Boer War of 1898 to 1902, British soldiers stood watch over the wasteland of the Karoo. The hotel was a hospital for wounded officers, and 10,000 troops were mustered on the outskirts of town. But Matjiesfontein survived. The town was never a garrison; it was a retreat.

Built by James Douglas Logan, a railway official and entrepreneur who worked his way up from carrying bags at Cape Town Station, Matjiesfontein offered food, drink, and fine lodging to travellers on the newly built line through the Hex River Mountains. The Sultan of Zanzibar stayed at Matjiesfontein, and so did Lord Randolph Churchill and the Duke of Hamilton. Some lingered. Olive Schreiner, the writer, rented a cottage from Logan, and she wrote: 'Now I am going to put my hat on and go out for a walk over the Karoo.' I looked around the Lord Milner, with its chandeliers and its red carpets and its wrought-iron balconies, spun as fine as Spanish lace. Then I went out for a walk over the Karoo.

It was like stepping off the edge of the world. The Karoo began where Matjiesfontein ended, and it went on for ever. The spiny sage bushes, wisely keeping their distance from each other, the tall eucalyptus trees with their peeling bark and rust-tinged undercoats, the hint of snow on the saw-toothed peaks of the Swartberg Mountains. I walked over to a small white farmhouse with a red tin roof.

There was no one around. A tractor lay defeated, tyres melted and cobwebs on its wheels. Like an undercover agent, a black-and-white cat roosted in the middle of a flock of busy hens. There was a barbed-wire fence with staggered posts, but it could not contain the landscape.

The bus driver was wrong. When you stop over at Matjiesfontein, in the middle of the Great Karoo, it is the easiest thing in the world to miss your train.

The sun set over the corridor side, and I

was Loin of Karoo Lamb and Ostrich Fillet Oudtshoorn. The Doctor of Mathematics from Birmingham was pleased about that, because he had been trying to take photographs of faraway ostriches from the window of his compartment all day long. I strolled down the carpeted corridor after the Black Forest Gateaux and the cheese and biscuits, and I wondered why the steward coming the other way was holding on to the brass rail for support. Then I saw the chamois cloth in his hand. He was polishing his way from car to car, and I suddenly understood why the tracks were gleaming whenever we took a bend.

Flashes of neon passed by my window, and we made up for Matjiesfontein. At 6.30 next morning, I watched the sun rise over the maizelands of the Western Transvaal. The land was in the grip of drought, and the husks looked as brittle as old parchment. The blood-red sun slipped through a pocket of cloud. No sign of rain today.

Leeudoringstad, Orkney, Klerksdorp: the mining towns rolled by, their spidery headgear standing sentinel over the plunging shafts. Since the gold rush of 1886, when an Australian prospector named George Harrison stumbled across the conglomerate on a small farm in the Transvaal, South Africa's mines have brought more than 36,000 tons of gold to the surface.

Today, that small farm is called Johannesburg. We were on the suburban main line now, cruising slowly past the mustard-yellow minedumps and sprawling townships of the Witwatersrand. Then the neat houses with their concrete walls and rose bushes gave way to smoke-stacks and silos, and the morning sun caught the glint of glass and steel in the distance. Johannesburg. In just over an hour, the Blue Train would ease into Pretoria Station, but I was home.

'I hope you are able to read my handwriting,' said Renier Koekemoer, entering my compartment as the vacuum brakes sighed outside the window. The certificate was bordered in gold, and was stamped with a cursive letter 'B'. It certified that I was a 'Graduate of the Blue Train, in a class of its own', and it was signed by Mr Koekemoer.

As I stepped on to the platform, I saw the sprightly old lady from Johannesburg. She was giving instructions to two porters, who were carefully seeking a hand-hold on a large, flat item of freight wrapped in copious sheets of brown paper. It was the Pierneef. All I had was my graduation certificate, but I suspected, somehow, that it would look just as impressive in a frame.

dimmed the lights in my compartment to get a better view of nightfall. Out here in the desert, the sky was blacker and the moon was brighter, and it glinted on the silver windmills and made woodcuts of the trees and mountains. Lights were burning behind the windows of the farmsteads. People were home. I found the Southern Cross and the Milky Way, barely visible from my home town, but here as plain as sequins on velvet. The Blue Train rushed on moonlit tracks, and the xylophone chimed three times for dinner.

Among other things, there

PRACTICAL INFORMATION

■ The Blue Train travels the 1000-mile (1608km) route between Cape Town and Pretoria three times a week, except in the winter months (May, June, and July), when the service is reduced to once a week. The trip takes just over 25 hours.

■ Passengers are advised to book up to a year in advance for the high season (November to February). It is a trip that is popular all year round, but the autumn light playing on the vineyards is particularly beautiful.

■ The train has four classes, ranging from a luxury suite with bedroom, sitting-room and private bathroom, to a coupé with shared shower facilities. Every compartment is fully air-conditioned and carpeted, and is equipped with hot, cold, and iced running water. Three meals are included in the price of a Blue Train ticket, and there is a lounge car for use throughout the journey. Valet service is available at the press of a button.

■ For bookings and further information, contact The Manager, Blue Train Reservations, Private Bag X47, Johannesburg 2000, South Africa.
Tel: 27 11 7737631.
Fax: 27 11 7737643.
In Britain the representative is SAR Travel, Regency House, 1–4 Warwick Street, London W1R 5WA.
Tel: (0171) 287 1133.
Fax: (0171) 287 1134.
In the US contact California SAR Travel Branch Manager, 1100 East Broadway, Glendale, California 91205.
Tel: 818 549 1921.
Fax: 818 507 5802.

Following the Nile from Cairo to Aswân

ROBIN NEILLANDS

❈

'Egypt', said Herodotus, 'is the gift of the Nile.' Its railways, on the other hand, are the gift of the British, who built them to nail down the country against civil insurrection and invasion between the time they entered Egypt in the 1870s and the time they left in 1953. It follows, therefore, that the railways of Egypt were built from strategic considerations and neither for speed nor comfort. A journey along the banks of the Nile by stopping train may require a certain resilience of spirit, but as a journey through the wonders of ancient Egypt it can hardly be bettered and as a journey through modern Egypt it simply does not compare with the traditional but now rather mundane experience of a cruise ship.

———

FAR RIGHT, *a graceful, tall-sailed felucca on the Nile*

RIGHT, *travellers on the platform at Qena*

CAIRO IS THE LARGEST CITY in Africa, the capital of the Arab world, but to the first-time visitor it much resembles an overturned ant-heap with people rushing in all directions, in a wide variety of Western and Arab dress, crowding the souks and the pavements, pushing you aside, selling you things you do not want, and demanding 'baksheesh'. The first requirement is patience, and nowhere more so than at Rameses Station where people are milling all over the place, sleeping in corners, feeding or changing babies, or simply lying comatose on the platforms or on benches, waiting for trains or for something to turn up – and where the ticket counter staff seem to live in a state of terminal lethargy. Be warned that the process of reservation and ticket purchase can take anything from a couple of hours to a couple of days, depending on the mood of the staff and how lucky you are.

The point of visiting Egypt is to see the ancient world, and for any visitor that is really the sole purpose of any journey down the Nile. There are two ways to make the journey by train. The first is on the special overnight sleeper trains operated by Wagons-Lits, which run from Rameses Station in Cairo to Luxor and Aswân. This is ideal for those who want to see only the main sites at Cairo and Luxor, like the pyramids and the Valley of the Kings at Thebes, before

travelling on to Aswân. The trains are fairly new, air conditioned Wagons-Lits Expresses, with plenty of white-coated staff to fetch and carry, overnight two-berth sleeping compartments similar to those used in Europe, and dining cars. This is a comfortable method of travel but not particularly exciting. Give or take a camel or two on the line, you might be anywhere.

Serious travellers, however – those who carry at least three thick guidebooks and several bottles of mineral water – will choose one of the day stoppers or local trains that link the small towns alongside the Nile. This is not a romantic train ride and even the First Class, air conditioned carriages are at best only adequate, but you can see the country, meet the people and get off where and when you choose.

Once you get the hang of it, getting down the Nile like this is easy. There are plenty of trains, including a surprising number of freight trains – though the freight wagons all seem fairly full of people. Decide which place you want to see, get off the train at the appropriate station and then shoot off by taxi or bus to visit it. When you get back to the railhead take a train along to the next town which has reasonable hotels and start the whole process again. It may sound hit-or-miss, but it works. And it seemed to me that to take the soft option of the Wagons-Lits special would be to miss the experience of a lifetime.

■ Most of Egypt is desert, so it follows that the centres of population are either on the coast, in the Delta or on either side of the Nile. The railway follows the course of the Nile, alongside the road, taking the visitor close to the places of interest.

From Cairo the train follows the western bank of the river south past the Sphinx and the pyramids to the ruins at Memphis, and then Saqqâra. It runs on beside the Nile with glimpses of feluccas and cruise ships through an almost biblical landscape. There are palm trees and irrigated market gardens around El Lisht, and after a while the ruined pyramid at Meidûm looms up on the skyline. Beni Suef is the first train stop, a market centre for the produce-growing Faiyûm district.

The railway runs south into El Fashn, a riverside town popular with cruise ships, and then to El Minya, another market town and the centre for a number of interesting sites. Asyût has the ancient city of Lycopolis as the main attraction, and is a centre for the production of cotton.

Railway, road and river now run on side by side to Sohâg, which has a Coptic cathedral as well as a bus station and an airport. Places to visit from here include the necropolis of Abydos or, on a slower train, the river town of El Balyana, another popular stop for cruise ships with a good souk, or market. The line passes the temples at Dandara, best reached from the railway halt at Qena or by coach from Luxor, and next are the temple of

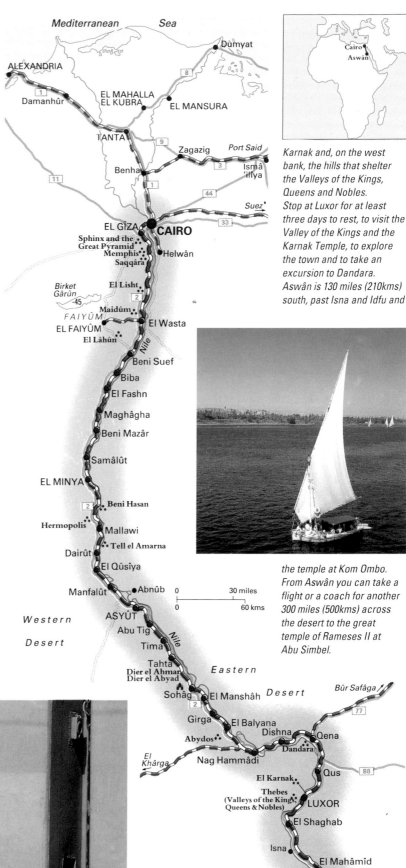

Karnak and, on the west bank, the hills that shelter the Valleys of the Kings, Queens and Nobles.

Stop at Luxor for at least three days to rest, to visit the Valley of the Kings and the Karnak Temple, to explore the town and to take an excursion to Dandara.

Aswân is 130 miles (210kms) south, past Isna and Idfu and

the temple at Kom Ombo. From Aswân you can take a flight or a coach for another 300 miles (500kms) across the desert to the great temple of Rameses II at Abu Simbel.

With the travelling arrangements in hand or taken care of there should be time to see a little of Cairo before bracing yourself for the rigours of rail. The first place to visit is the Egyptian Museum of Antiquities which is full of wonderful things, including the treasures of the young pharaoh Tutankhamun. The other essential sites are the Sphinx and the Great Pyramid at El Gîza, just on the southern outskirts of the city. It is possible to hire a camel here and most people take a ride on one, up from El Gîza and once round the Great Pyramid. Those who are getting a feel for this wonderful ruined land will also take a coach excursion south to Memphis and the ruins and temples at Saqqâra. Coffee, lunch or an ice cream at Groppi's in the Midan Talaat Harb is another tradition wise visitors will follow.

All this seen and done, it was time for me to check out of my comfortable hotel. I had become a kind of hero to the other guests, who viewed my intention to travel south by rail with the kind of awe that Stanley must have endured when he said he was off to find Livingstone. One gentleman, who told me that he had been down the Nile nine times, added that I would probably get my throat cut.

I had opted for an early train, hoping to avoid the crowds, but Rameses Station has a 24-hour rush hour. The confusion was increased by several score of people trying to carry my bag and a few more trying to sell me drinks, rolls filled with unspeakable foodstuffs, or hieroglyphic postcards.

THE SLOW TRAIN

The stopper trains are dented and dusty and usually carry far more people than they were designed for, and I have to say that my first reaction when I eventually fought my way on board was to wish I had settled for the cosy ride on the Wagons-Lits. Serious travellers seem to relish squalor and will probably enjoy this, accepting the crowding as part of life's rich pattern. The engines are French or Russian diesels left over from hauling concrete and equipment to the Aswân High Dam.

But there were already distractions. On the way out of city, rattling over innumerable sets of points, I could see the jutting triangle tops of the pyramids and the scattered columns of the temples at El Gîza, Memphis and Saqqâra. To

the west is Faiyûm, Egypt's largest oasis, and delightfully green after the noise and dirt of Cairo. Sugar cane grows here, and palm trees hang heavy with dates. I was sufficiently tempted to leave the train at Beni Suef, 75 miles (120km) south of Cairo for an overnight stop, to explore this district by bus and taxi, seeing the water wheels at Medinet el Faiyûm and the pyramid at El Lâhûn.

From Beni Suef the railway track stays close to the Nile to El Minya, 155 miles (249km) south of Cairo, which takes about four hours on the train. I breakfasted *en route*, on oranges supplied in quantity by my fellow passengers who

were carrying sacks of fruit, hens by the legs and at least one anxious goat. By midday we reached El Minya, a good base for visiting the tombs at Hermopolis or Beni Hasan, 12 miles (20km) further south. I got off the train (four or five hours on one of these trains is as much as the human frame can stand) but I chose to stay put for the day because El Minya has several good hotels for a meal, a good market to visit and excellent bus services up and down the river. It also has some very good beer. Hermopolis, a complex of temples dedicated to the god Thoth, lies near Mallawi, a small town 30 miles (48km) south of El Minya. South of here lie the remains of the city of Tell el-Amarna, built in the 14th century BC by the pharaoh Aklenaten and his famous queen Nefertiti.

From El Minya I took a 'commuter' train, somewhat scruffy even by local standards and full of more *fellaheen* on their way to market. Getting on board required a rapid deployment of the elbows and a total lack of compassion. These local 'commuter' trains are strictly for the peasantry and look as if they will fall apart at any

minute. However, it is remarkably easy to get used to squalor. With the chatter and the incessant questioning of the locals I was never lonely. I would have quite liked to be lonely, but the Egyptians are intensely interested in visitors and since many speak a little English or French you are kept deep in conversation. There is also the ongoing backgammon school in every compartment, and what with one thing and another it is often a relief to get off. Sometimes it is hard even to look out of the window.

There are temple ruins to be seen, however, on either side of the railway line, as the train rumbles on to the next stop, Asyût, which marks the dividing line between Upper (southern) Egypt and Lower (northern) Egypt. Asyût is the main town of Upper Egypt, an important rail stop and a great trading centre, standing astride the camel routes that come in from the Western Desert and the Sahara. The dam across the river here was built by the British in the last century to irrigate the country as far north as Beni Suef. The direct journey time here from Cairo is about six hours though it had taken me three days.

ABOVE LEFT, *local stopping trains generally carry far more people than they were designed for*

FAR LEFT, *dates drying in the sun near Idfu*

FAR RIGHT, *carving at the temple of Hathor, near Dandara – from one of the most photographed walls in all Egypt*

Another 60 miles (96km) further south, the train stops at Sohâg, a centre for Egypt's Coptic Christian community. The two monasteries, the Dier el-Armar or Red Monastery and the Dier el-Abyad or White Monastery, lie in the hills to the west and a taxi ride out there from Sohâg costs about £E10, or less if you haggle. I am not much good at haggling. The only time I tried it, the price went up. This hardly mattered because travelling like this may be dirty, but it is also dirt cheap.

I was now getting used to the journey and beginning to enjoy myself. My fellow passengers, the Egyptians, fell into two categories; friendly, and too friendly, as they offered me coffee, sweetmeats, fruit in various stages of disintegration and lethal bottles of orange juice and water. I even stopped worrying about my stomach and was eating platform food without a twinge – though getting a bad attack of the Pharaoh's Revenge on a rail journey through Egypt hardly bears thinking about. A bonus was that the demands for 'baksheesh' so constantly made in Cairo were not heard at all out here, away from the tourist centres.

From Sohâg the train trundles on, stopping and starting through this timeless landscape, some of the trackside scenes looking almost biblical. At Nag Hammâdi the line crosses the river on to the east bank. The great temple at Dandara stands just a few hundred yards from the Nile and is rich with hieroglyphs. It contains a temple of Isis and a temple of Horus, and hieroglyphs praising Nut, the sky goddess.

However you choose to travel, Luxor is the highlight of any trip down the Nile. The train gives a good view of all it has to offer on the way in from the north and passes beside the Karnak Temple. Not only is Luxor a very fine town, it is also full of fascinating things to see and do. Any wise visitor will allocate at least three days to it, and even then will have scraped only the surface of all it has to offer. Besides, after five days on tatty trains from the Delta, I was looking forward to a spot of luxury, hot showers and tea in a pot.

Follow the Sharia el-Mahatta, the main road from the railway station, and it will take you directly to the Karnak Temple, dedicated to Amun, the Sun God. Visit it in the daytime to admire the great columns and the statue of Rameses II and the Avenue of Sphinxes and all the other sites, and again at night for the Son-et-Lumière presentation. To get to Thebes and the Valley of the Kings you need to cross the river by ferry or *felucca*. Set on the west bank opposite Luxor, Thebes was a vast and splendid necropolis, where the mighty of ancient Egypt, the Kings and Queens and their children, their courtiers, servants and nobles were buried in great, gilded, and carefully hidden tombs.

The most famous of all the tombs to survive the onslaught of thieves of course, was that of the boy pharaoh Tutankhamun. It was discovered virtually intact by the British archaeologist Howard Carter in 1922, after six years of searching. The treasure, those '…things, wonderful things' that Carter saw in the funeral chamber, is now in Cairo, but the boy pharaoh still rests in his ancient tomb and a most wonderful sight it is, the walls rich with painted figures and hieroglyphs.

I took an evening *felucca* cruise on the Nile and I drank weak tea with buttered toast on hotel terraces and then I caught the train south again, down the last 130 miles (210km) of track to Aswân.

Places to see on this final stretch are Isna and Idfu and the temple at Kom Ombo. I must have caught a dozen or more trains on this journey, but not one completed the distance in the time the station master had assured me it would. These stopping trains are better at stopping than starting. We spent so long at Isna that, given prior warning, I could have left the train and taken a stroll around the town.

At my last night's stop, Idfu, the pride of the town is another temple, dedicated to Horus, the falcon-headed son of Osiris, a huge, grim building in the town centre, reached by *gharri* after crossing the river. Once the cruise ships had gone I seemed to be the only Westerner in town.

Further south, Kom Ombo is a dual temple on the riverbank dedicated to the gods Horus, the falcon-headed one, and Sobek, the crocodile-headed one. Crocodiles used to haul out on the bank at Kom Ombo, but the Nile crocodile has long since been driven from the Nile in Egypt.

BEFORE THE FLOOD

Aswân was and is a riverine port and railhead at the northern foot of the great Nile cataracts. These now lie under the waters of Lake Nasser, which spreads out to the south towards the Sudan. Aswân is a winter holiday resort, and among the local attractions are the famous Cataract Hotel, a *felucca* cruise to Elephantine Island or Kitchener's Island, or a visit to the tomb of the Aga Khan. Tired and dusty and in

sore need of a drink, but with a great sense of superiority over the river cruise crowd, I humped my baggage off the train for the last time and took a *gharri* to the Cataract Hotel. This is where Agatha Christie wrote *Death on the Nile* while her husband, the archaeologist Max Mallowen, was excavating in the area.

From Aswân it is possible to take a final excursion 30 miles (480km) south to the marvellously preserved temple at Abu Simbel. The rising waters of Lake Nasser would have

drowned it, but a mammoth rescue operation was mounted by UNESCO and the temple was cut into 2000 huge blocks of stone, transported up the hillside and reassembled where it stands today. Pharaoh Rameses II, who built the temple in the first place, could hardly have done better.

Seen like this, travelling slowly down the railway, hopping on and off the train as fancy took me, Egypt was revealed as a wonderful, almost magic land. Nobody bothered me for more than a cigarette and if I often felt dirty and weary, I never felt even remotely threatened. The country people are far too engaging and the towns and sites far too interesting. It is hardly possible to get to know this land and all it contains in one visit, but those who come down the Nile by train, seeing this land at a gentle pace, will have made a very good start.

■ The total distance between Cairo and Aswân is 453 miles (730km). Two special overnight sleeper trains go in each direction every day, stopping at Luxor, and take about 14½ hours. The carriages are all air conditioned and cabins have running water. There is a dining-car, and bottled water and wine can be bought on board. Tickets must be bought at least 48 hours before travel, particularly in the winter months, at the Wagons-Lits office in Giza Street, Cairo or through a travel agent.

■ The daily stopping trains and the local 'commuter' trains operating from larger centres are very much cheaper. These have First and Second Class air-conditioned carriages, as well as non air-conditioned Second Class. There is much less demand for these trains.

■ The timetable should not be depended upon and for this reason it is best to buy tickets locally.

■ The best months to travel are from October to March, when it is usually hot and sunny in the day but cool in the evening. In the summer it can be very hot indeed.

From the Centre of Madagascar

ROBIN NEILLANDS

Madagascar is not rich with railways, or indeed with transport facilities of any description. The local people manage well enough either on foot or ambling along with their ox-carts; the roads are few and dreadful. The only way to see the country is on the railway, though there is little enough of that either. Every rail journey in Madagascar, however, is interesting, partly because of the constantly changing scenery, partly because it offers a chance to meet the friendly Malagasy people, the real attraction of this most delightful and curious island. On the route from the capital Antananarivo (or Tana) to the east coast resort of Tamatave (or Toamasina) it is possible to stop off for the night at Perinet and visit the lemur reserve. This alone would make a visit to Madagascar worth while.

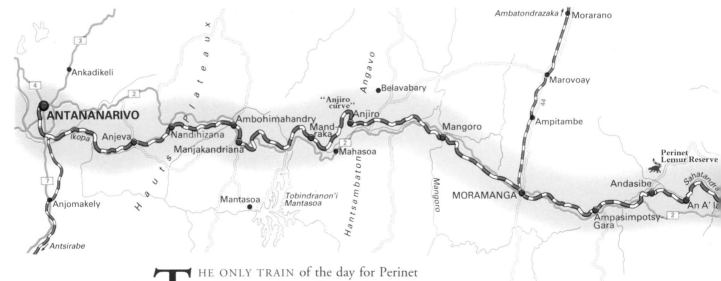

ABOVE, *the dusty cab of the Tamatave train*

FAR RIGHT, *a platform vendor offering fruit to the passengers*

THE ONLY TRAIN of the day for Perinet and Tamatave leaves Tana at six o'clock in the morning, not a time of day when I am normally at my best. But this train ride is one that no visitor should miss – after, that is, seeing the various sights of Tana and, above all, its Friday market. The Malagasy word for Friday is 'Zoma', and the Zoma market occupies all the main streets of the town, spreading right along the Avenue de l'Independence, with hundreds of stalls under a great network of white umbrellas.

You can buy almost anything at the Zoma market, from Zebu cattle and anxious goats to such items as toy cars made out of old fruit cans, spare car springs, and vast quantities of other junk. Only when you have seen the Zoma can you think of taking the train to Tamatave.

Madagascar is the fourth largest island in the world and is the size of California, yet has

An Early Start

My first task at the station that morning was to find the train, then the First Class carriage, and finally my seat. A few words in French, the *lingua franca* of Madagascar, had a friendly porter dragging me to the right platform, and after that finding the right carriage was easy; the First Class carriage is the one with glass in the windows.

I was glad of that because at 2600 feet (800m) Tana can be quite cold in the hour before dawn. I was also glad of the cup of tea on sale from a platform vendor. Most of my fellow passengers were foreigners like me. The locals cannot afford First Class travel and were already crammed like sardines into the Second Class compart-ments further up the train. I passed them and returned greetings and a few cheery waves as I went up to inspect the engine.

It was a small French diesel, 20 years old according to a brass plaque by the engine cover. The cab of this relic was already filled with Malagasys and

exactly 531 miles (855km) of track, all of it single. The line from Tana to Tamatave is still loosely maintained by the French, who built it between 1901 and 1913. The total distance of 233 miles (375km) is full of engineering marvels as the track runs through tunnels, over viaducts and across escarpment faces high above valleys full of bright green or muddy brown paddy fields, and on the very edge of cliffs overlooking rushing waterfalls and slow moving rivers.

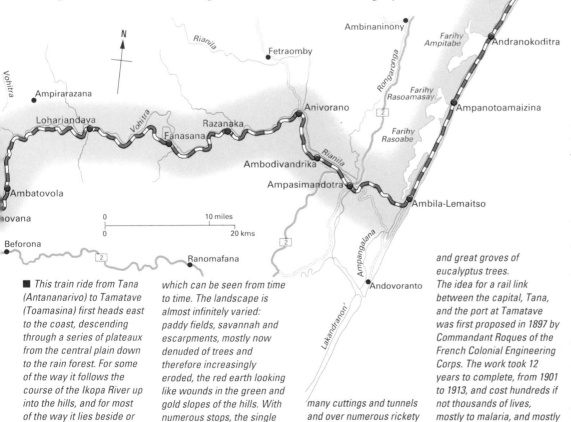

■ This train ride from Tana (Antananarivo) to Tamatave (Toamasina) first heads east to the coast, descending through a series of plateaux from the central plain down to the rain forest. For some of the way it follows the course of the Ikopa River up into the hills, and for most of the way it lies beside or close to the newly built road which can be seen from time to time. The landscape is almost infinitely varied: paddy fields, savannah and escarpments, mostly now denuded of trees and therefore increasingly eroded, the red earth looking like wounds in the green and gold slopes of the hills. With numerous stops, the single track runs through a great

and great groves of eucalyptus trees. The idea for a rail link between the capital, Tana, and the port at Tamatave was first proposed in 1897 by Commandant Roques of the French Colonial Engineering Corps. The work took 12 years to complete, from 1901 to 1913, and cost hundreds if not thousands of lives, mostly to malaria, and mostly among the thousands of

many cuttings and tunnels and over numerous rickety bridges, beside waterfalls

Chinese labourers from Canton and Shanghai who were indentured and brought here to hack out the railway line through mountain and jungle. It took two years to complete the first 30 miles (50km) which opened in 1903, and this was the easy bit, beside the Ikopa River. The most celebrated feature on the whole line is the famous Anjiro curve, an almost circular loop in the line just 262 feet (80m) in diameter, an hour or so before Perinet. The purpose of the Anjiro curve is to enable trains coming from Tamatave to pick up a little speed before tackling the steep uphill stretches leading to the central plateau. Going the other way, the train certainly picks up speed as it hurtles at 40mph (65kph) towards Perinet and then the sea.

ABOVE, *bright flower stalls at Tana's famous Zoma market*

RIGHT, *a patchwork of exposed, rich red earth – parts of Madagascar are in danger of being washed away*

more were swarming over the outside, hanging on to the handrails to give the window glass a final polish or dripping oil on to the wheels or into crevices of the engine cover. The engine looked far more suited to a spot of shunting than a journey through the mountains to the east coast, but the driver (or drivers) assured me that it was a very good engine and if I would like to travel in the cab for a bit later on that could be arranged. They only asked that I paid a small *pourboire* and waited until we were well away from the officialdom of Tana. This seemed reasonable and I went back to my seat (it is best to sit on the left) as the engine emitted a few warning hoots and the train prepared to leave.

At first the line goes south for a little way, circling the dreary and depressing slums on the outskirts of the city before heading east beside the Ikopa River through the varied scenery of the Hauts Plateaux, a mixture of hills and valleys, the slopes almost bare of trees, and the hills standing out starkly above the emerald green of the paddy fields. Here and there were small villages where the people were already streaming out to work, driving herds of long-horned Zebu cattle before them up to the slopes beneath the rocky outcrops that would become more prevalent as the train travelled on towards the mountains. With the coming of daylight I was able to take a closer look at my companions.

They were typical of the sort of traveller you expect to find on any famous railway journey in the Third World. There were two or three groups of students; there was a couple of Germans already muttering their commentary into a tape recorder; and a thin, bearded American with a cam-corder, cursing the lack of light as he attempted to get it all down on film, the better to bore the folks with back home. We were a very mixed bunch, from Australia and America, Europe and Japan, and in the best tradition of independent travellers we tried to ignore each other as much as possible. The one Malagasy in the compartment was Monsieur Joseph, proprietor of the Hôtel de la Gare at Andasibe, and from him I was happy to discover that I could have a room for the night.

After the savannah and paddy fields of the Hauts Plateaux comes an area of forest before the train climbs laboriously to the Angavo massif (Hantsambaton Angavo), clinging to the cliff-sides or running through tunnels and cuttings in the mountain wall. These mountains run up to 1500 feet (450m) above the plateau and overhang the Mandraka and Anjiro Valleys. Somewhere on the way the Ikopa River, which has been getting narrower and flowing faster, ends up as a waterfall spilling down a cliff. The Anjiro escarpment marks the gateway from the grass and eucalyptus trees of the Hauts Plateaux to the eastern rain forest which cloaks most of the country beyond the mountain ridge and down to the coast.

Here, as the railway reaches its highest point just before Anjiro, there comes the famous Anjiro curve, where the track makes a tight, 260 feet (80m) bend. As we leaned out of the window we could see the entire train, with the engine almost catching up with the guard's van as the bend tightens. The American with the cam-corder almost fell out getting it all in the shot.

From the Anjiro curve it is downhill all the way with frequent stops at the wayside stations, about 30 in all. Life on the stone and earth platforms is fascinating, with goats and chickens scurrying out of the way as vendors swarm up to the train to sell roast bananas and assorted meats and fruit.

VIEW FROM THE CAB

This train to Tamatave attracts the tourists but it is not a tourist train. It carries the local people to work and their produce to market. There was a great commotion and squealing at Anjiro while three large pigs were crated up and manhandled into the luggage compartment, and it was at this point that I was able to join the drivers in the cab. The tip was a dollar, which the other serious travellers thought so outrageous it was likely to inflate prices and wreck the local economy, but the drivers seemed happy enough.

The cab was quite small and very cramped. One man had the prime job of tooting the horn outside every station and at most level crossings and curves. Another held the oil can and the tea pot and was clearly essential, and the third man kept a careful eye on him. The fourth man talked to me, and the worry was that nobody seemed to be driving.

When you are rocking and swaying in the cab of an engine rattling along an 80-year-old, single track line in the middle of the jungle, this can be unsettling. However, nobody else seemed to be worried so I settled down to chat to the head driver, if that was his role, who was very

interested in the British Royal Family and said that he had met Prince Philip, Duke of Edinburgh. It appears that you see many famous people on the train to Perinet.

After Anjiro the scenery gradually changes, first to a deep belt of bamboo, then to moist and dripping rain forest. We crossed the River Mangoro and ran into the town of Moramanga about four hours after leaving Tana. Moramanga is a rail junction and the place where the Malagasy fight for independence from France began on 29 March 1947.

The American with the cam-corder took my place in the cab at Moramanga and after another half hour or so, just before eleven o'clock, we

rolled into Andasibe, the stop for Perinet. It is possible to carry on to Tamatave but wise people will break for the night here and continue next day. The train takes a leisurely lunch break here anyway, the locals eating at a platform buffet while the First Class passengers dine at the Buffet de la Gare. I found Monsieur Joseph and lugged my bag across to one of the thatched A-frame cottages that provide half his hotel's accommodation.

The Hôtel de La Gare at Andasibe is best imagined as a rather ramshackle tropical pension run by Monsieur Joseph and his cheerful staff with great charm and a certain vagueness. There was the small matter of dates for example. I arrived at Andasibe on 9 May. I know that because it is my daughter's birthday and I had phoned her that morning from Tana. The calendar behind the bar at Andasibe said it was 10 May. I thought nothing of it at the time but when I came in for breakfast next day the calendar read 11 May. Monsieur Joseph and Andasibe had gained a day somewhere, but it hardly seemed to matter. I had lunch, and then I set out with some others to visit the lemurs at Perinet.

The lemurs are the reason most people visit Madagascar. Madagascar has a unique wildlife and can boast 14 endemic

RIGHT, boy with a green chameleon

BELOW, clean washing adorns the wayside station house at Razanaka

species of lemur, 100 or more different species of bird, and more than 8000 plant species which are found nowhere else on earth. The most famous and most photographed of all the lemur species is the ringtailed lemur that appears on every book jacket and poster about Madagascar. It inhabits the Berenty reserve near Taolänaco (Fort Dauphin) in the south of the island.

The lemurs of Perinet are much more rare and much more shy. These are the Indri lemurs, who emit the most haunting cry to lure you on but are actually very difficult to see. We were lucky and saw three in the space of a couple of hours, admittedly after a flog through the wet and leech-infested rain forest. Through binoculars we saw them clearly, rather like cuddly teddy bears, with sticking-out furry ears. We also saw a marvellous green chameleon which was reluctant to change colour when put on a tartan scarf, and a great many beautiful butterflies.

Dinner that night was enlivened by the traveller's tales of my companions and bowls of what we came to call 'killer chilli'. After that and a bottle or two of wine the rest of the night was even livelier, but I was up at dawn for another visit to the lemur reserve, with two more sightings of lemurs, and was back at the station bar when the train arrived from Tana, ready for the last stage of the journey to Tamatave.

LAST STRETCH

Once again it is better to have a left-hand seat, and as a lot of people got off for a visit to Perinet this was not hard to arrange. After Perinet the railway finally strikes off on its own, leaving the road beside which it has marched since Tana, to follow the course of the River Sahatandra, or Vohitra. Most things in Madagascar have two

names, incidentally, so that Tamatave is more correctly but less commonly called Toamasina. The land is now falling away quite steeply to sea level and the views over the mountains and the rainforest are spectacular. So is the track, for this is the part of the route which kept Commandant Roques of the French Colonial Engineering Corps and his workmen busy for years.

The train rattles over bridges and through a countless succession of cuttings and tunnels which follow each other in rapid succession for mile after mile. There are more villages here and more stops, 20 or so between Andasibe and Tamatave. As the rain forest gives way to the flatlands there is more and more distressing evidence of how this vital asset is being stripped away for fuel or for pasture. Fires glow in the forest in the growing dark. The streams and rivers on this eastern side of the island are red with silt and above the villages the air is smoky with the fires of the charcoal burners. Slash and burn 'cultivation' is destroying the rainforest of Madagascar and when that is gone the whole island may slide into the Indian Ocean, washed away by the tropical rain.

The train leaves Andasibe at noon and just before dark passes through the little village of Bricka-ville (Ampasimanolatra), to reach the coast at Ambila-Lemaitso. Here the train turns north, heading up the coast through groves of fan-like wayfarer palms towards Tamatave, following the course of the Pangalanes Canal (Lakandranon' Ampangalona), a popular holiday spot for the Malagasy people. It was completely dark now and not much could be seen as the train rattled over a set of points and rolled at last into the station.

All journeys around Madagascar begin and end in Tana, so a return there is inevitable but many visitors will want to stay a little in Tamatave. Tamatave is a major port and a holiday resort – but those who wish to soak off the dust of travel with a quick dip in the sea should be warned that there are sharks about, and they are both close inshore and ferocious. One of the reasons for this is the presence of blood and offal from the town abattoir which has been thoughtfully sited close to the main beach. Those who wish to have a dip and survive the experience will use the protected area or stick to the hotel pool.

In the soft, warm air of the following morning, Tamatave revealed itself as a pleasant town, built mainly in the French colonial style, its attractive buildings set along tree-shaded avenues, the air redolent with the smell of the cloves that are grown near by. There are several hotels and many good restaurants. You can take a boat excursion to the Ile aux Prunes, an hour from the port, or a flight to the Ile Ste Marie, the archetypal tropical island, with drooping palms and sandy beaches, a warm sea and a reef to keep the sharks out. Or you can hop back on the train, return to Tana and take another train to see more of this fascinating and beautiful island before it all gets washed away.

PRACTICAL INFORMATION

■ It is 233 miles (375km) from Tana (Antananarivo) to Tamatave (Toamasina) and the journey takes about nine hours. There is one train a day in each direction.

■ There are three classes, First, Second and Third (in which livestock may be carried). There are no sleeping compartments or buffet, but plenty of food is on offer from platform vendors.

■ All First Class seats have to be reserved. There is usually enough room in Second and Third Class carriages.

■ It is a hot ride at any time of year, sometimes sticky and sometimes dusty. The dry season is from May to October, but the rain forests are blossoming in the wet season, November to April. The east coast has the most rain.

■ The trains are operated by Chemins de Fer Malagasy. It is not possible to book this journey outside Madagascar. Contact a hotel reception desk or travel agent in Tana for details, reservations and tickets. Tickets can be purchased at stations, of course, but this can be a time-consuming process.

About the Authors

Paul Atterbury divides his life between Britain and France, and is a writer and lecturer on art and antiques as well as travel – he is a familiar member of the BBC's *Antiques Roadshow* team of experts. An inveterate train traveller, he has explored and written about railways around the world, including *See Britain by Train*.

Ben Davies is a journalist and freelance photographer specialising in articles on business, travel and politics throughout Europe and Asia. Living in Bangkok, he has contributed articles to publications including *Euromoney* and the *International Herald Tribune*. He is the author of two recent travel guides to Thailand.

Timothy Jepson lived in Italy for some years, and was correspondent for the *Sunday Telegraph* newspaper in Rome from 1988–90. He has written and contributed to a number of travel guides, including *Rough Guides* to Canada and Italy, *AA Essential Explorer Rome*, and a new series, *Italy by Train*.

Mona King is a freelance writer and interpreter, and was formerly the UK Director of the Mexican National Tourist Council. She has travelled extensively in Mexico and Europe, especially Spain. She is the author of several travel guides, including most recently the *AA Tourguide Mexico* and *AA Tourguide Spain*.

Anthony Lambert is a freelance author and editor, whose lifelong interest in railways has taken him to over 40 countries – frequently to places where it is still possible to travel behind steam locomotives. The author of 12 books on travel and transport, he has also contributed to *The Times* and the *New York Times*, and writes regularly for *Geographical*.

Piers Letcher is a freelance writer and photographer now living in France. He has published some half-dozen books on computing and travel, including a guide to Yugoslavia. He has contributed articles to a wide range of newspapers and journals, and is currently publishing a collection of short stories.

Kim Naylor is a photo-journalist based in Stockholm, and contributes regularly to a number of travel magazines in Sweden. He has also written several *Discovery* travel guides – to Africa, India and Vietnam.

Robin Neillands is a freelance travel writer, and author of over 50 books covering travel, history and outdoor activities. Writing novels (some under the name Robin Hunter), he is also a frequent contributor to magazines and newspapers, including the *Radio Times*, the *Daily Telegraph* and *Harpers*.

Tony Pinchuck is a freelance journalist and designer, born in South Africa but now living in London. He has travelled extensively in southern Africa, and contributed articles to the national press on Zimbabwe. He is the

author of several books, and co-author of the *Rough Guide to Zimbabwe and Botswana*.

Christopher Sainsbury taught Fine Art before becoming a writer and photographer – now 'semi-retired', he works as a tour guide in South America. He has travelled and worked in 44 countries, largely in connection with the youth charities Operation Drake and Operation Raleigh, and circumnavigated the world twice.

Richard Sale and Tony Oliver are physicists with a particular interest in glaciology. Richard has walked and climbed throughout Europe, but concentrates chiefly on the Arctic. Apart from walking and climbing, Tony is also a keen cyclist, and is author of *Touring Cycles*. They have written and illustrated many books, together and separately – their most recent venture is *Arctic Odyssey*.

Dave Scott is a restauranteur and freelance writer on cookery and travel. Widely travelled, he has lived in Japan and studied the martial arts. He has contributed many articles on food and travel to magazines and newspapers, including the *Sunday Times* and *Here's Health*, and is the author of over 20 books, including the *AA Essential Guide Japan*.

Gus Silber is a South African freelance journalist, writing for a variety of magazines on subjects from sport to politics to travel. He has won awards for criticism, travel writing and feature writing, and is the author of *Who's Really Who in South Africa*, and *It Takes Two to Toyi-Toyi*, a survival guide to the new South Africa.

Roy Sinclair is a New Zealand journalist and freelance photographer with the *The Press* (Christchurch), and has been a keen railway enthusiast for as long as he can remember. He has written on many topics, including the national parks of Australasia, and is the author of several books, including *Rail: the Great New Zealand Adventure*.

Colin and Fleur Speakman run their own consultancy, Transport for Leisure, promoting 'environmentally friendly' forms of transport and tourism. They have published a number of walking guides to Germany and Austria, including *Walking in the Black Forest*, *Walking in Salzkammergut* and the *Green Guide to Germany*.

Richard Trillo has been travelling and writing in Africa for the last fifteen years. He is the author of two travel guides, the *Rough Guide to Kenya* and the *Rough Guide to West Africa*.

Ken Westcott Jones is a member and co-founder of the British Guild of Travel Writers. The travel editor of United Newspapers for many years, his column in the *East Anglian Daily Times* has been running for 40 years. His many books include *Great Railway Journeys of the World*, and he claims to have ridden trains in 52 countries.

Index

The Automobile Association wishes to thank the following photographers, libraries and associations for their assistance in the preparation of this book. (T=top, B=bottom, L=left, R=right)
Rick Godley/Ajax Silver Image Pictures 18(T); Jonathan Eastland/Ajax Silver Image Pictures 96(B); Alandalus Expreso 76, 77, 81(T); Bryan & Cherry Alexander Photography 58, 59(T), 63; J.Allan Cash Photolibrary 43, 47, 119, 133(B), 148(B), 149; Amtrak 102, 104, 106; The Blue Train 206; Britstock-IFA Ltd 66/7; Hilary Bradt 216, 217, 221; Countrylink 180/1; Bill Cousins 71,72/3, 73; Ben Davies 88, 89, 90, 91, 92/3, 93, 94, 95; Richard Elliott 56; French Railways 34(B), 36; Ffotograff 157, 176; Colin Monteath/ Hedgehog House New Zealand 197, 199(T); Nathan Secker/Hedgehog House New Zealand 174/5; Shirley Higgins 218, 220; Robert Holmes Photography 120(T), 123(T); The Hutchison Library 190, 198/9, 201(T), 212/3; The Illustrated London News Picture Library 7, 13; S.D.Jolly 28; A.Kraus 126, 128/9, 129, 130, 130/1; Anthony Lambert 82(T), 83, 84, 85, 86, 87, 133(T), 134/5, 136(L), 137(T); Piers Letcher 44, 46(B), 48/9, 48, 185(T), 186, 187; The Mansell Collection 9(B), 10; Mary Evans Picture Library 6, 9(T); Millbrook House Ltd 14/5, 153, 155, 156; National Railway Museum,York 8, 12(T); Kim Naylor 154, 158/9, 159, 160, 161; Dr.L.Nixon 136(R); Tony Oliver 57, 61, 62, 145, 147, 148(T), 151, 150/1, 152; Orient Express Hotels

Ltd 19, 20, 21(T), 21(B), 22/3, 23, 25; The Photographers Library 121; Rail Safaris 192(T), 194; Robert Harding Picture Library 115, 191, 192; The Robert Opie Collection 4(T), 4(B), 5(T), 5(B); David Rogers 14(B),70, 193, 194/5; C.J.Sainsbury 138, 139, 140, 141, 142/3, 143; Roy Sinclair 170, 171, 172, 172/3, 175; South American Pictures 134, 137(B); Spectrum Colour Library 18(B), 24, 27, 31, 99, 100, 101(T), 103, 109, 114/5, 146/7, 163, 166/7, 177, 179(T), 202, 203(T), 203(B), 205, 208(T), 208(B); The Telegraph Colour Library 122; Ian Thomson 142; Ian Yates 196; Zefa Picture Library(UK) Ltd 2/3,11, 12(B), 15, 26, 40, 59(B), 60, 60/1, 64, 65, 74, 80/1, 82(B), 104/5, 107, 108(T), 108(B), 110, 111, 116, 117, 128, 150, 169, 179(B), 182, 204/5, 207, 219.

The remaining photographs are held in the Automobile Association's own photo library with contributions from. ·
M.Adelman 32, 33, 34, 38, 39, 40, 42, 50, 51, 52, 53, 54, 65, 67, 68(T), 69; A.Baker 29, 30, 68(B); J.Carnie 74; J.Edmanson 80; R.Elliott 114, 118, 120(B), 123(B); D.Hardley 75; P.Kenwood 101(B), 112, 113, 183, 184, 185(B), 187(T), 188, 189, 196, 199(B), 200, 201(B); J.Lloyd 37(T); D.Noble 55; D.Robertson 78, 79; A.Souter 40/1, 41, 49; R.Strange 1,35, 37(B), 96(T), 98, 99, 211, 212, 214, 215; R.Surman 45, 46; P.Timmermans 124, 125; P.Wilson 127, 131.